Celtic Islands.

D1629669

SIXTY YEARS AT SCHOOL

SIXTY YEARS
AT
SCHOOL

by

A. L. IRVINE

WINCHESTER :
P. & G. WELLS, LTD.
1958

MADE AND PRINTED
IN GREAT BRITAIN
BY
WARREN & SON LTD.
THE WYKEHAM PRESS
WINCHESTER

CONTENTS

TO ALICE

PREFACE

THIS book owes its existence to the importunity of my niece, Alice Tanqueray, one who has always rated me far above my deserts. She insisted that my memories would be of interest not only to her generation but to her children's. If it has found its way into print, that is due likewise to family pressure ; and, outside the family, my friend Raymond Robertson-Glasgow has given generous encouragement. Still, it is a venture which I make with apprehension. I have pleasant links with the publishing world, but could not ask any publisher to take a thing so unimportant, so personal, and I fear so egocentric. I am not so much afraid of dulness as of giving an impression of complacency, which I think would not be true. I am no Freudian searcher of the subconscious, have no great thoughts on the subject of education, and seldom exercise myself in great matters which are too high for me : this is mainly a record of people and things I have enjoyed. Recalling the past has certainly been a pleasant occupation, at a time when such occupation was much needed.

The intended title was *Fifty Years at School*, which would have been an understatement. Oxford after all is school with a difference : one is still *in statu pupillari :* and if to the Oxford years is added my St. Martin's summer at Prior's Field, the sixty years of my title go very little way beyond the truth : and I have enjoyed them all. The last time I saw my old friend A. B. Ramsay, he said, ' I have been a lucky man '. And so have I, and hope that these pages may show it.

CHAPTER I

COLCHESTER, FOLKESTONE, RADWINTER

I was born on 18 September 1881 at St. Mary's Rectory, Colchester, the fifth of the seven children of John William and Catherine Maria Irvine. But for most of our lives we have been a family of four, since two died in infancy and the eldest at school in his fourteenth year. He was the most promising of the family, with a sweetness of disposition which not all of us have possessed.

I have no precocious memories and if I had should not wish to write them down. Biography and autobiography have long been my favourite reading, and I know too well how wearisome the well-meaning tales of babyhood can be. So the *puerilia*, or perhaps I might say *infantilia*, will be few. The first public event that I can recall, local but literally earth-shaking, is the Colchester earthquake of 22 April 1884. The date is given me by an article in *Country Life* for 6 March 1957, which records that 1213 houses and 31 churches were damaged and gives pictures of some of the ruined buildings. My brother Lionel and I were in the nursery, mowing the lawn as the gardener and his boy, with a horizontal chair, when I found myself, as I remember saying, ' tipping, tipping ', and I *think* I saw Jumbo, the huge four-legged water-tower in the adjoining precinct ' tipping ' likewise. Certainly someone saw that sight. My second memory is the death of General Gordon. I remember being in Crouch Street with my nurse and hearing it talked of : that must have been at the end of January 1885.

My father was a great builder : he rebuilt the church, built the rectory and school, and had much to do with the building of the hospital. And if when I have returned to Colchester with more sophisticated eyes I have found the sight of them a little embarrassing, my father could only take what Victorian architects offered him. The garden was large enough for a tennis lawn and even for cricket, and for some years an annual match was played there in which at least two distinguished county cricketers took part in their boyhood. But it had its limitations. A full pitch to leg was not much use when the drawing-room windows, well protected by a

net behind which sat scorer and spectators, was within a few yards
of the wicket, and when half the fielders, on the tennis lawn,
had a gravel path between them and the batsman.

The western boundary of the garden was the Roman wall, over
which we looked down on the roofs of the small houses of Balkerne
Hill.   To the north a high hedge separated us from the precinct
in which stood Jumbo.   When I had to squander the lovely spring
of 1896 upon scarlet fever in my old nursery and an airgun was
borrowed for my amusement, my favourite target was a spade which
stood against the nearest foot of Jumbo.   He, or it, was my contemporary, built in the year of my birth, to be the second largest
water-tower in England.

The ground was full of Roman remains, and we were told that
when the flower beds were first made there was always a chance of
picking up a Roman coin after a shower of rain.   I remember a
coin of Carausius coming to light when a swing was being erected
in the nineties.   And when a garden drain was being cleared its
floor was a Roman pavement.   We really had too much of Roman
remains, and the jumble of a Victorian museum gave me a distaste
for them.   The perfect set-out of a modern museum—Colchester
or Verulamium or Silchester-at-Reading—is a very different
matter.

It was while I was contemplating that drain that an elderly
clergyman, coming to see my father, entered into conversation with
me about the ' gyarden '—the only time I can remember hearing
that good old-world pronunciation.   My mother always said ' jest'
for ' just ' and called a herb a nerb (until we laughed her out of it).
Far into this century, old Mrs Foster of Salcombe, who visited us
at Lord's Meade, would talk of taking cawfee with an awficer, and
an old man who died in 1927, when I wrote a notice about him to
The Times, still called a bomb a boom.   He remembered talking
to a man born in 1753.   But most of the once familiar words—
yaller, and cowcumber, and chany, and obleege and the rest I have
only heard as conscious archaisms, which don't count.

A good view of Colchester on its hill may be enjoyed—I truly
enjoy it—from the railway, and the two objects on which the eye
fastens are the Town Hall, built just after our time to the designs
of John Belcher R.A., in whose office Will Green worked in his
early youth, and the huge form of Jumbo ; and just to the right of
him is the tower, the only ancient part, of St. Mary's, where we used
to carry up rugs on August nights to study the heavens and watch
for meteors.   In the siege of Colchester by Fairfax in 1648 the

church tower was occupied by a one-eyed gunner who gave great annoyance to the besiegers : that is why the church had to be rebuilt later—though it didn't wait for my father for that : his was a second rebuilding, in 1871. The church, by the way, is known as St. Mary-at-the-Walls, and the lower part of the tower alone survives from the medieval building.

My grandchildren will read half incredulously of that secure Victorian world where from a decent household a good servant seldom left except to get married or as too old for service. We left Colchester in 1897 and until that time, while pleading guilty to a capricious and selective memory, I can only remember one cook and two parlourmaids, and when one nurse left there was her understudy to succeed her. When on 30 December 1938 a notice of our Silver Wedding appeared in *The Times* newspaper, it brought me only two letters, and one was from the nurse I had known as Flora Appleby : she might herself have kept a Golden Wedding since I had seen her last. A cook in those days was always prepared to bake, and no ' baker's bread ' was seen in the dining room. Further, we had two kinds of bread, for a special ' baking-powder ' bread was prepared at the end of the week for sacramental purposes. We had the reversion of it, and delicious it was. When the practice of using wafers at Holy Communion began to come in, I cannot say. Our bacon came from the grocer, but no ham would have appeared in the dining-room that was not home-cured.

Colchester was, and is, a garrison town, and in days when, apart from church and the drawing room, music could hardly be heard except from the itinerant ' German band ' or the barrel-organ, the military band was a thing of real importance. On a still summer night, from garden or open window, we could faintly hear the band playing after mess, and it truly was Horns of Elfland. The rectory lay pleasantly in a cul-de-sac, the only western exit being down a flight of steps where once had been a postern gate in the Roman wall ; but when on rare occasions a regiment had surmounted the North Hill and the band struck up at the top of it, we might just be in time to see them go past. When we began to attend Church Parade I cannot remember, but in our last Colchester years and later as visitors, or revenants, we regularly did so : the Abbey Field was about a mile away and we could easily be back for church at 11. The Queen's Birthday review on 24 May, for which we always had a hired landau, was one of the great days of the year, as between 1890 and '94 it was at Shorncliffe. Our grandchildren can still see in Whitehall what the Victorian soldier looked like, and the variety meant much to us when hussars were succeeded by lancers and lancers by dragoons. After 1918 Sir Winston Churchill tried to put the army back into colour. It could not be done, but with the band it *had* to be done : a band in khaki got so few engagements.

The prejudice against the army was still very strong in some quarters. My father's old cousin Sir John Murray, who had raised a famous regiment in the Mutiny, had given me some military equipment in which I paraded the streets. One of the good nonconformist ministers asked my father if I, or my brother, was destined for the army. My father said he had not heard of it, but he would be well content if it were so. ' Rob him of his freedom ! ' exclaimed Mr Batty—or Mr Spurrier : ' Rob him of his manhood ! '

I was sent to school at the Grange, Folkestone (the Rev. A. L. Hussey) when barely turned of eight, very small and for a year and a half the youngest boy in the school : no wonder I went by the name of Dolly. On the previous Sunday I had been sent, alone, in my first Eton jacket and top hat, to pay my respects to friends at the far end of the town. I am not sure it was a very kind errand to be sent on. I must have been a ridiculous spectacle, and certainly some of the populace thought so. There was, and I expect is, a certain mark-book kept by our good governess, Miss Lee, in which our marks appeared under the three headings of Punctuality, Conduct, Application. Years later we used to derive much amusement from looking to see on how many days I did not get 0 for Conduct. No doubt I was a more than usually detestable small boy, and perhaps that was the chief reason why I was sent to boarding-school at least a year before the usual time. But I gained much by my early start.

The Grange has no records in print and I do not know of any reference to it in literature except in Sir Harold Nicolson's *Some People*. He hated it, but I daresay he would have hated another school equally. I enjoyed it. I met no bullying—though there was some, once a very bad case—if much teasing, and thoroughly enjoyed the life, perhaps because I enjoyed the work. Besides the new boys, there was a new master in charge of the lowest class, the Fourth—E. W. Moore, a scholar of Christ Church, as I was to be ten years or so later. His first experience of a schoolmaster's life was a very small boy being sick beside his table. I spent the rest of my first day in the matron's room, more homesick than I ever was again, attempting to read a book about Grace Darling, the lifeboat heroine. I had been taught that I must eat what was set before me and next morning was addressing myself to a breakfast sausage when Hussey came along. ' No sausage for you who were sick yesterday ', and the sausage flew out of window. Hussey certainly had not the gift of doing things graciously.

The education, it need hardly be said, was severely classical. I had done a little Latin with my father, but his mid-Victorian pronunciation was already out of date, so I had to start afresh. But I was well rewarded for my early start and, till I reached the First, was top of every class while the youngest boy in it. History and Geography were included, but French and the Mathematics at which I was wholly imbecile were done in divisions by themselves. I had begun Greek in the Lower Third before I was nine. I was never head of the First Class. The head boy was older than myself, but in our last term we dead-heated for first place and when I next saw the school seven years later, I found my name on the board bracketed as head boy. I never was head boy, and it was simply favouritism.

There was no teaching of English and I don't in the least regret it. The arts were no doubt as little regarded as elsewhere. Some doubtless learnt drawing and the piano and performed their piece at the school concert. I had learnt the first rudiments of both, and enjoyed the lessons at the Colchester School of Art. All this was dropped when I went to school, but I found I was expected to resume music at home, and the instrument took a good deal of kicking before I was allowed to give it up. Whether perseverance would ever have made me a competent pianist I can't say. I doubt it ; but I believe I could have drawn passably well, and at least I could have saved other people an infinity of trouble in teaching me my songs.

Hussey, who had taught for a brief period at Bradfield, and then at Radley, was no doubt a good teacher, with a bitter scorn of slovenly and careless work, and carelessness was not tolerated for long. I remember being warned that I had reached the limit in one particular mistake, and it seemed prudent not to make it again : those who were caned by Hussey were not generally amused. But my real debt was to the teaching of Moore when I met him again in the First Class : he could give one, even at that tender age, some idea of what scholarship without pedantry really meant. And we had to face our difficulties with no help but a dictionary. In the First Class no editions with notes were used. I started on

Homer and Horace the week I turned eleven with an ugly plain text, and can still remember the first lines of the Iliad I ever puzzled out, with a dim sense that here was really something rather wonderful.

The First Class often worked in the study which was also the library, with a rich store of the works of G. A. Henty. We sat at a table by a large window that looked across the gravel playground and the cricket field to the railway line and the trains approaching or leaving Radnor Park station, and the sight of a fire-breathing train in the darkness still carries me back to the Grange. The whole, or most, of a Saturday morning was given to the making of Latin verses, and when I went up for a scholarship at the age of twelve and ten months it seemed quite natural to turn out sixteen very passable verses with no aid from books. I believe I still have them somewhere, for we were required to bring out our rough copies to show to Hussey—a most unwise proceeding, which could only produce discouragement if they were bad. Mine certainly were not, but there was one mistake, an intransitive verb used transitively, of which the old man made the best. 'Ah well, perhaps it might mean '—what it certainly might not, and I had never supposed that it could ! Such is the force of favouritism.

On a few occasions as we worked in the study a boy would enter with a note from some master and would be caned then and there. How the school compared in this practice with other schools of the day I cannot say. I should think that a majority of boys, like myself, remained unscathed. Some offences always met with summary treatment, e.g. dressing in prayer time. We required three bells to get us up and downstairs in the morning, and the second commanded a few minutes of stillness for our private devotions. I think the prefects were expected to go round occasionally and listen for undevotional movements. Anyhow I remember the head of a general who is also a member of the House of Lords appearing round the door one Sunday morning, and a colonel, R.E., with a long string of letters after his name (as I gather from *Who's Who*) was summoned to the study afterwards with a companion in misfortune. Many years later the general walked into the colonel's mess in France and was reminded of the incident. We rather went in for distinguished soldiers at the Grange.

I suspect that Hussey in his last years before retirement became rather an old brute, and in retirement he was a sore trial to his successor, once a favourite pupil. He lived for his boys, and perhaps a little for his horse, and when he retired all too late he took a house close by and, resenting every change, might be seen glaring over the gate like a spirit exiled from Paradise. But I cannot be ungrateful to one who gave me my first nights in London —in lodgings which he took every winter—my first theatre, which was also my first Gilbert and Sullivan, my first (and nearly my last) circus at Olympia, and my first Drury Lane Pantomime, with much that was good besides. Further he was on the best of terms with my parents, even with my mother, though he found it hard to be gracious to a lady. No doubt he often remembered the promising scholar, my brother, who had died at the Grange on 1 June 1889.

A bachelor with grizzled beard, red-veined nose and rather bloodshot eyes, it cannot be said that his manner was winning, and his furies were formidable. But parents trusted him, he had a good school and I am grateful for having been there. It had the Victorian stability. All the masters who were on the staff when I arrived in 1889 were still there in 1894, though at that moment two of them, Campbell and Reece, left to found a well-known school, Doon House at Westgate-on-Sea. Nearly fifty years later I was astonished to rediscover Campbell as a wartime neighbour at Guildford, and to learn that Reece, his brother-in-law, was also vigorously alive. Schoolmasters on the whole are a long-lived race : they live a wholesome life and have good holidays.

I have said that there was no teaching of English literature. The nearest we came to it was this. On a top shelf of the study was a row of scrubby little Miltons, and occasionally, when a lesson had been finished early, they might be produced and a bit of *Paradise Lost* read aloud—quite meaningless to us though perhaps useful as a reading lesson. And once when Good Friday fell in term, we of the First Class were set to learn by heart Samson's lament,

' O dark, dark, dark, amid the blaze of noon '.

Further, on Sundays we were given eight lines of English verse translated into Latin Elegiacs which we had to commit to memory—brief memory, I fear, for only two isolated couplets have remained with me. One of them came from the old ballad of *Giles Collins* :

His mother she made him some water-gruel
And stirred it round with a spoon

De mensa cochleare capax rapit anxia mater
Farraque cum tepidis mollia miscet aquis.

But for that I should certainly never have known that *cochleare* was the Latin for a spoon.   Yet there was no excessive insistence on learning by heart, though I can still say a good deal of the battle canto of *Marmion*.   I was seventy before I read the rest of the poem.   If learning by heart, whether the poets or the gender rhymes, has in latter days been crowded out, it is a great loss, except to the few, the very few, who genuinely cannot do it.   Sometimes on a Sunday the whole school would have to draw a map : that was very good for us and set a premium on neatness.

One valuable byway of knowledge came to me through a short-lived cult of tracing, to which the woodcuts in the Classical Dictionary lent themselves.   Naturally one read a good deal of the text too, and it proved most useful.   Some years ago a wise Cambridge examiner told me he thought a classical General Paper should always contain a mythology question, and that it should be an obligatory one.   After all, there is a great deal of English poetry —let alone Latin and Greek—that one cannot read without such knowledge.   I have not possessed a Classical Dictionary for forty or fifty years, and if I have seldom needed one it is because I learnt early who Orpheus and Perseus and Oedipus were, and what were the Labours of Hercules.   If the announcers of the B.B.C. had had the same training, their utterances might have been less trying to listen to than in fact they are.

I had a brief passion for the yellow-backed military stories of one Captain Peacock, till Hussey to my great indignation seized them and flung them into the fire.   How good or bad they were I cannot say, but the blurb (to anticipate the arrival of that useful word by at least a generation) made a high claim for them : ' Captain Peacock has long passed Mr Rudyard Kipling and with a little more experience will rival Hawley Smart in depicting military life '.   (Who *was* Hawley Smart ?)   But for most of us Henty was the man, and a very good man too.   I know all too little of history, but of that little I am sure that Henty taught me most. He brought out two books a year and good friends gave us these two every Christmas, and the family ultimately possessed not less than fifty.   For the excellent practice of matronly readings in the drawing-room Rider Haggard was already established as a classic, and this was the period when Sherlock Holmes was appearing monthly in *The Strand Magazine*.   The stories were preluded by Miss Lawford reading us *The Sign of Four*.

One other good thing that I carried away from the Grange was an early enjoyment of wine.   I suffered from bad sore throats and

Burgundy was prescribed : so for a considerable time I had the unique privilege of a glass of Beaune (in a coarse school tumbler) with my dinner. Otherwise I did well in the matter of health. I shared mumps with my brother in the sanatorium—to Hussey, the Cottage—and much more memorably chickenpox with the admired head of the school and captain of games, J. L. Stow, universally known, not then but for sixty years afterwards, as Daddy. I was already in the First Class and on the verge of the cricket eleven, but the discovery that such a being treated me as a friend and equal did much for my self-respect. Later he visited at my home and I at his. After his death the son who succeeded him at Horris Hill told me he had endless stories of ' the incredible Hussey ', and I wish I had seen him more often to recall them.

It was a characteristic of Jimmy Stow, as of many of us, to be highly contemptuous of anyone who did not know something that he did know. I remember being humbled to the earth because I had never read Macaulay's *Lays of Ancient Rome*. How I first became acquainted with them is a little bit of Victorian history. There was an old lady in my father's parish to whom I used to be sent on the last Sunday of my holidays for the purpose of receiving that desirable object, a gold half-sovereign. We understood that she had once been kicked in the chest by a cow, I cannot say how many years before, and never again left her bed—though from her appearance and her talk it was not clear that anything was the matter with her. On a round table in the pleasant drawing-room which she never visited was a copy of the *Lays*, the same handsome edition which I afterwards inherited from a godmother ; and while I waited to be taken upstairs I used to read as much as I could. I have never undervalued the odd minutes in odd places to get through an extra page or two of some book.

I suspect that the Grange was old-fashioned in many ways, and certainly it was so in the matter of games. Our elevens still played football in long white trousers when their opponents had advanced, if not to shorts, at least to knickerbockers buckled below the knee. And changing for football might mean putting on additional garments. If there was a cold wind the notice would be given out at dinner ' No leaving off vests or drawers '. I could not leave off the one without the other, for I was equipped with combinations, always derisively referred to by Hussey as pengatherums, a magnificent word which I have not met elsewhere. I can't remember that we always left off our shirts either, and whatever we wore was covered by a thick blue fisherman's jersey. While other schools

B

had their teams disposed as they are today, we still, at least in my earlier years, played two centre-forwards and two half-backs. Yet we usually played as well as our opponents.

In Athletics also we lived in the past. The Pole Jump still figured in our sports, a relic of earlier days, very many years before it reappeared as the Pole Vault in the Varsity Sports. Those who entered for the so-called Steeplechase sported coloured scarves of their own choice.

I was small and weak and never reached the Football XI, and I cannot remember any race in which I came in higher than last. But when it was a question of hitting a ball with a bat or a racket, or even a stump at rounders, it was a different thing, for I had a good eye, as I still had fifty years later. I had two years in the Cricket XI, following a year as scorer, an office I enjoyed. In my last year the Captain of games was Geoffrey Lawrence, now known as Lord Oaksey : he made most of the runs and I got most of the wickets, 53 to be exact in eight matches. But I also received from Eddie Moore a bat for the only 50 of the season, made against new opponents from Walmer, a school called St. Clare.

It was many years before the game of Squash, then always called Squash Rackets, had anything like a regulation court, and our two courts adjoined each other with only three and a half walls apiece, so that really only one could be used at a time. It was the game I played best, and I recall a desperately close semi-final with Lawrence, after which in the final I beat one Blackwood, who later played for Rugby at the parent game of Rackets.

Much in the life of those years is vividly fresh in memory, nothing more so than certain sounds. I hear the creak of the roller on a breathless night in July '94, with a thunderstorm coming on, as Eddie Moore rolled the pitch for the last match of the season, against Bradnack's. The school was called Sutherland House, but we nearly always spoke of our rivals by the master's name. It was a school with a good cricketing reputation : twelve years later I met Bradnack in Guernsey, when he told me that shortly after my time he had two successive captains of Cambridge in the XI. But on this occasion fate delivered them into our hands. We made a respectable score while the going was easy, and then on a baking wicket nearly got them out twice, and seventeen wickets fell for 14 runs. In the second innings my vis-à-vis, the Rev. E. P. H. Pardoe, took five wickets for no runs.

The other sound I can still hear is the howl of the great gale of November 1891, when the three-masted *Benvenue* went down off

Sandgate, leaving only her masts above water.   The whole school struggled down to see the sight, with survivors of the unfortunate crew clustered behind some sort of canvas shelter on one of the yards.   I remember a boy, one of the numerous tribe of Kempe, setting off in pursuit of his cap and seeming to fly, carried through the air like the cap itself.   I remember too the welcome appearance of old Hussey with a great box of Fry's Sweet Chocolate that was our regulation issue, sometimes produced after dinner on wet half-holidays—' Seniores priores, first round ', my first experience of a queue.   Those flat oblong slabs of chocolate, rather coarse and gritty but very palatable, have long since been superseded.   The last time I met one, to my great satisfaction in days when any chocolate was rare, was when cycling through the little North Oxfordshire town of Charlbury in 1917.

The wreck of the *Benvenue* had a comparatively happy ending. We were told that the rocket apparatus could not reach the ship in face of the gale and that they were bringing up a field gun from Shorncliffe.   We saw the flash of the first shot as we started for home in the gloom, but the discharge broke the rope every time. At prayer time, when of course we sang the appropriate hymn, A. & M. 370, we were reminded that it was not likely that those men would ever come to land alive.   As a matter of fact they did.   The wind began to fall at night, and the Dover lifeboat did what others had failed to do.   The masts disappeared one by one, but it was a matter of years rather than months before all were gone.

Another convulsion of nature that lives in memory is the Sandgate landslip, of which I cannot recall the date.   We visited a half-deserted town where coastguards patrolled with cutlass drawn.   I still possess a souvenir of it, a small white triangular tile from the conservatory of a partially wrecked house.

I came of a family markedly clerical and markedly Carthusian. So I had always assumed that I should follow my brother to Haig Brown's house, Saunderites, and remember retiring to a secret place to weep when I was told that I was to sit for a scholarship at Winchester instead.   The Grange seemingly had only just discovered Winchester, for Stow had been our first Winchester scholar only a year earlier.   Afterwards there was a pretty regular procession from the Grange to the College.   When I paid my first visit to the school as an old member in 1901 the head boy was Dick Gleadowe, afterwards Art Master at Winchester and designer of the Stalingrad sword.   And when in July two years later I came back as an examiner in succession to Daddy Stow, I brought out two future Wykehamists at the top of the list. One of them was A. P. Herbert, Hussey's prime favourite, though by that time Hussey had retired in favour of my good friend Charles Jelf.

So to Winchester we went in July 1894, Joe Lane-Claypon, head of the school, and I, and Hussey. I thoroughly enjoyed the experience. Except for Greats ten years later I have always enjoyed an exam. I had been assured that if my classical papers were good my mathematical imbecility would be tolerated, and so it must have been, since I eventually appeared third on the roll : No. 2 became Lord Chancellor and No. 4 sailed round the world in a boat of his own design. Though Eton and Charterhouse were examining at the same time, there were 105 candidates, and my number was somewhere in the seventies. The examination took place in School, that fine building attributed not certainly to Wren, which till well on in the nineteenth century served as a general classroom for the whole College. In those days, instead of an allowance for age, candidates were divided into two lots, senior and junior, and the senior papers were considerably harder. I expect I was a better examinee than my companion, but at the Grange we ran neck and neck, and only the greater difficulty of his papers can have brought me out thirteen places above him. It was the Winchester custom to eliminate the weaker candidates after the first day and others after the second, and it was Hussey's first task of the morning to go down before breakfast to see that our names were safely on the roll in the window of Wells's bookshop. If your name was still there on the third morning your chances of a place on the roll were bright, yet not necessarily of a place in College ; there were always twenty names on the roll, but there might be only ten or a dozen vacancies in College. Finally the roll appeared in *The Times* on 16 July. My parents were drinking the waters at Ems, but returned in time for the concert and prize-giving ; and as I sang a solo with something less than the usual panic, and dead-heated for the first place in the school, and received the ball for my bowling average, I ended up momentarily as a V.I.P.

Holidays were usually spent at home. The time had not come when it was thought necessary for children to be taken to the sea, though I have a dim memory of Bournemouth, and a dimmer one of seeing a hornet at a tiny place on the Suffolk coast, Sizewell. And anyhow the males of the family had the sea at Folkestone. We came of a highly clerical family as I have said : both my grandfathers and two uncles were in orders, and if I were to carry it further and include my later Lloyd connections, starting with two brothers-in-law, the number would be beyond my power to calculate.   So from very early days time not spent at Colchester was likely to be spent at Radwinter Rectory, my grandmother's home near Saffron Walden.   There my uncle Fred Bullock and his father and grand-father before him held the family living for 110 years, 1806 - 1916. My mother then was a Bullock of Radwinter, my grandmother a Bullock of Faulkbourn—that noble house near Witham, home of the family since 1637, the sale of which in 1897 was so deplored in the clan that we were never encouraged to go and see it.   I was about 70 before I did so.   By that time one could be thankful that no one in the family had the responsibility of trying to keep it up.   Nor Radwinter either.   The new Rectory was built by my great-grandfather in 1808, a pleasant late Georgian house in white brick, recalling the days of window tax in the windows that had never held glass.   And history was to be read in the drawing-room too.   When my uncle retired to Oxford in 1916, the original wallpaper was still on the walls.   I was told it had been there for 108 years, but it was in such good condition that the new incumbent did not have to remove it.   The paper was made in squares because there was a Napoleonic wartime tax on rolls of paper.   The family had made over the presentation of the living to Keble College, and that body had the wisdom to find yet one more Bullock to hold it, a remote cousin : but he was the last.

When I read Kilvert's Diary or *Larkrise to Candleford*—both books to be heartily recommended—I have a strong sense of Radwinter life as I remember or have heard of it.   The Rectory family were not rich people and lived simply enough, but a family with its feet firmly planted in the eighteenth century naturally possessed lovely plate and china, and in those easy days they had a gardener and two boys to keep the garden with its wealth of flowers and fruit and vegetables ; an old coachman, Potts, in a livery coat by no means smart, two elderly horses, Sally and Cocoa, and a pony, ' the Little Beast ', who had no intention of being ridden by a small boy.   The rectory, long superseded as such, was a mile from the village, just the right distance for the church bells to have the true romantic appeal—but I forbear to quote Tennyson.   My bachelor uncle and his sisters lived for the parish as my parents did for theirs.   The removal to Oxford followed the death of my younger aunt : the elder, Aunt Margie, declined to die till she had completed her century, which occurred in 1947. Towards the end of her life I once asked her what was the earliest public event she could recall, and she spoke of the Great Exhibition. And when I asked what she remembered of the Crimean War, she said it was getting a letter which complained that one of hers had arrived so damaged by rain that he—' I think it must have been one of the Irbys '—couldn't read it. Cicero if I remember right made a similar complaint 2,000 years earlier, when his brother was serving under Julius Caesar in Gaul. I only know of one Irby with whom we can claim kinship, but as he was the great eccentric of the family I feel tempted to say something about him. I can't remember that I ever saw him, and only know him by repute and by a delightfully sentimental photograph of him with 'Aunt Emily', my grandmother's sister. To us he was ' Uncle Llewy ', to the world the Hon. and Rev. Llewellyn Irby. He was uncle to the Lord Boston whom we knew well in later years at Godalming, where we annually visited Maidenhatch on the south side of the Hogsback to find the wild orchises which he protected so carefully. We could be sure of finding four or five species as well as a dwindling patch of woad, a plant which I cannot remember seeing elsewhere. Uncle Llewy was rector of Whiston, with a lovely church (which I saw for the first time in 1942) some six miles from Northampton. The only one of the family who could write of Whiston life is my elder sister and I have often urged her to do so. For when selfishness and unreasonableness had led to a crisis in their domestic affairs, it was she who would be wired for to clear up the mess. ' They're so stupid ' are the words I always associate with the old man : they represented his views of the rest of the world. One old letter survives which describes the Whiston method of ordering fish for dinner : ' Mervyn (a manservant) went with his cycle by train to Northampton, where he sat at the fishmonger's and waited till a telegram arrived to say what fish was the day's choice. The telegram had been sent from Castle Ashby, the gardener having walked a mile to despatch it. Then Mervyn cycled back six miles with the fish.' But the story I treasure is of the pills. For a slightly disordered digestion the doctor had prescribed two pills, one to be taken after meals, the other at bedtime. No improvement followed, till finally the old man (with my sister), denouncing doctors and chemists alike, entered his carriage, drove to the chemist's in Northampton, deposited the two pill-boxes on the counter and expressed his views. The chemist looked at them and remarked quietly. ' You've changed the lids of the boxes '. This

I understand was the only recorded occasion on which the uncle did not have the last word : he returned to his carriage without it.

Some years ago, lunching with me at 7 Albemarle St., which is close to Brown's Hotel, my sister recalled her last lunch at that place of entertainment—entertainment indeed. The uncle walked into the dining-room followed by Mervyn carrying a light overcoat on one arm, a heavier on the other, to give the old man his choice, while she brought up the rear, carrying a small decanter of whisky.

My memories of Radwinter are not all childish. I revisited the place in the blessed interval between school and college in 1900, when I learnt for the first time how very ' high ' the local churchmanship was : how my uncle escaped disturbance by Kensit I cannot imagine. Cambridge was within cycling distance and I enjoyed my first rather bewildered sight of a place I have come to love only less than Oxford. My last stay at the Rectory was as late as July 1912 during a windfall of extra holiday, when I cycled during a fine interval in a far worse summer than 1956 through that deep unspoilt country to places of beauty like Thaxted and Finchingfield. One afternoon I spent in the company of a docker who used the enforced leisure of the 1912 strike to cover great stretches of the eastern counties on his bicycle. It is strange that in all my visits I never saw Audley End, which was very few miles away. The family had left their mark there, for my uncle Lowndes Bullock, who had been in ' Lord's ' at Winchester in 1864 and must clearly have been a mighty hitter, is recorded to have broken the stable clock.

I saw what had been the rectory a few years ago, a melancholy sight, but at least it was being prepared once more for human habitation. The paddock before the house had been a wartime camp, but already the traces of that were gone. I have revisited in recent years the three rectory gardens that I knew in youth, all places of beauty and civilised life, and all gone to ruin and desolation. Nothing has impressed upon me more the need to re-house the clergy.

CHAPTER II

WINCHESTER

I find it difficult to write about Winchester because I have done so once already : I cannot do it better and can only do it worse. When George Blore's admirable little book, *College in the Eighties*, appeared in 1937, I remarked to him that I hoped someone would soon follow it with *College in the Nineties*. His reply was ' Why not you ? '. It seemed an absurd notion : there were a dozen reasons why not. But the idea stuck in my head, and no one else seemed to be doing a thing which really needed to be done. So one morning in December 1946, when the weather seemed too foul to go to the University Soccer match, in which a former Pageite was playing, I sat down at my table and began to write on the spur of the moment, and once begun I had only to borrow from P. & G. Wells volumes of *The Wykehamist* covering the period in order to go straight ahead. I have never enjoyed any writing so much. When the book, a pamphlet of 62 pages, appeared, it brought a stream of letters of most interesting criticism. Oddly enough, the most copious commentator was a Commoner, not a College man, who was once at the Grange, though he didn't know I had been there. This was L. G. Wickham Legg, Fellow of New College and till lately Editor of the *Dictionary of National Biography*. His notes were so valuable that I later handed them over to the Winchester archives. The little book was written for Wykehamists : anything I write here is for those who cannot have the memories that all Wykehamists, or at least all College men, share in common.

I entered College on my thirteenth birthday, knelt before the aged Warden Lee for formal admission, and found myself placed in Seventh Chamber. That was because my cousin Arthur Grove was head of it, and by good luck Stow—by this time Daddy Stow— was there as a ' second year man '. This meant that he became my ' pater ', whose task it was to teach me my ' notions ' before I came in course as a junior at the end of a fortnight. As he was not very diligent in teaching nor I in learning, I was ' croppled ' in Notion Examinâ and my pater spanked ; and I had to pass a second test a week later. I am glad that neither of my sons let me down, for I had two : it was possible to have a son in one's third year as well as one's second : it depended on what chamber you were in. My first son became Dean of his College at Cambridge and then a Bishop in Australia ; my second became Viceroy of India. It so happened that I never met him, Wavell, in later life except once. But my little book brought me a delightful letter from him and a reproach for not saying how many of our contemporaries gave the service of their lives to India. That certainly ought to have been said, but his own roll was exceptional, with no less than four I.C.S., one educational, and two who served her for many years as soldiers. Wavell himself was a square, silent, self-contained youth who left for Sandhurst and the Boer War at the earliest possible moment, too soon to have taken his rightful place as a leader in College. I have been told that the most original mind among the dons of that day, who taught what there was of an army class, said of him that he never did a stroke of work but that nothing would keep him from the top of the Sandhurst list. And in due course he came out second. He certainly was using his mind at Winchester : the notes to *Other Men's Flowers* are evidence of that. When his son, the lamented Archie John, was getting together information for the use of some future biographer, he asked me if I could tell him why his father was four years in the Corps (not yet of course an O.T.C.) without attaining the rank of lance-corporal. As a matter of fact I could answer that one. When induced by a keen soldier to enter the ranks, he said that as he was going into the army he would have quite enough of drilling later on, so he did the minimum that had to be done. And the minimum of those days, one parade a week, was very little indeed.

But to return. The test in ' notions ' served a double purpose, to see that we knew about people and things that we ought to know and that we were sufficiently grounded in the curious language of the place. No doubt there were far more notions current sixty years ago than there are now, and many of them such lively forcible expressions that I should be sorry to think that in a latter-day Notion Book they might be labelled *obs*—which stands for obsolete, not obscene. Who that has worn a babylonitish would wish to call it a dressing-gown ? Any fool can make a face, but only a Wykehamist can sport a duck. And often we were using good old English words really obsolete elsewhere, such as to brock (badger or bully), or poser (examiner), or watching out, for fielding at cricket—a term I recently met in Gilbert White of Selborne.

So, as I have said, when the fortnight was up, ' junior sweat ' began. The word ' fagging ' was not in use : it would have been

reprehended as a ' bad notion '. It began too at 6.15 a.m. (First
Peal) in all but a few weeks of winter, when ' junior in chambers '
left his bed, had his cold bidet (bath) on the cold lead floor, and
filled baths in readiness for others. I need hardly say there were
no bathrooms in the modern sense : till I became an usher I had
never inhabited a house that had one, except the Grange. The
four parsonages I knew best had many amenities, but none of them
a fixed bath, nor yet electric light.

At 6.25 calling began and continued at five minute intervals
till 6.50. The junior went round to each bed and announced ' five
past half-hour ' or whatever it was, and everyone below Sixth Book
had to get up and go to his bath promptly at the prescribed time,
to avoid crowding. For more than one chamber used each bidet-
room, and I can only remember one boy who was excused his cold
splash or shower on grounds of health. In me it formed a habit
which for much of the year I still enjoy. At 6.45 he had to back up
(shout) ' Three Quarters ', and the last call was five minutes later.
But he also had to light the miniature faggot, known as Bill-Brighter,
which gave a pleasant little blaze for a few minutes, but served no
other purpose that I can see. ' Morning Lines ' were at 7, followed
by Chapel, so a junior had been up for at least two hours before he
had breakfast. I believe there was tea in Hall before 7, but I
don't know who went to drink it.

Other duties of a junior were washing up tea and cocoa cups,
always in cold water, and lighting bedroom fires in the interval
between toy-time (preparation) and the brief evening prayers in
Chapel at 9. The fire of course was laid in advance by the loyal
and friendly ' sweaters ' who served us, generally for most of a
life-time. But some guidance to an incompetent child would
have been a good thing. There was no supplementary store of
newspaper for use if the fire proved recalcitrant, and I remember
using up sheet after sheet of the beautiful paper known as John
Des without even knowing that paper used to light a fire should be
crumpled. This paper was named from the first mathematical
master to be appointed (in 1834), John Desborough Walford,
brother of that Oliver Walford, whose name, or rather nickname, is
perpetuated in Verites at Charterhouse. I only gave up using this
paper some fifty years later. Every junior was also valet (pronounced
as an English word, please) to a prefect, carrying up his books
in the evening and down in the morning, and keeping his washing-
stool (table) tidy. And in his second year a junior might be ' writer '
to one of the five ' officers '. I had the good fortune to be writer

to H. T. Baker, Prefect of Hall, a most distinguished scholar and a Liberal politician who gave up office and his career when his chief, Asquith, was displaced by Lloyd-George. Later he was Warden of Winchester, a very high honour. It was a hard life but a most enjoyable one, and I cannot remember any prefect who used his authority vexatiously to make it harder. But with chalky cold water, I have an abiding sympathy with those who had chilblains. We had a pretence of a hot bath once a week, when a Sixth Book inferior, i.e. a member of the lower division of the Sixth, carried a ' toe-pan boiler ', heated on the chamber fire, into bidet room and emptied it into one of the saucer baths, where it was at most an inch deep and was cold in a minute or so. It was a notion that the bearer should carry the heavy vessel in one hand. Hot water was laid on the year after I left, and it presumably became less difficult to be clean.

Some years ago a disgruntled Old Carthusian attributed to a lack of studies the intellectual inferiority which he professed to find in Carthusians as compared with Wykehamists and Marlburians. Inquiry showed that his house at Charterhouse was better provided with studies than Marlborough, while at Winchester there were no studies at all. We lived by day in four chambers and slept by night in seven, and every ' roll ' was represented in each from senior prefect to first year junior. We had not even the privacy of cubicles. Prefects had their washing-stools, tables with bookshelves adjacent, sometimes fitting pleasantly into a window recess, while the rest occupied ' toys '. These were mostly ' horse-boxes '—a desk with partitions behind and before, and cupboard and bookshelves at the side : they gave one a delightful sense of comfort and privacy. College provided one ' tolly ' (candle) a day, but most found it advisable to procure a second at their own charges. Electric light arrived my last year, to me of all modern conveniences the most indispensable. Only one of the four chambers, and that the least attractive, had a coal fire. The other three were warmed by a daily ration of faggots. While they lasted they gave a glorious blaze, with a useful little secondary conflagration of ' backings-up ', i.e. unburnt ends, a bit later. A whiff of wood smoke, like the smell of lime trees in flower, may at any moment carry me back to Winchester.

The feeding was unquestionably bad, and we were too dependent on ' cargoes ' from home and on School Shop. But in one matter I must supplement *College in the Nineties*. Till 1904 College still brewed its own beer, and the spicy breezes were wafted at brewing

time into our chamber windows.   But very few of us were educated
to beer or attempted to acquire the taste, and we assumed no doubt
that College swipes was as bad as College food.   I now know what
we missed.   I have a long letter from Sir Robert Ensor, who comes
nearer to omniscience than anyone known to me, in praise of the
excellence and wholesomeness of College beer, ' the real drink of
old England before tea and coffee came in '.   There was no limit
to the amount supplied, but when ' vulgar brewer's stuff was
substituted the whole system had to be altered, and free beer came
to an end '.   And I am left with one more regret for wasted chances.
Brewery was then abandoned to ignoble uses, and it was many years
before Sir Herbert Baker converted it into the most beautiful of
libraries.

I cannot write here of the work.   That it was predominantly
classical goes without saying, and the liberal system which makes
it possible for almost anyone to study almost anything belongs to a
much later period.   Half-rems (half-holidays) were Tuesday and
Thursday.   On Saturday we still had a chapel service at 5.30 after
an hour ' up to books '.   Thursday in the summer (Cloister Time)
was a glorious day.   We did not go up to books after breakfast
at all : we had two hours of ' Books Chambers ', writing tasks or
reading, and then, if not required for cricket, were free till toy-time
at 7.30 to be as idle or as energetic, and in any case as free, as we
chose.

My career in College was very undistinguished, for besides
silliness and shyness which one might hope to outgrow, I suffered
from the two curses of mathematics and scarlet fever.   In almost
every Division below Sixth Book a weekly order (called cuse) was
produced, while the marks of the Mathematical and French—or
later German—divisions were only added in the final order at the
end of the Half.   In cuse I cannot remember ever being lower than
third and was often first.   Mediocre French did me little harm,
but the mathematical marks robbed me of promotion more than
once : in those days classes did not move up almost bodily : I
remember getting the last place for promotion in July 1895 from
eighth.   Yet to be completely without the mathematical faculty
does not necessarily make a fool.   Readers of that delightful book,
The Puppet Show of Memory, may remember how Maurice Baring's
career was imperilled by a like infirmity.   Then on Easter Eve in
1896 I came out with scarlet fever, a formidable disease in those
days, with a minimum of six weeks confinement, which I spent
not unpleasantly in my old nursery, in the charge of the kindest of

nurses, with a sheet steeped in carbolic draped over the door and no visitors but my father and the doctor. Then later, as it was the year of the Gloucester smallpox epidemic, it was thought a good moment to vaccinate me, and the thing took only too well. My arm produced what the authorities called proud flesh, to my no small discomfort : and then, perhaps as the result of a chill, I finished up with a quinsy. It was well into July before I was set at liberty. I had missed a whole golden summer term. But that month at least gave me my first visit to Charterhouse. My father took me there on Old Carthusian day, and we lunched with the Haig Browns. Queen Victoria's Carthusian grandson, Prince Albert of Schleswig-Holstein, was playing in the match and lunched at Saunderites, where Mrs. Haig Brown disposed of a superfluous small boy by appointing him page to His Highness : as such I walked in at the tail of the procession.

A fortnight before the end of the next term—Short Half as we called it—a week after my confirmation by Randall Davidson, Bishop of Winton, I started a bad sore throat. It was scarlet fever all over again, not without complications. I spent a rather miserable holiday in Sanatorium, not as good a place as home for incarceration, and missed half the following term, Common Time. Where competition was so severe, there might have been no recovery from all this. I had only five terms in Sixth Book, Senior Division, where worse scholars but better all-rounders sometimes had three years. But here came a great piece of good fortune. Old ' Dick ', the Rev. George Richardson, who had been Second Master since 1873, resigned in July 1899 and was succeeded in College by Monty Rendall. If I owed nothing to Rendall but the revelation of Italian art that would be debt enough. But he saw that I was a good deal better than my place and took me at once, out of my turn, into his own compos division—and he was far the best teacher in that line that I have known. I caught fire, and after a time, Fearon, the Headmaster, could write to my father that he had never known a boy come on so fast ; and when I left, Rendall noted that in ' Goddard ', the formidable July examination, I was ' in unprepared work, practically second '. And that meant above all my own roll, for the first two in the list were really outstanding scholars of the 1895 vintage with still a year to go. Is it surprising if I worshipped Monty ?

George Ridding, our ' Second Founder ', Headmaster from 1867 to 1894, when he left to become the first Bishop of Southwell, had ordained that every don should teach one subject outside his

regular range.   Charles Griffith, who taught the vitally important
division just below Sixth Book, chose Geology, and taught it for
the rest of his long, too long, career.   I enjoyed the subject, and,
in illustrating my notebooks, found the only encouragement to
draw that I have had since the age of seven.   It so happened that
it was this year (1897) in which we left Colchester for Littlemore,
and the Oxford country is very good ground for the geologist :
so is the chalk round Winchester.   So for two years or so, before in
our new home we fell into the routine of cricket and tennis, I had
an admirable hobby which carried me about three counties on my
bicycle, getting to know country I should not otherwise have known,
and on rare visits to London gloating over the cases in the Natural
History Museum as eagerly as later on I did in the V. and A. next
door.   In 1914 I left my collection on loan in ' Corridor ' at
Bradfield College and what became of it I cannot say ; efforts to
unearth it in the thirties failed.   It is a pity, for if most of it was
commonplace enough, there were some specimens of cretaceous
echinoids hardly, I think, to be surpassed at South Kensington.
The Griff was always pleased when a boy shared his interests and
he was my first friend among the dons, who took me and a more
scientific geologist, Conor O'Brien, the circumnavigator, on delightful expeditions to the Isle of Wight and elsewhere.   Further, at
the back of his house, Norman Mede, was a good tennis lawn, and
his step-daughters were players above the average.   And when it
appeared that I was above the average too, I was invited into higher
circles and played on the Bursar's court.   The Bursar's son,
Walter Kirby, had played for Oxford in his time, and I once found
myself a fourth with three half-blues, one of them the famous
Corinthian, W. N. Cobbold, ' prince of dribblers '.

Which brings me to the inevitable subject of games.   The
nineties were a decade in which, without any loss of intellectual
standards, College had greater success in games than at any other
time.   For the purposes of Winchester football, played throughout
Short Half, the seventy of College were matched against the four
houses of Commoners, and the five which without explanation I
may call O.T.H.   Yet in these ten years College won more matches
than they lost, only two less than Commoners and nine more than
Houses.   This too was the time when Soccer, played after
Christmas, first took root.   Here, as was usual in house matches,
College was divided into two, East and West.   The House Cup
was played for first in 1896, and till 1900 one or other College team
won it every time, and twice East and West met in the final.   The

second time was in 1899, and I have a photograph of the two elevens. There were not yet enough decent soccer players to go round and some of us were deplorably bad—as I was. Of the twenty-two, one went to Woolwich, first in and first out, and one deviated to Cambridge, where he took a ' one-one ' in the Classical Tripos : the other twenty proceeded to Oxford, only two of them as commoners, and of these at least nine represented the University in some form of sport, even if they did not all actually achieve a blue. It seems a good record for two teams of scholars. Indeed in every form of sport except the rather exclusive game of rackets and the young but thriving golf club, College took their full share. They had one or more representatives in Lord's every year except 1894. College East won the House Cricket Cup in 1898 and it was my own fault that I was not in the team. In a previous round I made 0 and missed an easy catch and deservedly lost my place. Generally speaking I made plenty of cheerful runs, but as a bad, disgracefully bad, fielder I could hardly enter the best company. And I was never regarded as a bowler at all : in six years at Winchester I took two wickets, forty-three years later in the last match I ever played I took nine. Indeed I was only once put on to bowl in a match and that was near the end of my last term when, ' to oblige ', I was filling a gap in a College West team that was short of a man. But the occasion and its distant sequel live in memory. There was a young batsman on the other side, of the highest promise, who came it to bat just when I came on to bowl, and I still can see the ball that whipped across to hit his middle stump before he had scored. Two years later, on the day he left school, I went down to Southampton to see him play in his first match for Hampshire against Surrey and in 1914 he headed the first class averages. Many years afterwards I was bowling for Brooke Hall against a team from Sandhurst, when a middle-aged man came in, lame from a war wound. I at once bowled him (not intentionally !) a full pitch to leg which he hit as such things are hit. But short leg's hand shot out and the ball went no further. I don't think my friend J. D. Bennett (another Wykehamist) would have claimed to be a Lock or a Stewart : it was one of those things which make cricket a matter of everlasting surprises. So I had the great man's wicket twice for no runs, once deservedly and once not : for when I looked in the score book afterwards I read the name, Col. A. C. Johnston.

Two other matters which I cannot wholly omit are Chapel and Music : they come near to being the same thing. It must be difficult for a generation which has great music available on wireless or gramophone every day of the week to realize how musically benighted the Victorian school was. Such music as we had was almost purely vocal. Glee Club, conducted by a housemaster who was the father of Francis and Geoffrey Toye, and much given (I am glad to say) to the singing of Handel, gave the two school concerts of the year. Apart from these I recall only one concert in six years. Otherwise all music to be heard was in Chapel, where we had three full choral services every Sunday at 9, 11 and 5. Those who attended the early service, as a good many did, could hardly have spent less than four hours in Chapel. We had, one might say, everything possible : full psalms of course, choral settings of the canticles, sung litany and ante-communion service, anthem, and two sermons. As my voice was slow to break and quick in beginning to return, I was in choir for most of my six years, and because I enjoyed the music I did not find the services too long. No doubt I had a real music hunger, for when I was not in choir, which practised on Friday evenings during toy-time, as soon as I heard the anthem begin I used to ' put up a roll ' and go to listen outside. But one term of Magdalen and New College was enough to teach one how crude Winchester singing was. There was no orchestra till in my last year a keen and ambitious Commoner got together a little group who practised assiduously and were actually allowed to perform a homely little piece in the July concert of 1900. In that concert I was required to sing the small bass solo in Mozart's *Splendente te, Deus.* I have never heard the little work again, but am humbly glad to have had that early introduction to the beloved composer. The new century brought, in Dr Sweeting, the first musical director, a trained musician and an educated man, and that was the beginning of a new musical life. And what directors Winchester has had since ! Sir George Dyson, Sydney Watson, Henry Havergal, and now Christopher Cowan.

I came a year too late for the Quingentenary celebrations of 1893, but enjoyed those of the Diamond Jubilee in 1897, when I was privileged to witness the great Naval Review from the deck of H.M.S. *Alexandra*, in which my mother's cousin Cresswell Eyres (afterwards Admiral) was serving. In that same term Memorial Building was opened, that is, the Museum and Art Gallery, which meant a real renaissance to me. I used them constantly, both as a geologist and an incipient art-lover. I must tell the story of my prize fossil—bought I regret to say in the first instance, not excavated by myself, but the men in the great chalk cutting at Micheldever working six days a week had advantages over a boy who might go there once in three months. Anyhow I acquired a lovely specimen of the Echinus *Cidaris Clavigera*, still half imbedded in chalk but obviously of rare size and perfection. My fellow geologist Conor O'Brien, whom I have referred to elsewhere as the circumnavigator, had wonderful hands : did he not on one occasion, having a puncture, remove the tyre with two pieces of stick and mend it with paper and gum off a fir tree ? He undertook to complete the cleaning of the treasure and to photograph it : but unfortunately he began by dropping it on the tiled floor. Or perhaps I should not have said unfortunately, for from inside the ruin emerged most of the teeth and plates of the apical disk (if I may use a technicality) previously invisible, and the last state of that specimen was a great deal better than the first. I deeply regret the loss of it.

But I found my real inspiration on the other side of the building, in the great wall cases of autotypes (as they were then called) of the great masters of painting. Here Rendall would often be found discoursing on a Sunday morning after Chapel, and I was generally there to look and listen. For some reason Correggio was my first love, and how many hours I spent poring over Claude Phillips's *Titian* I would not venture to guess. One very small repayment I was allowed to make. Once when I came on a visit during my last year at Oxford, Rendall showed me a recent acquisition, some specimen lantern slides of Old Masters, and asked if I would like to present some to Museum. So I gave a set of Botticelli slides chosen by him, and believe they were the foundation of his collection. Three or four years earlier I would hardly have believed that anyone who professed to like Botticelli could be sincere.

The Wallace Collection was opened in my last term and I remember cutting out all that the newspapers had to say about it, and in 1900 there were a good many more civilized dailies than in 1957. And as soon as the holidays arrived and the pang of parting —and it was a pang—was over, I was allowed to go to London to see it. I spent a few days with a cousin in the Temple, the only time I have lodged in that romantic quarter. I gave most of my time to Hertford House, where I made acquaintance with Watteau and Fragonard, and such treasures as The Lady with a Fan, and The Laughing Cavalier, and Kitty Fisher, still to me one of the most fascinating of Sir Joshua's female portraits. With the National Gallery I was already pretty well acquainted, far smaller

c

in area in those days and far more crowded, packed rather than hung with pictures, like those minor Italian galleries where the whole wall is a jigsaw puzzle of frames rising almost to the ceiling. If a lover of our galleries and museums could see them as they were sixty years ago he would realise how much we have to be thankful for now.

But I have become an Old Wykehamist before my time : there are two events which cannot go unrecorded.

My father was now turned sixty, had been nearly thirty years in his Colchester parish, and felt the need of change and relief. In 1896 he came near to accepting the living of Ardleigh, a few miles away, in which case it would have been an exchange, since it was from Ardleigh that our friend Greville Hales came to succeed him at St. Mary's. In 1956 I found myself the guest of my friends James and Margaret Farmiloe in the Vicarage which had so nearly been my home. Some were surprised that my father should leave the diocese of St. Albans, in which he was an honorary canon and the whole of his ministry had been passed, but no doubt it was the magic of Oxford and the name of Newman which drew him to Littlemore. He hoped for lighter work in his old age, but that he hardly found, and I am ashamed to think how little help I ever gave him. When I came home for the summer holidays of 1897 I found the family installed in the pleasant vicarage which was our home for nine years.

Secondly, there was the question what should be done with me when I left school. The average level of our roll was high, much higher than the 1893 vintage, though not equal to that of 1895, which was outstanding ; and there were more presentable candidates than could possibly be taken by New College. So I welcomed the suggestion that I should sit for my father's college, Christ Church. I thoroughly enjoyed my November days in Oxford, staying with my Wykehamist uncle Lowndes Bullock, who had returned from a long career in the East to become Professor of Chinese ; and in due course my name appeared first on the list. And if I ever enjoyed idleness it was during the closing weeks of that Short Half, while the rest of Senior Div. were engaged in the laborious New College exam, for which the whole division sat, not the candidates alone.

My roll numbered fourteen, of whom I find that only six now survive : after all none of us is less than seventy-six years old. The war of 1914 took only two, but those I should call two of the three best—W. R. H. Merriman, the ideal Civil Servant, and

Geoffrey Smith the zoologist, whom I have heard one qualified to speak call our greatest single loss of all that the war claimed.

It is quite certain that the nineties were a golden age for College, less tough than the decade which followed, despite the rosy glow in which my dear friend Spencer Leeson sees it in the little book that is a sequel to mine. I am thankful to have been there in Victorian days, before College became a breeding ground of the left-wing intelligentsia, in days when the fees of a Commoner were £120 and of a College man £21, and when a strawberry mash cost fourpence, or sixpence if you felt bulky. That was Winchester language for rich, and the corresponding term for hard up was brum—a much more familiar word to us ! I use them deliberately. Perhaps because of the little book I wrote ten years ago, my memory is surprisingly well-stored, and in thinking of the Winchester of the past it comes natural to me to use its language.

CHAPTER III

OXFORD

A summer holiday that extended into October was indeed a delight. The only weak spot was that I had not yet passed the petty examination which gods call Responsions and men Smalls, and without that I could not go into residence at Oxford. The days of the School Certificate were not yet, but once in three years the upper divisions at Winchester took what we called Certificate, without qualification, which opened the necessary door. This came round in 1899 and I was ploughed in Mathematics (as was R. W. Livingstone) and a year later had to disturb the pleasant idleness of August by cycling over to Forest Hill, the village where John Milton once found a wife, to do sums with the Vicar. Fortunately this served the purpose, but by the narrowest margin. That holiday gave me my penultimate visit to Radwinter, and my first to Walsingham Abbey, where another great-aunt lived with her son Henry Lee-Warner, another great eccentric. It was a thrill to stay in a spacious country house with the lofty arch of the ruined abbey on the lawn and a Van Dyck of Charles I over the drawing-room mantelpiece, and I only learnt later how desperately tight were the family finances. My cousin Henry dined with the party in a dressing gown which I understand to have covered a kilt, but otherwise lived his own life, lunching at 4, settling down to a book towards midnight and going to bed some time in the small hours. There were other Lee-Warners in that part of Norfolk, and the Rev. James of Fakenham and Henry of Walsingham had a limited appreciation of each other. Each in talking to me of the other had recourse to a Latin poet : the one quoted *Impiger iracundus inexorabilis* from Horace, the other Virgil's *Monstrum horrendum informe ingens*. That of course was my cousin Henry, a huge man indeed. Readers of that enchanting book, *A Victorian Childhood*, will meet him (with other cousins of mine, Halls and Headlams) as I never saw him, in the red velvet jacket and knee-breeches, red stockings and scarlet slippers, which apparently he wore when he dined from home. Like me he was a Christ Church man and like me an inadequate mathematician, in days when that subject could haunt one even after matriculation. I understand that he never took a degree because rule of three (whatever that was) defeated him. It was at Walsingham that I first met that excellent and undervalued wine Marsala : one small glass was the ration at dessert and I never saw any other wine in the house.

October arrived and I went into residence at Christ Church. Francis Paget was still Dean, and in my first term the universally loved Mrs Paget died. In the following summer Paget became Bishop of Oxford, and Tommy Strong succeeded to the Deanery. As senior scholar I had free choice of rooms, and my brother, who finished in that summer, had applied for ' drawing-rooms ', i.e. first floor, with a balcony, in Meadow Buildings, the more studious and less aristocratic part of the College. In those spacious days I had, subject to good behaviour, security of tenure for three years, so it was worth having the rooms redecorated and the furniture, taken over at a valuation, re-covered. My scholarship was worth £80, a Winchester Exhibition £40, and my father allowed me £100. My brother had done well enough on £200, and in those days £20 went a long way. With my home only three miles distant I had no travelling expenses : it generally meant a half-crown cab with my ever-serviceable sister inside it, while I rode my bicycle. I don't think I ever occupied quarters that I enjoyed so much. To wake in the morning and hear the scout's boy lighting the fire, and not get up to keep a chapel but go to sleep again, ministered only too much to complacency. Many years later a furious young socialist, himself an Oxonian, who came to preach at Charterhouse, said to me that there was nothing like Oxford (or Cambridge) to breed selfishness : and certainly one was in danger of taking the good things of life too much for granted.

For some ten or twelve years I kept a diary, beginning I believe in 1899, though the earliest surviving volume covers the year 1902. I have recently read through what remains of it for the first time since it was written, and truth to tell have found the Oxford years extremely dull reading—a factual record of work done, games played, music heard and social events. To read it has been a rather humiliating experience : if I ever thought of anything beyond the daily round I find no evidence of it. One thing that did impress me in the record was the evidence of endless hospitality. I walked or cycled out to Littlemore almost every Sunday, generally taking Wykehamists or House men with me, and that did not exhaust the number of young Oxonians I met in that most hospitable of homes. For Eights Week and Commem there were likely to be decorative young women staying there as well.

In College the commonest time for entertaining was breakfast, a portentous meal of three courses, usually fish, bacon and eggs, and omelette.   But if the guests were ladies it would of course be afternoon tea, and grateful memory must pay tribute to the bread-and-butter and jam sandwiches sent over from the J.C.R.   Living as I did on the fringe of Oxford and being a very active member of the Parks Club—of which more hereafter—I knew a great many dons and their wives, and in Eights Week a tea party would some-times run into double figures, which my pleasant balcony helped me to accommodate.   But I liked best to entertain a friend or two at dinner.   We had in Hall an excellent guest table, next the fireplace on the south side, and I cannot remember that the dinner cost more than half-a-crown.   I made coffee for some of my neighbours most nights after dinner, for my coffee was better than theirs—my only culinary art.

In general we lived simply enough.   We had all meals in our rooms except dinner, and I never ate meat for lunch, unless it was a sandwich in the J.C.R.   My first headmaster, Gray of Bradfield, who loved rhetoric, would warn scholarship candidates not to ' imbibe the sherry of their emancipated schoolfellows ' ; but I cannot remember ever seeing a bottle of sherry in an undergraduate's room.   When we dined with our tutors they did us extremely well, but there were no alcoholic preliminaries.   I never possessed any wine.   For luncheon parties claret cup from the kitchen served in summer, mulled claret in winter.   It is strange that convention should require the offering of sherry when it costs about £1 a bottle, when we felt no need of it at 3/6.   That too I fancy was the price of whisky, which I did keep : also sometimes *crème de menthe*.

My acquaintance among married dons involved a good deal of Sunday afternoon calling, with bowler hat in winter and straw in summer : we did not yet go about bare-headed.   The straw hat was universal, and I was recently surprised to realize from a photo-graph that as late as 1914 it was still the commonest summer headgear even in London.   I never heard the derisive term ' gent's boater ' till years later than that.   It was an Oxford of absurd little horse-trams and streets never crowded, though in winter they might be a sheet of greasy mud.   Cowley and Headington were villages.

On my staircase I found Eric Maclagan, now in his third year, a floor above me.   I had known him well at Winchester, when for one half we sat together at the top of a division taken by a much liked and respected don whose foible was the use of French words and phrases. I remember him asking why we always smiled when he spoke French. I could not reply that though I knew little French I could tell a thoroughly British accent. Maclagan was passing through a very aesthetic phase and gave little hint of his future eminence as Director of the V. and A., though he already knew a great deal about art, and I am grateful for what he taught me. Thirty-three years later I induced him to give a course of lectures at Charterhouse : I found him delightful company, and the lectures were masterly. On the top floor, in ' garrets ', were two freshmen, Leonard Bennett and Okey Belfour, who soon became my friends and are my friends to-day. Both were consistently hard workers and I wish I had emulated their consistency.

At the beginning of my second year, October 1901, there was a new name on the door opposite mine, Mr C. R. Stone, a first year scholar from Eton. My earliest memory is of listening outside the door to a voice singing *Plaisir d'Amour*. But I spent a good deal more time inside the door than outside it : indeed I doubt if there was any place where I wasted more time more pleasantly in the course of the next two years. It became common form for some of us to drop in towards midnight and drink tea and eat the admirable Opera Wafers (do they still exist ?) which he was alleged to order from the J.C.R. by the dozen boxes at a time. Sometimes when his friends Tom Spring-Rice and Timmy Jekyll came in from Balliol, we had a quorum, or company, to go through a Gilbert and Sullivan opera almost from cover to cover. For Christopher Stone rightly fancied himself as a soprano, and his baritone voice was light and high enough to manage a tenor as well. His singing had a wonderful charm, like Angela Thirkell's Lord Silverbridge, ' with the kind of heart-rending voice that two singing lessons infallibly ruin '. A less military man one could scarcely conceive, but when after a gap of some years I met him again at his home near Steyning in Sussex, he had D.S.O., M.C. after his name. And in the early days of the B.B.C. his voice must have been as well known as any in England.

The scholars of my year were not a very scholarly nor for the most part a very attractive lot, and the two Westminsters who were my friends did not read Greats. I should have been in much better company with those of the next year. The three outstanding scholars of my time were all Westminsters : M. L. Gwyer, afterwards the first Chief Justice of India ; H. L. Henderson, for many years a tutor at New College ; and Wilfred Greene, who became

Master of the Rolls.   He was two years junior to me, but I knew him pretty well and liked him immensely.   Afterwards I scarcely saw him till I met him in 1947 as President of the Classical Association, when I found him just as natural and charming as fifty years earlier.   All these men were pupils of the great John Sargeaunt, the centenary of whose birth on August 12 1957 was marked by a leader in *The Times*, an extraordinary honour for an assistant master. I am not sure that his death in March 1922 did not produce a leader too.   I may have occasion to mention him again.

It was the custom of the House in those days to offer annually two scholarships to I.C.S. Probationers for the year in which they had to qualify in the necessary Eastern languages.   They were usually, or always, graduates of Scottish Universities, and others tended to follow the scholars to Christ Church.   By some chance or other I was drawn into their company, and it was no doubt good for me to be with men—some of them a bit uncouth—four or five years older than myself.   But such a friendship can hardly go very deep, and there was only one of them of whom I heard again after they had departed for India.

The work of my first two years was a delight, something I could do with fullest zest.   All scholars took a four year course for granted, with Honour Mods (First Public Examination) in the fifth term, leaving seven for finals.   During my first vacation I took on an extra task and wrote for the Chancellor's Latin Verse prize.   The subject, *Mycenae*, was a congenial one, and at the beginning of the Summer Term I was told that I had been placed second to Sir Richard Livingstone (as he now is).   It brought £5 from my father, and I acquired the Temple Shakespeare in the good leather binding of those days, still sound after nearly sixty years' use, and a better text than the later edition.   At the beginning of our second year we had ' Collections ' on a big scale, with a £40 prize that was generally divided between two.   But I suppose my papers were the best, for it was all given to me, a boon indeed, since it made my first visit to Italy possible after Mods in the following spring.   When the Mods list appeared and my tutor, Sidney Owen, was told that I had got one of the two best Firsts of the year, it was decided to send me in for the Hertford, the Latin scholarship open to men in their first two years.   It was really too late to do much in the way of preparation, but I enjoyed the exam as usual, though quite out of my depth in the general paper.   There I was reduced to writing an essay on an author of whom I had never read a page—nor have I done so yet !   An examiner wrote to me that I had been placed sixth, and one of the three had voted for giving me an hon. mention, but I am quite sure I had not deserved it. I had welcomed the task as postponing the evil day of Greats, for I had never supposed that I should be anything but a fool at philosophy. But my delayed start was not a good thing, for it put me behindhand, and ever afterwards I was working not only against the grain but against the clock. Greats needs all of seven terms and two Long Vacations.

So far as Greats consisted in reading Latin and Greek historians I was quite happy, though the complete exclusion of poetry was a privation : I could hardly fail to enjoy Herodotus and Thucydides, Cicero's Letters and Tacitus, though when it came to treating them as a serious study of ancient history I was at best mediocre. And on the other side, if I hated Aristotle I could love Plato, while understanding the one just as little as the other. Yet I appreciated my philosophy tutors much more than my historians. They soon discovered that modern philosophy meant as little to me as mathematics. Professor J. A. Stewart, officially my tutor, with his beautiful old Scottish face and beautiful Scottish speech, after a few words of comment on my thin and barren essays would often turn to poetry or some more congenial subject of discourse. H. W. Blunt, a far abler man, frankly advised me not to read modern philosophers, but to make the most of my ability ' to translate Greek without understanding it '. So Bacon, because I had to read him in Latin, was the latest author with whom I could make contact at all. I revered both these men, and Stewart I loved. He too was a lover of Cicero's Letters, and thirty years later I dedicated the appropriate book to him, just too late for him to read it : I found the copy on the little table by the armchair from which he had retired to bed for the last time. Both men were full of kindness and gave me credit for what I could do instead of scorning me for what I couldn't. A First in Greats is a really formidable thing : of our excellent Charterhouse scholars I can't think of more than half a dozen who achieved it ; so I had every reason to be thankful for a good safe second. If my philosophy and logic papers were more than mediocre, in translation I was informally given to understand that only one man did better.

It must not be thought that I underestimate Greats, which for those who are fitted for it I believe to be the finest of schools ; but unless a man has some stomach for philosophy, while wishing to take his degree in classics, he might think seriously of the claims of Cambridge.

The Summer Term of 1903 was my last term in College and, before it ended, Mr Turner of Gillman's came to photograph my my room, and wonderfully pleasant it looks to-day. It must be almost impossible for any undergraduate's room to be worth photographing now. Mine, it is true, contained too many pictures and too much china, but I always kept it scrupulously tidy and everything in it had a meaning for me. Rather out of focus on the corner cupboard is the bust that was in those days called Clytie, from an obscure lady in Ovid's *Metamorphoses* : but she is more beautiful under her real name as Antonia, daughter of Mark Antony and mother of the Emperor Claudius. I must have made her acquaintance through the effusion on the second page of *Trilby*, so wallowing in sentiment that I am rather ashamed once to have known it by heart. I hope the lady is known to many. To meet her, you have only to enter the British Museum and turn to the left.

For my fourth year I moved into digs in the Old Palace, the residence of Bishop King, first Bishop of Oxford, a little lower down St. Old's (St. Aldate's), rooms I had secured a good two years ahead. It was a potentially fine house, shamefully disfigured by an ignoble sweet-shop stuck onto its corner, now for many years, with its dignity restored, the Roman Catholic equivalent in Oxford of the Anglican Pusey House. Monsignor Knox presided there formerly and now it is Monsignor Elwes. I shared my quarters with Okey Belfour, not only the best of companions but an intensely hard worker at his subject, in which he early showed the rare gift for languages and comparative philology which made him, after some miserable years wasted on the Stock Exchange, a professor at the age of 26. He concerned himself with the arrangements not at all—except once. I was passing through a phase of ridiculous pedantry about sugar, a theory that it should be left out of cooking and added later by those who required it. My landlady applied this to the first rhubarb of the year. On tasting it Okey fell off his chair, rolled the length of the room and back again, sprang up and inverted the sugar bowl into the dish. I soon recanted this folly, but if at my mother's table, and my sister's and my wife's, the milk puddings have always been delicious, it is because in that matter I, and my family, have been right. I must record that in digs, without neighbours to drop in at any moment, I found work a great deal easier to do.

I suppose that if one repeated one's life one would also repeat one's follies. But at least I now realize that had I worked regularly for six hours I need never have worked for nine, and that if the chief session of the day had ended at 1 p.m. it need never have ended at 1 a.m. or later. And if one goes to bed unwholesomely late at night, one is not likely to be up in good time in the morning. On the whole, vastly as I enjoyed my Oxford years, I would not claim to have made the most of them. I only once listened to a University sermon, and only once attended a debate at the Union, when Lord Hugh Cecil was the principal orator. Yet it was a period of notable speakers, and I don't think they took themselves quite so seriously as undergraduate debaters too often have done since. And though I was a regular chapel-goer, it was often to Magdalen and New College that I repaired, ' not for the doctrine but the music there '. And I joined none of the Debating or Play-reading societies, which might have done something to enlarge my mind.

It would be a strange thing if a son of Oxford, and loving the place as I do, were to regret having taken his degree there. But in fact for purposes of academic distinction I was far better suited to the Cambridge type of scholarship, and (with compensating advantages in term) it was a disadvantage to have my home only three miles away. It meant insufficient change from the Thames Valley climate and, in vacation, an almost daily habit of drifting into Oxford and spending hours in the Union or browsing, some-times expensively, in bookshops or antique shops or (better) in the Ashmolean—though that was far from being the wonderful treasure house that it is now. But heaven forbid that I should seem ungrateful to Oxford for all that it gave me, and has given me ever since.

Many Oxonians look back with special pleasure to the reading parties of their undergraduate days. That good thing never came to me till my very last vacation before Greats, in April 1904. Then I went down to West Malvern and joined a group of third year men, two of them greatly superior to anyone of my year. If I had been more in contact with the massive brain of John Murray and the lively wit of ' Sonners '—I decline to give any other name to so well-known a Principal of Brasenose—I might have been convinced that it is possible for a young man to be interested in philosophy. Two memories stand out. One is of a walk with R. H. Charles, later a colleague of John Murray at Exeter, when we came on a clearing in a wood so breathlessly lovely with gorse and blackthorn and violets that the vision of it is with me yet. The other is of walking over the hills to Great Malvern, while the rest were studying humanity at the Colwall races, to hear a young violinist named Kreisler. The hall was half full, and it throws a light on provincial musical education fifty years ago that every time the artist lowered his instrument the audience began to applaud. It was forty-five years before I saw Malvern again : since then I have visited it annually.

I had arrived at Oxford with an eager appetite for music and a profound ignorance of it. It sounds a strange thing to say, but one could actually hear more music performed in the Oxford of those days than one can now. For the Musical Club, nearly all professional, with a meeting every Tuesday in the room at the back of Rowell's, the jeweller, which afterwards became the Friends' Meeting House, had not yet amalgamated with the Musical Union, which used the famous Holywell Music Room. I was a member of the Club but never of the Union. And the admirable Balliol concerts then took place every Sunday in term. Further, in my second year the coming of H. P. Allen to New College brought new life to Oxford music. I heard the first Oxford performance of the B Minor Mass in February 1904, an overwhelming experience ; but if I had been better advised I might have sung in it. As it was the only time I contributed my quota of noise was when six or eight of us were got together to provide a chorus for Plunket Greene when he sang Stanford's new *Songs of the Sea* at the Club. It is the only time I was rehearsed by Allen, though I knew and revered and laughed at him for many years. I owed much to a delightful and critical friend from Dublin, J. E. Geoghegan, who had real knowledge of music. He took me to a memorial concert after Queen Victoria's death, my first visit to the old Queen's Hall and my first hearing of Beethoven's Violin Concerto, which long remained my favourite work. It was played by Ysaye, who then, I suppose, occupied the place of the first violinist in Europe between Joachim and Kreisler. Later my friend took me to hear the Saxe-Meiningen Orchestra, under Steinbach, when I was vaguely conscious that I was hearing something better than I had ever heard before, but could hardly anticipate the joy that Brahms's Third Symphony and the Enigma Variations, then three or four years old, would be to me half a century later. In those days we could still hear old Joachim (Uncle Joe) with his Quartet, and at ballad or ' celebrity ' concerts not only the contemporary favourites such as Clara Butt and Kennerley Rumford, but an earlier generation in Albani and Patti and Santley (best of them all). Harry Plunket Greene came not infrequently

and gave song recitals, as he was still giving lecture recitals twenty
and more years later. His voice was not good, nor well used, and
at some time in every performance he sang flat—generally at the
beginning—but the charm of his personality, the excellence of
his diction, the vitality of his rhythm, were truly spirit-stirring.
To hear him sing *The Fairy Lough* was something one could not
forget : even with Kathleen Ferrier it was only a lovely song :
with him it was a thing of magic. I did not know it at the time, but
a new singer, Gervase Elwes, and young Campbell McInnes came
to mean more to me than any of the famous names I have given.
The D'Oyly Carte Company came to Oxford annually and that
claimed most evenings for a week. But the rage for Gilbert and
Sullivan began only five or six years later : in my time it was
seldom necessary to book in advance. Opera was rarely to be heard
and, I suppose, by modern standards the Carl Rosa Company
was far from firstrate. Still it gave us what we could hardly hear
otherwise, and in February 1904, with Greats all too near, I had
my first hearing of *Don Giovanni* and *Figaro* on successive nights,
with a matinée of *Carmen* in between.

I never played football or cricket at Oxford, except for a match
on the last day of my last summer term. But I played regularly
the game known as Fug Soccer, four a side in a racket court, with
tennis shoes and a small-sized football. I wonder how long this
excellent game survived. We generally played the same four
against teams from our own or some other college, and from
habitually playing together we seldom met with defeat. It is a
really good game so long as there is no roughness or clumsiness
and few would want more than the one hour of concentrated
exercise.

Otherwise all my efforts were devoted to lawn tennis. I had
come up with legitimate ambitions and the intention of playing on
the hard courts in winter as well as the grass in summer. And in
my first term I was very lucky. In the Freshmen's Singles I drew a
Worcester man named Crawley, who proved to be in a different
class to anyone I had played against before : one can say confidently
the best freshman who had yet come up to Oxford. He had had
what in those days so few ever could have, a thorough drilling in
style and tactics by a brother, also a notable player, a good many
years older than himself. I may add here that in four years against
Cambridge he won eleven matches out of twelve. Crude as I was,
he thought me just good enough to give him practice, and I learnt a
great deal in the process, including ultimately a style. When the

summer term came I was again lucky. In a very thirdrate College side there was one good player, already a half-blue, but a scrubby and unattractive little man with whom none of the others wanted to play. So the freshman was told off to partner him and learnt a good deal more. In my second year I became secretary and for the two years after that president. And as keenness generally has its reward, we built up a six which very nearly won the Inter-Collegiate Cup in 1903, won it in 1904 and again in 1905. When a challenge came from Trinity, Cambridge, in 1903, we looked to be having the best of it when rain came to spoil the match, as it did most things in that disastrous year, when Oxford had three floods in eight months, and a fourth and worst in the following February. For three years my College partner was another Wykehamist, Clive Pawson, a versatile games player who got his cricket blue in 1903 and only missed a football blue through injury. We went through three seasons on two defeats and in our last year won the so-called College Pairs, the University Doubles Competition. In that year Christ Church might well have challenged the University.

Meantime in my second year I had found a place in the Varsity team, was secretary in my third year and president in my fourth. In those days most inter-Varsity matches took place at Queen's Club—Football and Athletics as well as minor sports like Lawn Tennis. It was well worth becoming an undergraduate member at two guineas a year in order to watch these events in comfort, perhaps with a guest. The lawn tennis match always came in the week after Wimbledon : three singles players played each other on the first day and three pairs on the second.

My first partner was J. A. Barrett, brother of Roper Barrett and like him in figure and in activity, but hardly so in skill. Our match against Cambridge began on the lowest level with an ignominious defeat by the Cambridge third pair, 0—6 2—6. We went on, feeling rather desperate, hit at everything, and, but for a wrong decision by an umpire on the winning stroke, would have beaten the second pair by exactly the same score. Still 6—0 6—3 was a sufficient revenge. More important, we then took the first pair as far as six-all in the final set, and came as near as that to saving the day for Oxford. That is characteristic of the immature player : he may perform deplorably at two o'clock and very well at three, or the other way on : consistency comes with experience. Barrett forwent his fourth year, to take a post offered him in Morgan's brewery at Norwich, so my Oxford acquaintance with him was limited to that one term. But we had taken to each other and corresponded and occasionally met till he was killed in action. A brewer with Left-wing tendencies, who thought for himself in an ultra-Tory family, writing letters full of enthusiasm for Chaucer and other poets, classical and modern, the best of companions, with his own individual sense of humour, he was, I think, of all friends whom the war of 1914 claimed, the one I missed the most.

In my first and third years Cambridge won by the closest possible margin, 10—8 : in the intervening year, with a good team, Oxford won handsomely by 14—4. That was the only year in which I won all my doubles, partnered by Geoffrey Smith, the zoologist, who had entered College with me in 1894. In that year I had induced the whole Oxford team to enter for the Reading tournament in the previous week, with excellent results, both there and at Queen's Club. If the great Crawley had played in the doubles as he did in the singles, we need never have lost in any of those years. In singles he played under an iron control ; in doubles he was extremely temperamental and too often there were two players in court but not a pair. In 1904 I confronted the great Tony Wilding for the first time, three years before his first victory in the doubles at Wimbledon. He was not yet good enough to beat Crawley, but more than good enough to beat me ! I reckoned a score of 2—6 3—6 as quite good enough. That was the last year in which the match was played at Queen's Club.

In the Summer Term of 1903 I was invited for the first time to play for Essex in the County Championship, against Middlesex. The opposing team was to consist of three pairs of brothers, Baddeleys, Dohertys and Simonds : in other words it contained the doubles champions of every year except one from 1894 to 1905. But the weather washed out the match, and when it was actually played the Middlesex side was so impoverished that Essex won, with no player of any note in the side except Roper Barrett. About the same time the secretary of the All-England L.T.C., Archdale Palmer, wrote that, to stimulate interest in the game, he would like to bring down the full strength of the club for a match against the Varsity. The team duly arrived, with the Dohertys in it, but once again the weather intervened and the visitors went home, prematurely as it proved, after lunch. So twice in a month I lost the chance of discovering what it felt like to be on the opposite side of the net to the best pair in the world.

Having achieved a half-blue I felt myself entitled to acquire that superior article a blanket coat. It cost two guineas, and now, dyed navy blue in the twenties on the advice of that inveterate lawn tennis player Lord Pethick-Lawrence, it still serves me as a good warm ' babylonitish ' and will do for someone else hereafter.

In my last term I felt myself ripe to play at Wimbledon, and my experience of the old simple friendly amateurish Wimbledon is so unlike anything that could happen to-day that I propose to put it on record here. The date coincided with Commem at Oxford and I could not enter for the singles, which began on the Monday, because I was (for the first and last time) going to the House ball. That I did, and went to bed at 6 a.m. Then in the early afternoon I left for Wimbledon, where I was to stay with friends, but went first to the club to deposit my bag. I had believed that no doubles were played till Wednesday, so it was a shock, when I reported to the referee, to be told with some asperity that I had been down to play at 3.30, as I could have seen on the front page of *The Sportsman*. The day's programme was always published in that long extinct daily. My partner was F. W. Goldberg, a good player in the Oxford side of the previous year, but we had never played on the same side of the net, and when we met he confessed that it would be his first double of the season. We were drawn against Hillyard and Cazalet, one of the four best pairs in the country, but they seemed quite undisturbed by the lateness of an insignificant undergraduate and we had an excellent game, and actually led 4—3 in the first set. We got one more game off them than Crawley and Wilding did in the next round. I am glad to have played that year, for the opportunity never occurred again.

Looking through a Wimbledon programme I find that I have played with or against seventeen Wimbledon winners, and that but for those two wet days in 1903 the number would have been twenty. They cover just fifty years, ranging from Lottie Dod, whose first victory was in 1887, to Raymond Tuckey, who won the Men's Doubles in 1936.

In my fourth year I got, rather surprisingly, a little more experience of indoor play on wood. A wealthy parson had just built a covered court, the first private one in England, at his remote vicarage on the top of the Chilterns, and as there were no local players he had to import them from a distance. The first time I went there I found the reigning champion, Miss D. K. Douglass, afterwards to be known as Mrs Lambert Chambers. I had forgotten the fact, but my diary tells me that I played her a single and that I was glad she made me give her 15, because she would have beaten me without it. On a later occasion she did play me level and won three sets to none. But it leaves unsettled a question I have often wondered about : what is the difference between a second class man and a first class woman ? Games such as ours, in winter, on an unfamiliar surface, with neither in practice, do not answer the question.

For play in the Long Vac we had what I will for convenience call the Parks Club. It still exists, but it was sad to read lately in *The Oxford Magazine* a letter from the secretary appealing for more members. I was moved to write a letter telling what the club offered to our more fortunate generation in return for a single guinea, or a family subscription of two guineas. For three months the club had the use of the Varsity cricket ground and pavilion, six days a week, with tea provided—and a particularly good brand of dough cake—two tournaments without entrance fee, and the right to introduce guests without payment. In August the club grew rather languid, but filled up again in September, and July was a very busy month. There were a number of good players and a few enjoyable matches, of which the chief was against the corresponding club in Cambridge. There were ample courts and balls were provided. Croquet players were equally well catered for. The club, I understand, really lived on the subscriptions of a large number of non-playing and indeed invisible members.

It is not surprising to re-discover with the aid of my diary what a delightful time was the summer of 1904, when the burden of Greats was laid aside, while so many of my contemporaries were giving July to an intensive course of coaching at Scoones's, and then sitting the long Civil Service examination, a worse Greats, in London during a fine hot August. But I am surprised to see how conscientiously I kept up my reading for a Greats *viva* which when it came was a formal affair of five minutes. A *viva* was only formidable if your class was doubtful, and mine was quite clear. When it was over I returned with fresh appetite to the Greek poets, and to lawn tennis. Then in mid-August I went up to Moffat, new country to me, where Rendall had suggested me as tutor to the captain of the Haileybury Eleven, who aspired to a Cambridge scholarship. His parents were in India and my hostess was his aunt, widow of an I.C.S. man, living with her uncle, also I.C.S., and her father who had commanded a merchant ship in the Crimean War. They occupied Moffat House, an Adam house if I remember right, and rented some 3,000 acres of rough shooting, of which a certain area was given over to the youth. So there I had my only shooting, of a highly unconventional sort, since it involved a good

D

deal of running to keep the birds from flying onto forbidden ground. I shot a few rabbits, but no one should shoot unless he can shoot well, and I really preferred walking with the guns on more conventional occasions. The Scottish Lawn Tennis Championships were played at the beautiful Beechgrove Grounds, and I received a cordial invitation to go up the next year to play in them : indeed I did so a number of times.

BRADFIELD

CHAPTER IV

THOUGH my four year course was completed and my scholarship had expired, I had not yet done with Oxford. It was thought that I might improve my qualifications as a schoolmaster by wider and more congenial reading and by learning properly the German which I had only played with at school. I was to spend the winter in Dresden for that purpose. Rendall strongly advocated this course, and my father generously agreed, though all the expense fell on him. But I am genuinely glad that my fifth year was limited to one term, still in the Old Palace, though sorry to keep only a smattering of German and never to have seen the Sistine Madonna or heard the Dresden opera. After all I had already had fifteen years of schooling and it was high time to earn a living.

It was also possible that I might get a Fellowship, and indeed in the next two years I was twice second choice for one. Years later, when I met my successful rivals I greeted them as unconscious benefactors, for I am truly thankful to have lived the life of a schoolmaster and not a college don.

On the last day of October 1904 I went to the office of the Appointments Committee to register my name for employment in the following September. The secretary told me that he had news of a rather attractive job that morning : a certain public school wanted a Sixth Form master, though he was not at liberty to name the school : but he advised me at any rate to let my name be sent in. A few days later I had a letter from Dr Gray of Bradfield inviting me to go and see him. I took train to Pangbourne, hired a bicycle, and rode the four miles of pleasant country I was to know so well. It was not my first visit to that delightfully situated school, for Rendall had taken some of us to see the *Agamemnon* in 1900. On that occasion too I had arrived by cycle, but from the other side, from Newbury : a ten-mile ride by Cold Ash and Bucklebury Common, a lovely region which I have traversed on foot or bicycle or by car a great many times over a period of fifty years and more. The Warden and Mrs Gray were most friendly, and very soon I received an offer of the post. My salary was to be £200 resident, a good one for those days, better I fear than some colleagues much senior to me enjoyed. I have no doubt that I owed my appointment to Claude Blagden, Junior Censor at Christ Church and himself a Bradfieldian. When fifty years later I met that dear man, the Bishop of Peterborough, for the last time, he greeted me as ' his first scholar ' : for as a very junior don he had examined for entrance scholarships for the first time in November 1899, and I was at the head of the list.

At the end of December I spent a night with the man to whose place I was succeeding—a night of wild storm in a house much exposed to it, on the high ground of Buckhold, near Dr Watney's big house that is now St. Andrew's School. He was A. E. Crawley, elder brother of Cecil Crawley, who had learnt his tennis from him. He was an able but strange man ; a scholar, a parson of sorts, an anthropologist, and a student of ballistics. He was a notable lawn tennis player, and at this stage the writer of long and technical articles in *The Field* on the flight of balls. I learnt with astonishment that he proposed to become curate to Robson at Lacey Green, while taking pupils and continuing his study of ballistics on the covered court. But the Vicar was not an intellectual man nor Crawley a very tolerant one, and the arrangement did not last long.

Crawley was not particularly encouraging. He said that his hours of teaching were far too long and that, as he had so much work to do in school, he made it a rule to do none out of it and took all his lessons unprepared. That seems to me an astonishing confession from a Sixth Form master. In forty-two years I cannot remember ever taking a lesson unprepared. But he did me a great service in writing to Dr Gray urging that a Sixth Form master ought to have more freedom. The Warden accepted the advice and I had a time-table which allowed for preparation and correction, and never had to live from hand to mouth. And a Sixth Form master of twenty-three has everything to learn.

I commenced usher, as they say, on 19 January 1905. The term had a tragic beginning when we heard that two boys, twin brothers, had been killed in a railway accident. I thought that Gray's manner when he asked me if I had heard the news was very strange, and later, Kyrke, the senior mathematical master, had a weird story to tell of a meeting in the Warden's study. A gentle tapping, several times repeated, was heard, and as no answer came, a maid's head appeared round the door. The Warden put his hand to his head and asked ' Is anybody dead ? Is anybody dead ? ' Then advancing upon the maid behind his eyeglass

he addressed her, ' I would have you to know that the privacy of
this sanctum is not to be violated except in the case of immediate
death '. Gray was a man of great force who, if he had left Bradfield
after twenty years instead of thirty, might have left a name as one
of the great headmasters. He came to Bradfield in 1880, just before
the Founder, Warden of the College, Lord of the Manor and Rector
of the Parish—in fact the Squarson—went bankrupt for £160,000.
With fifty-five boys and few masters, hitherto irregularly paid,
he brought out a balance on the right side in his first year and built
up a school which was latterly only too full. And it was he who
conceived and created the Greek theatre in a neighbouring chalk
pit, which has now been an inspiration to thousands for two-thirds
of a century. With spade and wheelbarrow he led the work himself,
much more effectively, I feel sure, than Ruskin in his roadmaking
at Hinksey. In his later years, with his outside interests, which
ultimately included a ranch in Alberta, he lived in a state of
continual nervous strain. He was even chairman of his own
Governing Body, there too, I have no doubt, as autocratic as
everywhere else. In the spring of 1910 he returned from a visit to
Canada too plainly ready for a breakdown, and a few days later
we learned that the doctors had ordered him away, not to return.
I must add that he and the very able woman who was Mrs Gray
were uniformly good to me.

I was fortunate in my work, and in my form, which contained
boys of real promise. I must have been as crude as any of them,
and only four or five years older than some. It is a startling thought
that my earliest pupils are now past seventy. I have no written
records, but in my first year can recall scholars-to-be of six Oxford
colleges, and three of them have been my friends from that day to
this. Through Crawley's intervention I had been spared some
probably tedious Army Class work, and outside the Sixth had only
Roman History with a form very pleasant to work with, the Upper
Remove. Many years later I was told that, finding myself expected
to teach *The Student's Gibbon*, I began by asking if anyone knew
anything of the subject, because I didn't. Anyhow, I enjoyed
learning it with them, and the master can generally keep a page
or two ahead. In those days specialization had hardly begun,
and the two or three boys who aspired to study history remained,
as much later at Charterhouse, members of the classical side.
With them I read some Greats books, as I may call them, which
may have been good for them and certainly was good for me.
One boy I remember, son of the proprietor of *The Sportsman*,

who got his scholarship at Cambridge without reaching the Sixth at all. Another who never reached the Sixth, R. N. Carew Hunt of the Foreign Office, is now a leading authority on the depressing subject of Communism.

It was the good fortune of the Sixth to work in the Library, a first floor room looking westward over the cricket ground and the rectory glebe, known as Privilege, and northward over the church to the woods half a mile away. For most of the year school began at 7 a.m., and on a fine morning I never failed to walk to the end of the room to enjoy the view. The lot of the Bradfieldian had certainly fallen to him in a fair ground, and after a hundred years the surrounding country still remains wonderfully unspoilt.

My father died in July, 1906, after long illness, though he had the courage to take some part in the church services almost to the last. He was buried at Colchester, and the service in St. Mary's, crowded to the doors with those who had loved and honoured a good man, is a proud memory. In September my mother was able to buy a house known as The Lodge at Eynsham, six miles west of Oxford, on the Witney line, and moved there at the beginning of November. I got leave to spend a night there, and recall vividly the sense of well-being as I read Fielding in bed that first night. My diary says nothing of that, but much of the journey. Fielding was new to me and I began *Joseph Andrews* while waiting for the train. Its impact was such that I got into the train without my bag—it was before the day of suitcases—which some kind person observed and handed it in. A few minutes later I left it in the train at Reading and had to retrieve it from a siding. I write this to suggest, not my own futility, but the enviable gift of being able, at that time, to become wholly absorbed in a book. I seem to remember that at an earlier day *The Prisoner of Zenda* caused me to leave my hat in the train.

From the first we loved the new house, which of my eight homes is the one I look back to with the warmest feelings. It cost my mother £1,800, about what the gardener's cottage might fetch to-day. It was our home till her death twenty years later, and if there was no electric light, it had a bathroom, filled with the morning sun. Where my mother was there was sure to be a lovely garden and animals of highly developed individuality, including one Curly, a remarkable Russian goose.

But at Eynsham we did not inherit perfection : the old part of the house, with its great sun-inviting windows had the best rooms, but additions were needed, and a new wing was designed by a clever and amusing young Cantab, then at the beginning of his career, Clough Williams-Ellis. A fragment of dialogue will suggest that a cheerful impertinence helped him on his way to Portmerion. ' The firm has come to tea.' ' Oh, but we had tea long ago.' 'Another word, and the firm will stay to dinner.' Some thirty years later I entertained him when he came to lecture at Charterhouse and found him wonderfully good company and very like his youthful self.

The year 1907 was for me a very eventful one. In April I paid my first visit to Italy not in someone else's charge, but in charge of someone else. To that end I went daily in the Christmas holidays for lessons with Signor Coscia, the Reader in Italian at Oxford, and when my friend Vince and I went to Rome and elsewhere, I was capable to some extent of understanding and making myself understood. Any visit to Italy, given normal health, can hardly fail to be enjoyable, but this time the bad weather made it the least enjoyable of my nine visits, and in particular gave me a distaste for Rome, so that I never attempted to go there again till 1939—when I learnt what a mistake I had made.

More important perhaps, for the first time I saw a Bradfield play from the inside and learnt much from the patient devotion of Vince. My only share was scholastic, not dramatic—to edit the verse translation which in those days the Sixth were always required to produce. With the work of George Rostrevor Hamilton and F. R. Barry (now Bishop of Southwell), I am sure that this was the best of Bradfield translations. I can quote some of it still. The *Antigone* produced two notable performances. At the very last moment we lost our Coryphaeus (leader of the Chorus) through the illness and death of his mother, and Dr Gray, who had once played the part many years before, undertook it again at 24 hours' notice. Wisely he took no part in the singing, but his declamation was masterly—a remarkable *tour de force*. But the most notable performance was the *Creon* of Guy Garrod, now Air Chief Marshal, a good friend of mine whose name will appear again. The Bradfield play has a tradition of good weather, and after a cold and cheerless spring we were lucky again. Only one brief but heavy shower taught us what an astonishing roar rain can make on a thousand umbrellas in that auditorium. Luckily it was soon over. But I learnt a useful lesson which I have only once had to put into practice—that if rain threatens it is best to carry two raincoats, one to put over head and shoulders and one to tie round the waist. Rain if heavy cascades down over the seats, and this is the best protection.

I saw two more Greek plays from inside, the *Agamemnon* of 1911 and the *Alcestis* of 1914, and after attending all but two of the Bradfield plays over a period of 55 years always maintained that the performance in 1911 reached the high watermark. But after seeing the wonderful performance of *Oedipus Coloneus* in 1955, the first production of David Raeburn—once a member of my House and of almost my last Sixth at Charterhouse, as his father had been of my first—I was prepared to change my view. That was good, but not so good was the thought that to act a Greek play notably well it was not necessary to know Greek. In fact there was not one classical specialist in the cast : in the *Antigone* of 1907 the eight principals included six future scholars of Oxford colleges.

In 1912, amid protests from some who should have known better, the theatre was for the first time used for something other than a home-made Greek play. Harley Granville Barker brought his company to give performances of Gilbert Murray's version of *Iphigenia in Tauris*, and very good they were. In 1955 I received two letters from America asking for information about the production, for a treatise on the work of Granville Barker. What I remembered best was the shouts of delight from the company when they saw the lovely place in which they were privileged to perform.

One attraction of life at Bradfield was the proximity of Mapledurham, not more than six or seven miles away. There, with no need to give warning, before the day of universal telephones, I was sure of a welcome at any time in the beautiful vicarage with its beautiful garden and the murmur of the weir audible day and night. My uncle StJohn Thackeray, first cousin and godson of the novelist, had long been an Eton master, and the stories about him and his disciplinary difficulties are on record, and very funny they are. But he had been an excellent tutor. I have never known a parsonage with so interesting an entry : a long passage with glass all down one side and the garden beyond it, and his Eton honours boards on the other, and on both sides the glass-topped cases that held his collection of fossils, some of them acquired in remote and little-known places. I wish I could remember more of the distinguished names on the boards, but they included those of A. J. Balfour and W. R. Inge. The old man was always the scholar, liable I believe to quote Greek to the assembled rustics in church, but from our similarity in tastes I got on excellently with him : one of my cousins remarked that I always saw him at his best. And when in earlier days I had the good fortune to geologise at Bridport and Lyme Regis, it was in his company.

On the first Sunday of this Summer Term of 1907 I cycled over to lunch, when my cousin Ada Thackeray told me that a man named McInnes was giving a song recital at University College, Reading, and was he worth going to hear ? I replied that he was, and two days later we went. In the audience I noticed a Christ Church man who was a friend and persistent follower of this singer. He told me that McInnes was coming down to teach at the College two days a week. Dr H. P. Allen (not yet Sir Hugh) had taken over the musical directorship and induced one or two men of mark to come and lend distinction to the teaching staff. I arranged to go for a trial lesson a week later, little knowing what was in store for me. I had had many lessons at Oxford from a lady who, as I came to understand, had taught me not singing but songs. With Mac it was to be quite the other way : it was a good many months before I was allowed a song at all. He asked me to sing something very sustained and, after looking through a volume, chose that lovely song of Doctor Blow, *The Self-banished.* Neither was impressed with the other. I thought how he banged out parts of the accompaniment—he was of course trying to discover how much tone would come through—and he told me that my noise was four-fifths breath. Later he said that, hollow and lugubrious as my voice was, he was sure there was another voice behind it. This was rather strong meat for one whose *forte* (perhaps a suitable word) was in songs like *King Charles,* or *To Anthea,* or *The Old Superb,* but who had also a large repertoire of Schumann and Mozart. Next week he told me I was in a pretty poor way, but that if we went very gently he thought I might yield to treatment. By the end of term I was launched on an entirely new course, really beginning to feel the difference between tone and noise, ready to slip away at every available opportunity for an extra five minutes in the horrible music cells, and generally going late in to lunch for the sake of a little more time of practice. Years later McInnes spoke of me to a friend as the keenest pupil he ever had.

So once a week for the next three years I mounted my cycle after morning school and rode off to Reading, or to catch a train at Theale, eating something on the way, and despite checks and setbacks enjoying the lessons and the rare new songs, and sometimes the old, more and more. The worst setback was when McInnes had to be away for a few weeks and his place was taken by Frederick Keel. Keel was a charming man, composer of that lovely setting of Masefield's *Trade Winds* and editor of the well-known first volume of Elizabethan songs which preceded the great edition of Dr Fellowes. I had a number of them in MS before their publication in 1910. Keel encouraged me, or at least allowed me, to ramp through many of the old songs, and Mac when he returned was not pleased. He said the ' old toothbrush noise ' had come back, and for a while songs were once more forbidden. The patience and thoroughness of McInnes were wonderful, and if I was not patient I was at least persistent—and for a long time the road did seem to wind uphill all the way. And of course I was constantly warned by compassionate friends that I was ruining my voice. I remember a remark in a moment of gloom : ' I don't care in the least if you can't sing now : I'm thinking of fifteen years hence '. And so it was : my voice got to its best, impervious to tobacco and quite untiring so long as I stuck to the right kind of song, in the 1920s.

We had all inherited a singing voice from my father. I rarely, heard him sing, but his voice for reading or intoning in church or speaking on a platform was as beautiful as I ever heard. I remember that the first time I ever attended a political meeting, at Colchester early in 1895, I was accommodated with a chair at the back of the platform, and my father was to come in after another engagement if he could : suddenly I heard his ' Hear, hear ', from the back of the hall, and ' the very word was like a bell '. And at the age of 70, a dying man, the beauty of his voice was quite unimpaired. But only one of our family could be called a musician, my sister Margaret, a most expressive singer—she too became a disciple of McInnes—and a pianist with a wonderful touch. But she let her gifts wither too early from overwork.

The most formidable of family critics has told me that I have not a note of music in me. That in a sense is true, if it means any sort of technical comprehension of the art, a power to read music or to understand anything of the mystery of its creation. And it is the same with all the arts. I have looked and tried to see, I have read and been told, how some painter gets his effects, but it remains for me wholly a mystery and as such never loses its magic. After all, to love and enjoy it is the one thing that matters. Let me be, like Wordsworth, ' contented if I may enjoy the things which others understand '. I sometimes feel like the unsuccessful painter in *Pippa Passes*—' No end to all I cannot do '. I have nothing but a smattering of any modern language, a blank ignorance of science in every form and of all things mechanical, which is why I hated driving a car and thankfully gave it up, never to be resumed, in 1939. The only mechanism I ever mastered was a rifle, and I doubt if I

ought to use the word ' mastered ', for though I taught musketry
for years I found it advisable often to revive my knowledge. A
reluctant and incompetent gardener, limited to the menial tasks of
mowing and weeding, my hands have never been of much use
except to hold a pen and to hit a ball. I cannot, like R.L.S., ' pickle
with the manly and melodious forefinger ', and that has no doubt
meant a lot of work for other people in teaching me my songs.
But I have never felt that they grudged the time, and anyhow I
have acquired an enormous and varied repertoire.

I was wonderfully fortunate in my friends outside the College.
The Common Room was a bachelor establishment, and such places
are at the mercy of the loudest voice ; and here two voices were very
loud indeed. It was in the summer of 1907 that I first met the
best of them all. One day I had a letter from an unknown Mrs
Hughes, at Yattendon, saying that an old friend of our family had
become engaged to her stepson, and inviting me to visit her. I
went, rather bored and reluctant, little knowing what sort of home
was to be opened to me for the next seven years. It was the kind
of family the world will not see again, one in which every son gave
the service of his life to India as if nothing else were possible, and
two daughters lived their early married life in Bombay. The father
was Lord Roberts's most trusted artillery officer, and had just
reached the exalted position of Military Member of Council when
he died, leaving this wise and great-hearted little woman with two
stepchildren and five of her own. Three sons entered the Indian
Army and one the Political Service. Only one survived the war
of 1914. He had been compelled by deafness to leave the army and
had devoted himself to Lord Roberts's national service campaign.
He made a most happy marriage, but a charming wife went out of
her mind, and worry and strain led to a breakdown and a nursing-
home, where his life was ended by a fall from a window. Of his
three brothers, the eldest died of pneumonia on his way to the
Mesopotamian Front in command of the 14th Bengal Lancers, the
' Murray's Jat Horse ' raised in the Mutiny by my father's cousin :
the other two were retained in their posts on the North-West
Frontier, where one was shot in his camp by a fanatic, the other in a
petty action as he carried in a wounded man. Fortunately the mother
had gone first, after a stroke in August 1915. The sole surviving
member of the family remains one of my most valued friends.

Yattendon, three or four miles from Bradfield, was a remarkable
village. It might have been a forcing-house, but I do not know

that it was. A little earlier it had harboured three resident poets—
Mrs Alfred Waterhouse (a Hodgkin by birth and of course in the
Studbook), her son-in-law Robert Bridges, and the Rector, H. C.
Beeching, later Dean of Norwich. The only divorce between simple
and sophisticated, so far as my knowledge goes, was over the
Yattendon Hymnal of Bridges and Wooldridge, which the village
could not stomach : it was used at matins, but not with a different
congregation in the evening. Miss Waterhouse was then and for
many years afterwards the inspiration of the local music, and she
built a concert room as a first instalment of what was to be her home
when the time should come to leave the great house built by her
father. I was at the opening concert in 1910, an astonishing performance indeed for an Edwardian village. It began with Bach and,
when I had to leave, the orchestra were going strong in a Haydn
symphony. Yattendon Court is gone, but the family still live in
the place, a third generation of eminence in the architectural
profession. For Michael Waterhouse, like his father Paul, has been
President of the R.I.B.A.

When the Hughes family moved into a modern and much less
attractive house, the Grange lay empty for some time and then was
tenanted by one Emery Walker, who became a dear friend of mine.
But of him I must speak elsewhere.

Among my own colleagues I made a number of pleasant
acquaintances and three very good friends, all much older than
myself—Thomas Steele, J. H. Vince, and C. E. Nicholl. Steele, with
a very happy home life, mellowed into as wise an old schoolmaster
as I have known, and his letters were so good that I have never
thrown one away. He had a wonderfully light touch with his pen,
and it was a great day when I managed to wheedle an article out of
him for the school Chronicle which I edited. Vince once said that
there were two writers whose style might be called unique—
Charles Lamb and Tom Steele. Anyone who lights on a little book
with the title *Musings of an Old Schoolmaster* will understand why
he should have said so. Of Mrs Steele I think as one of the bravest
women I have known. For some years she suffered much as the
result of a carriage accident, which led in the end to the loss of a
leg. Quite soon afterwards I paid them a visit, expecting to find
an invalid on a sofa. Not so : my hostess was down to breakfast
at 8 o'clock. The pair needed, and showed, all their courage when
their gifted daughter was killed in a road accident.

Steele lived to be 87. But Vince went beyond that : he was in
his 91st year when he died, all in a moment, as he carried a pail of

water into the house, in the late summer of 1955. Vince is one of
the men to whom I owe most in life, including unfortunately a
permanently injured right eye, from a post-prandial missile which
went straight, as such things so seldom do. He was a beautiful
scholar, setting a standard one had to try to live up to, with wide
interests, well read in philology and anthropology, a real understanding of architecture, some knowledge of birds and much of
flowers, and from 1898 to 1914 the inspiration of the Greek play.
He taught me, and how many others, to walk and know the unspoilt
Berkshire country in the best possible way : and not Berkshire
only but the Oxford country and the Cotswolds and Bredon Hill,
and above all the Lakes. My first approach with him to the Lakes
in the April of 1910 is so vivid in memory that I hope to say more
of it elsewhere.   Lastly we went twice together to Italy and once to
Greece.

In 1919 he wearied of ' ushing ', as he called it, or of the regime
under which he did so, married the matron of the sanatorium,
one almost as much esteemed as himself, and retired, unpensioned,
to a cottage in the Duddon valley. There, at a rent of 2/6 a week,
he had as much beauty and even of comfort as he wished, and from
that vale of peace he seldom emerged. He had still 36 years of
life before him, and was never more to be admired than in his brave
old age, still self-sufficing as cook, houseman, gardener, and nurse
to an invalid wife : and to the last he wrote an admirable letter.

My third friend, the Mole, sometimes known as Mr Nicholl,
still lives in his native land of South Wales, bearing the trials of old
age with a characteristic humour, deaf and incapacitated for
strenuous gardening or fishing, and till lately finding his chief
occupation in rather amateurish watercolour painting. As teacher
and housemaster he was only too conscientious, and till middle age
a good bowler and footballer. In youth he shot in the VIII as well
as captaining Elevens, and I never allowed him to forget Dr Gray's
rhetorical picture of him before a large assembly on a public
occasion—' C. E. Nicholl, double-handed he, who with one hand
held the willow, with the other the musket-butt '. I doubt if he
generally held the willow very long, for he was not much of a
batsman. Nor can he have forgotten the time when the Warden
described him as ' a strong plain man '. I may add that I have
seldom seen a leg without wanting to pull it, and his I have pulled
for half a century. He had a happy turn of phrase and is the only
captain I have known to address an inadequate footballer as a white-
livered hound. He was one of those who carried the burden of

Bradfield through precarious years, and in any gathering of Bradfieldians was likely to be the central and best-loved figure.

These three men all possessed an admirable and individual sense of humour—no doubt one of the things that drew me to them, and for the memory of their sometimes sorely tried friendship I am deeply grateful.

Two other matters belong to the year 1907, perhaps too absurd to put on record here, but I rather enjoy absurdity. Like my father and my younger son I went bald very early, and some friend persuaded me to consult a certain Professor of Trichology, as he called himself, with an establishment somewhere behind Burlington House. The Professor diagnosed bulbular atrophy and prescribed herb shampoos, little bags of dried simples which smelt delicious at every stage, dry or wet : but of course they could not prevail against nature.

The other is a scholastic matter. At the beginning of the year the three-year-old Classical Association induced the Headmasters' Conference to accept a ' reformed ' pronunciation of Latin. The motion, by the way, was put by Frank Fletcher, later my revered chief. Even after fifty years there are those who inveigh against a change which was in fact the only alternative to chaos. I would not have mentioned this but for the absurdity that hitherto my form had used one method of pronunciation and I another : they a Continental manner of some sort and I an Anglo-Victorian, complicated by one Wiccamical idiosyncrasy or ' notion '.

Yet again, I saw in this year a football match which I am glad to have seen, because it closed an era. It was the Dewar Shield match, the last of its kind, between the Corinthians and Newcastle United. Just before the end of the old century an annual Charity Match had been instituted between the best amateur and the best professional team of the year. The Corinthians were always chosen, except once when preference was given to the Scottish Queen's Park. In 1904 Bury were selected, as the Cup Holders, and were two goals up in ten minutes : but when the match ended the Corinthian score was ten. If in this last year the Corinthians were defeated 5—2, it was only that three goals were scored while their famous centre-half, Morgan-Owen, who played repeatedly for Wales, was off the field, injured. Next year came the split, and the great amateur clubs were debarred from playing against professionals : then came the war, and since that time no amateur side has, except on very rare occasions, been a serious competitor with the pros.

I write elsewhere of my appetite for Chinese porcelain, but put it on record as belonging to what I have called an eventful year that on 3 September 1907 I lit by accident on a tiny newly-opened shop, 377 Oxford Street, with the name A. E. Bluett over the door. As a collector in a humble way that meant much to me, but belongs to another chapter.

At this time there was a remarkable inn, *The Boot*, at the beautifully named village of Stanford Dingley, two miles up the valley, where later I enjoyed a happy eight months in 1914 as my first married home. Some of us found it a delightful refuge from communal life. Mrs Cox was a supremely good cook, and it was a great loss when she and her husband migrated to a farm in Cambridgeshire and later, I believe, to Canada. For once I quote verbally from my diary, for Sunday 12 July 1908. ' The Mole and I had ordered a duck at Stanford Dingley, so we sallied forth to eat it at 12.45. Not only a duck but new potatoes and priceless peas. Not only these but raspberry and currant tart and cream : not only these but strawberries, and beer, and coffee ; and at the end we had to pay two shillings each. We reeled away at 3.30.'

After *The Boot* was lost to us I made another happy discovery. One day at Cold Ash I had stopped to enjoy my favourite view and found myself sharing it with a middle-aged man of pleasant appearance. He told me he was retired from the Metropolitan Police and lived close by and came almost every day to enjoy the view. Afterwards I, alone or companioned, several times begged a meal at his house. On 19 September 1909 I note that ' the Osgoods did us excellently for lunch : shoulder of mutton and green peas and apple tart, one shilling '. And again, ' Tea with excellent strawberries cost sixpence '. I also found that at University College, Reading, if I could arrive early enough, I might lunch well in the Buttery for sixpence. No wonder that in those fortunate days one was passing rich on £200, or later £250, a year. I always kept good cigars for the entertainment of friends and regularly drank Pol Roger on Saturday nights, when we kept up the civilised habit of dressing for dinner, and could afford to go abroad once every two years. Also in days when telephones were rare and unreliable I was surprised to learn from my diary how freely we corresponded by telegram, when one telegram cost the same as two letters do now. I don't know what a telegram costs to-day but I doubt if I have sent one for twenty years. Then again, books. In my youth a novel, or storybook as my mother always called it— and I use the word for convenience now because it would include

Henty—normally cost 6/- in the bill or 4/6 cash. I don't know when the so called Net Agreement came in, when discount for cash ceased to be allowed. Early in the century came Everyman and the World's Classics, both at a shilling, and in 1912 volumes of the Home University Library began to appear at the same price, and better produced than they were after 1918 at a very different cost. These were the most remarkable of all the shilling issues, for a distinguished author had to be paid for writing them, a Trevelyan or a Herbert Fisher, a Hadow or a Gilbert Murray.

It is only too easy for a schoolmaster to play games if he wants to, and at Bradfield I returned to both football and cricket and played them throughout my ten years, the one a good deal better than the other. Further I found the Common Room much given to golf on their own rough and ready links ; and as in my first term the death of a neighbour meant the loss of these, new ones had to be made by our own unskilled hands in the fields round the Rectory. But after three or four years these too were surrendered. But to me, of course, lawn tennis counted most. The masters' courts were bad, but those of the Reading Club excellent. At Bradfield Hall lived a retired Civil Servant who, after not too strenuous a professional life, retained his fitness and considerable skill. What is more he possessed a car, in which he was always ready to give me transport and made possible a great deal of play which I could not have managed otherwise. In those days of easy money and ready labour there was a wealth of lawn tennis available and, though I was not often free to attend their meetings, I much enjoyed the Crimson Ramblers, a very pleasant Mixed Doubles concern centred mainly round Baughurst on the far side of the Kennet valley

After 1909 I found the best of tennis at Newbury. In January of that year I had for the first time Mac's permission to sing at a concert, at Yattendon, and there I was introduced to a Miss Dod, who proved to be the famous Lottie Dod, the first great woman player ; she won the Ladies' Singles at Wimbledon in 1887, at the age of fifteen, and retired after her fifth victory in 1893. It is more to the point that I met her in court in the following July and found a first-class modern player, the best lady volleyer I had encountered except Mrs Larcombe : at Victorian Wimbledon it would have been thought barely decent for a woman to volley. After giving up competitive lawn tennis she became lady champion at golf, played for England at hockey, won an Olympic gold medal for archery, skated with the best, and when first I had the good fortune to go to her home at Newbury, I found her and one of her brothers in the paddock before their house engaged in mastering the boomerang. My information is derived from a treasured number of *Lilliput*, for June 1950, with a truly astonishing photograph of the lady in her schoolboy's cricket cap, holding a square-headed racket. I wonder if that racket was a Tate. For at one time the possession of a Tate racket marked the player as belonging to the very highest circles. The maker, I believe, did all the work with his own hands, and would (or could) only serve a very small and select body of customers, while the frames were so good that they could be restrung over and over again. At any rate when first I played with Miss Dod she told me she had used her racket at Wimbledon twenty-one years earlier.

She lived with her two brothers till the younger married. He too was an excellent player, and I think that perhaps the best day's lawn tennis I ever had was when I played set after set against them with Mrs Luard, who as Miss C. M. Wilson had been for some years, if never a winner, yet always in the first flight at Wimbledon. My annual week-end at Newbury was a great privilege. I may add that Lottie Dod was an excellent musician, and above all what one inevitably calls ' a great dear '. The family moved to Devonshire a little before we moved to Surrey and I never saw her again. But thirty years later a letter in *Country Life* showed that she was very much alive and led to a pleasant correspondence : she wrote of herself as ' in the sere and yaller ' ; but she is still alive to-day.

My ten years at Bradfield were bisected by a change of head-masters, or perhaps I should say by a change from Warden to Headmaster. The summer term of 1910 opened badly, with the second master and the two leading mathematicians ill. Next morning we heard of the death of King Edward VII, and after a few uncomfortable days came the news of the sudden departure of Dr Gray. The appointment of a successor might have been a difficult matter : it was in fact the simplest thing in the world—had the obvious course been taken. The Warden, as I have said, was Chairman of his own Council, or Governing Body, and as he was doubtless an autocrat there as elsewhere, few men of distinction cared to assemble in order to register his decrees : so the Council of that day was not a notable body. And now the Chairman was not there, or the course taken would have been unthinkable. There was one man,

E

Claude Blagden, so obviously suited to the position that there was really no need to consider other names. He had always kept in touch with his old school, he would have been acceptable to the staff and to the whole body of old boys, and as his charming autobiography *Well Remembered* tells us, it was a keen disappointment to him to be invited to come forward and then to be rejected. But one member of the Council took the view that the man appointed must have been a schoolmaster, not only a College don, and they decided accordingly. That was not wise, but the separation of the office of Warden from the Headmastership *was* wise, and so was their choice of the new Warden. And Bradfield has been highly favoured in her Wardens ever since. Four years after his appointment the new headmaster had to resign because the numbers had fallen by fifty per cent. and the school was on the verge of bankruptcy. It was not, I think, the headmaster's fault, and I believe he left a better school than he came to ; but he was not the right man for that place and that time. For Costley-White and his admirable young wife it must have been a bitterly anxious time, but a Headmaster of Westminster and Dean of Gloucester cannot consider his career a failure.

Had Blagden been appointed, the history of the school would have been different. He would have bridged effortlessly the transition from autocracy to constitutional government. For the trouble with Bradfield was that it was almost a proprietary school. Parents sent their sons because they were impressed with the personality of Gray, and he took a good deal of trouble to impress them. He received them always in person and showed them round in cap and gown. He regarded College as ' my house ', though it contained two sorely tried and ill-paid housemasters. All new boys were ushered into his presence. I wish I had been there, as one of my colleagues was, when the butler introduced ' Masters Fairlie, Gawne and Dunnett '. The responsibility for the troubles of Bradfield really lies at the door of one member of the Council.

The summer of 1910 was not wholly disastrous. Gray had always favoured rifle shooting and in his absence Bradfield won the Ashburton Shield, after a lapse of thirteen years, with a score that beat the record by no less than twelve points. The captain and coach was my friend Guy Garrod, and there are few of whom I have more affectionate memories. He developed very early and was only fifteen when he entered the Sixth, with a formidable moustache, and stayed there four whole years. But for the necessary postponement of the play in 1910, he would actually have appeared in a leading part twice, which, not surprisingly, no boy has ever done. He went up to Oxford as a scholar of Univ. and, though he had no skill at ball games, I cannot think of anyone who did more things well. He persevered with his shooting and as a freshman won the bronze medal for the King's Prize at Bisley, and shot habitually for England. He led the best undergraduate quartet of the Musical Union and was an admirable Coryphaeus in an O.U.D.S. production of *The Acharnians*. He got his half-blue for cross country running, rowed for his college at Henley and got his Leander. It is not surprising if reading was a little crowded out, and he hardly took his rightful class in the Schools. I met him in August 1914 as he came away from the place where commissions were being dispensed, and his parting remark, ' Rather a brick, Greats ', were the last words I heard from him for many years. When I wrote to Air Chief Marshal Sir Guy Garrod on his retirement from the service, he wrote back : ' Now I can unpack my Homer and my violin '.

From him, at a date I cannot recall, came a suggestion which has borne abundant fruit. He proposed the foundation of a Classical Society to have lectures on Art and Archaeology, and very suitably Monty Rendall was induced to give the first. From that suggestion sprang the Art Lectures which I got started at Charterhouse in 1919 : they have gone on ever since.

But the summer term of 1912 was much more obviously disastrous. To begin with, the weather : it was the wettest summer of my lifetime, though that might have been consonant with much good fortune. The headmaster was ordered away for an appendix operation which did not prove so easy as sometimes ; and during his absence three boys died from three different causes in three weeks. And that was not all. In July we were told that grave defects had been found in the College drainage system and that the school was to break up forthwith. That no doubt proved a source of satisfaction to many, and certainly to me : it gave me that last visit to Radwinter and quickly cleared away the hideous cough which had made me a nuisance to my neighbours. It proved that the worst of the drains were under the passage where I slept.

But the year between, 1911, I have long reckoned as my *annus mirabilis*. The year 1909 was the last in which I kept a continuous diary, but for two years more I made a record of some outstanding events. I summed it up on December 31 : ' What a year ! The Coronation, the great strike, . . . my visit to Greece and all that came of it, the wonderful summer, the St. Matthew Passion, the *Agamemnon*, and I don't know how much besides '. That would

include my first visit to Lichfield and Stowe Hill, and my first
acquaintance with the juvenile family of Will and Cicely Green.
I could hardly guess that I should find in their endless kindness
one of the greatest blessings of my life. And there can be no
doubt which of the year's events had the most momentous results.
I spent the night of 11 April as the guest of McInnes and Graham
Peel, who shared a most civilized bachelor habitation. Peel that
night gave me an MS copy, which I still treasure, of his not yet
published ' *In Summertime on Bredon* ', certainly one of his best
songs : McInnes remarked that it had in it all the bells in the world.
Next morning I was at Charing Cross by 8 a.m. and joined my
travelling companions there. They were Vince, as in the past three
Aprils, twice for Italy, once for the Lakes—and Colin Eddison,
a Bradfield Oxonian who had just become President of the O.U.D.S.
(He died in this summer of 1957.) Into our carriage got three
ladies, one of whom I seemed to know by sight and connected with
Yattendon : she proved to be Ruth Fry, who a few years later
was to achieve wide fame as the Secretary of the Friends Relief
Fund in and after the war of 1914. The second was Jean Alexander,
whose noble home, Aubrey House on Campden Hill, where she
still lives, must be known to many people. It reappeared in two
numbers of *Country Life* in May of this year. The third was ' a
rather attractive girl with a mouth that turned up at the corners
like a Correggio '. Subsequent acquaintance has taught me the
meaning of that, that Mildred Lloyd, travelling with a highly
intellectual cousin whom she did not know very well, was shy and
homesick. We also, as it chanced, shared a carriage with them from
Calais to Paris, but whether we got into their carriage or they into
ours is a question that will never now be settled. Further, when we
boarded the *Dunottar Castle* at Marseilles we chose at lunch time
the end of a table which filled up rapidly from the other end, so
that when our trio entered, the three places next to us were among
the few still vacant, and once more they became our neighbours,
together with a friendly old gentleman who, as it proved, had been
at Charterhouse when my father was a master there in the early
sixties and had affectionate memories of him. And when nearly
two years later I became engaged to Mildred Lloyd, the old boy
wrote, ' I remember how we all wanted to sit next to her '. Of the
cruise I cannot write more than a string of names, but what names !
Syracuse, Ithaca, Aegina, Athens, Delphi, Delos, Cos, Cnidos,
Rhodes, Halicarnassus, Cnossos. And if I may select one perfect
day where almost all were perfect, it would be that of our walk

across Ithaca, from our landing in Polis Bay, via Anogi 1700 feet up, to rejoin the ship in the Bay of Molo. From that day, with the cistus and the bee orchis and the fritillaries, I have found in the wild flowers of a Mediterranean spring one of the chief joys of travel. The *Dunottar Castle*, by the way, was the more commodious successor of the *Argonaut*, and my berth cost me £26. Recently I asked a friend what a similar cruise in 1956—but a summer cruise without the spring flowers—cost him, and he said there was little left over from £200.

When we reached Marseilles on our return I found a letter telling me that McInnes was to be married almost immediately to the brilliant Angela Mackail, whom so many of us know and delight in to-day as Angela Thirkell. In London my first act was to hurry to Powell's, not yet in Wigmore Street, but still in their original Whitefriars, and buy a wedding present. I knew Powell's lovely re-creation in glass of the Minoan lily vase which I had just seen in Crete, and that seemed to meet the case.

Of the other things my diary refers to, I remember nothing of the Coronation and not much of the railway strike. It gave my mother a difficult journey, with a carefully shielded engine-driver, to Grimsby for a cruise to Norway. When I travelled from Moffat on 21 August it had ended at most places, but not at Carlisle. There my luggage departed to Manchester while I was helping Miss Cecil Leitch to cope with hers. Miss Leitch had been playing in the Moffat tournament, but she would not claim that her tennis was on a par with her golf. The reference to the St. Matthew Passion, had it been written later, would have read ' My first Three Choirs Festival ', the first of more than I can reckon. The great works of Bach were not so often heard in those days, nor nearly so well performed. I had only heard the Passion once, at the Queen's Hall, and remember telling Graham Peel that I had been disappointed. His reply was that I ought to hear it in a cathedral. I did so now, and it was indeed a memorable experience, with Gervase Elwes, and McInnes (his first appearance at the Three Choirs) and Agnes Nicholls, and Muriel Foster, with a voice that, as Ernest Newman wrote at the time, was a ' pageant of golden splendour '. There was no such contralto again till the ever-to-be-lamented Kathleen Ferrier. It was followed in the evening by Kreisler in Elgar's Violin Concerto, a new work of which I contrived to hear three of the first four performances. And McInnes gave the first performance of Vaughan Williams's Five Mystical Songs. It suggests the easy money or the lavishness of those days, that Kreisler himself should have been engaged to play the obbligato in the Bach. And that year at Worcester saw an experiment that remained unique : twice in the day wind-players of the orchestra climbed the great tower and on its roof played arrangements by Elgar of Bach chorales—heavenly music indeed. But it is not surprising if that experiment was not repeated. Everything that summer took place in perfect weather, another long ' pageant of golden splendour '.

I have said nothing about the work of the school, nor of what interested me most, the arts. The school as a whole was pretty deeply Philistine : literature and music counted for very little. An Edwardian Army Class was hardly an abode of sweetness and light, though it produced some very good fellows, and a really successful Navy Class had disappeared when the Britannia yielded place to Osborne. For most boys there were only two easily available occupations, work and games. The latter count for far less in school life to-day, because so many other things have come into it. I recently noticed in *The Bradfield College Chronicle* (of which for eight years I was editor) the reports of fifteen societies— which may well be too many. Only one of them existed in my time, the Shakespeare Society, and that had room for only eight boys, with four masters. (After the meetings Vince often brewed the most excellent rum punch.) There was, as I have said, really promising scholarship in my early years, better than a few years later, but the only contact with English literature was through the rather blighting medium of the Higher Certificate. I had fortunately not outgrown a Victorian taste for Tennyson, and in my first year offered a prize for a paper on most of the *Idylls of the King*, in which it is still possible to find much of excellence if one looks for the merits and not the defects. There was no obligation to read them, but the work was most encouraging : and it was at least a beginning. After that I always managed to get in a little English literature besides the prescribed books, and it certainly paid dividends.

The chapel services were too much coloured by the dominating personality of the Warden, who even composed what the school called ' Sporting Litanies ' and, what is worse, sang them himself. A feature of the building was the pulpit on rails. Gray disliked having the choir behind him when he preached, and the pulpit therefore, when we came in, would be found placed centrally just below the communion rail, and during the last hymn would be pushed back on its rails by two prefects. I have so often told, or been told, that the preacher used to be drawn forward in the pulpit like Agamemnon in his chariot that I have sometimes almost believed it was so : but it is not true ! He claimed, in his own words, to ' speak straight from the shoulder ', and the best of his sermons were very powerful and even inspiring. But, as Vince remarked, he never recognized fustian, and where a man is a phrase-maker it is always the worst that are remembered. A letter to my father quotes ' the strings of the nervous system on which the psalm of life is played '. ' It isn't good enough to go to church on a Sunday morning with a gardenia in your buttonhole and sing " *I was a wandering sheep* ".' And I remember a reference to ' those who plaster their hair and bespangle their socks in imitation of some aristocratic dude '. Dude ! really and truly it was the word ! Any personal adornment was likely to draw fire, except in one boy of whom he made rather a favourite, calling him ' my fop '. But it was not in chapel that he told someone it was a bad thing to stand in the way of an express train, but worse to stand in the way of the Warden of Bradfield. And I could give the name of the boy who on some complaint about food (which was generally good, far better than at Winchester) was asked if he was accustomed to live on meringues and maraschino in marble halls.

To return to chapel. My diary records a morning when we of the choir, surpliced always, processed into an empty building, while the congregation with commendable discipline—there was seldom indiscipline where Gray was—waited outside for the door to be unlocked. And believe it or not, the hymn that morning began with an address to One ' standing outside the fast-closed door '.

Costley-White was a music lover, but the director was a poor thing and not much could be done. His first appointment was F. H. Shera, and it is odd to think of the late distinguished Professor of Music in the University of Sheffield as an ordinary hack form-master. If he did anything for the cause of music, it had to be done unofficially, almost clandestinely.

The Victorian and Edwardian sense of security had become less absolute by the time that George V ascended the throne. Lord Roberts, Lord Charles Beresford, and Robert Blatchford did a good deal to shake it, and Lord Haldane's creation of the Territorial Army and of the O.T.C. was a great stimulus to the various school corps. In 1912 as a matter of conscience I entered the ranks as an extremely crude recruit, though I had not the lurid experiences that my old friend Tom Steele recounts of his own days in the ranks. I did once drop a rifle on parade, but I never let one off during the solemn ceremonial of an Inspection, as he did. In due course I proceeded to a commission, and efficient N.C.O.s generally protected me from my own incompetence. My friend Shera took a commission at the same time. He was a man of almost historic plainness and for a musician strangely awkward in his movements. When I took him on the river at Eynsham he didn't quite go into the water, but his hat did, twice. I don't know how unmilitary I looked, but I know how unmilitary he did. I remember returning from firing some elementary course on the range with him and the huge Falstaffian figure of our C.O., Major Wyndowe, when we met Tom Steele. He stopped and with extreme gravity, but with devilry in his eye, murmured in his confidential voice, ' Go and look at the Fourth Act of *Henry the Fourth, Part One* '. (I hope I need not explain that the reference is to the troops with whom Falstaff declined to march through Coventry.) Though it is anticipating, I must come here to my first Camp. It was at Mytchett, that strange Camp of 1914. Even when we met there, very few had any suspicion of what was to come. At mess the first night I chanced to sit opposite the War Office representative and overheard the words, ' If we have to mobilize '. No later than the Sunday, after five nights in Camp, the deluge descended. The army cooks were recalled and we were told that the Camp would break up on Monday and, practically speaking, the troops would have to find their way home. Some officers who were already Territorials were mobilized at once : the rest of us were told to go home and wait for orders. When these orders came, they were that we were to remain with our own units. And by that time my unit was the Charterhouse O.T.C.

For to Charterhouse I must now come. Prudent friends had long been warning me against staying at Bradfield too long. I had discussed the question with Monty Rendall and others ; but I was happy at Bradfield and diffident of my own capacity, and had done little beyond writing to a few headmasters, who sent the usual non-committal replies. Only twice did I apply for a definite vacancy. One required qualifications which I did not possess : for the other, a Sixth Form mastership at a school better known than Bradfield, but without its classical tradition, the salary proposed was £150. When the chance came I owed it, like so much else in life, to my wife and to Will Green. Frank Fletcher had gone to

Charterhouse in 1911, leaving Marlborough reluctantly because the Archbishop of Canterbury, chairman of the Governing Body, had convinced him that it was his duty to do so. Where Mrs Fletcher was there would also be a garden, and wishing to build a garden house for amenity and privacy she consulted her cousin, Mrs Hugh Arnold, about an architect. Two names were given her, and of the two Will Green was called in because his home was close by, at Farnham. Next he was asked to design a delightful holiday home at Woolacombe in North Devon. In the summer of 1913 he told Fletcher that he had a prospective brother-in-law who would like to come to Charterhouse, and was invited to bring him over for inspection. So on a lovely Saturday afternoon in early October I came to Farnham, and with Mildred Lloyd (henceforth to appear simply as M.) and the Greens was fetched over in the Fletchers' car for inspection. That must have been the first time I was driven by Humphries, now in his fiftieth year of service with Lady Fletcher.* Like most people our hostess took to M. at sight, and no doubt that helped. Fletcher said that there would be a vacancy in September 1914 by the retirement of a senior master, but that he was not happy about the arrangements in the Sixth Form and might want to make a change in them : but he could not *promise* the position, and anyhow the matter must be strictly confidential. He asked if there were any Bradfieldians at Oxford whose opinion of me he might seek, and I named two Oriel men, F. R. Barry (now Bishop of Southwell) and Kenneth Armitage, who entered the I.C.S. and died young through a fall from his horse. Fletcher naturally approached them through the Provost, Phelps, a Carthusian of Carthusians. In the following February one of my referees was at Bradfield and told someone that I was going to Charterhouse. I wrote to him and asked for an explanation and was told that the two of them were walking with the Provost when he remarked, ' Well, we've taken your man '. It was a foible of Phelps to regard himself as next door to being headmaster : and indeed a man who serves on the Governing Body for more than forty years without missing more than one meeting—so he once told me— has a right to take himself seriously. I wrote to Fletcher and said I had not betrayed his confidence. A reply came from Mrs Fletcher to say that the Headmaster was ill with pneumonia and unable to answer letters. And that was the last I heard till the end of April, when we returned from Italy to find a letter inviting me to Charterhouse in September, but warning me to say nothing about Sixth

* Lady Fletcher died on 21 March, 1958.

Form work. It was only after the Summer Quarter had begun that he finally told his colleague that he proposed to transfer him to another form.

My engagement to Mildred Lloyd had been officially recognised in February 1913, with marriage to follow before the end of the year. Even in those days it might be difficult to find a house, and it certainly was to us, till at last we were offered ' Brookside ' at Stanford Dingley, two miles from Bradfield, further up the valley of the Pang. It was a beautiful little Georgian house, with a rent of £32 and, as far as I remember, no rates ; and of course no light, and a cesspool that was periodically cleared at night by a one-armed tramp in consideration of five shillings and a jug of beer. Close by was a watering-place of cattle, water avens grew in the field opposite, and from a southward-facing slope not far away we had daffodils and primroses and cowslips and oxslips and once even *narcissus biflorus*. It was a perfect home for one summer and tolerable for one winter, but really too far from the College to be a permanent home in days when school began at 7.30 in the morning. Later generations, knowing only the roads of to-day, can hardly conceive what a side lane could be like in winter fifty years ago. When I had come off my bicycle once or twice in the dark I found it simpler to push it the rest of the way. There was a delightful riverside path, but that took too long. Still for a limited tenancy of eight months it was a charming home. We had the help of an excellent maid, Milly Ennew, who had been with the family at Eynsham. She did not accompany us to Godalming except to settle us in, having decided on what proved an unhappy marriage with a worthless young farmer next door. Our united income was professedly £500 a year, quite sufficient for a start in those times ; but we were greeted on our first arrival by a letter asking me to wait for part of the salary due to me : Bradfield was already in deep waters.

We had been married on 30 December 1913, a day on which bright skies and a thin coating of snow on the ground made Lichfield Cathedral more beautiful than I have seen it before or since. M. with her gift for going all lengths had invited the whole tribe of her nieces, nine or ten of them, with two seniors, to be bridesmaids and two small nephews to be pages. One of them, my friend Michael, very reasonably went on strike half way. The best man was my Oxford friend Okey Belfour. The more conventional members of the clan were mildly shocked at the substitution for Mendelssohn's Wedding March, which I appreciate now more than I did then, of Vulpius' *Gelobt sei Gott*, a glorious tune for a cathedral organ played by the young Dr Harris, later Master of the Queen's Music. Who could have guessed that eight months later Okey would be a prisoner of war ? Knowing twenty languages, he had gone out with the B.E.F. as an interpreter, and in the stress of August 1914 had been used also as a despatch rider. He was made prisoner because he was exhausted to the point of going to sleep on his motor-cycle, when he fell off and sprained his ankle. I will add that he used his captivity to master Hebrew and Russian, and when the polyglot camps were divided up into national ones, he applied to stay with the Russians to complete his mastery of the language. He was with them for two years. Northern Ireland became his home and still is. We have not met for thirty years, but an excellent letter can be elicited on occasion.

Furnishing had been good fun. It is possible to use that word of days when a decent chest of drawers might with luck be bought for ten shillings and £50 went a very long way. M. possessed some charming bedroom furniture, but I cannot remember that I owned anything but an armchair. But at least I possessed the books and the china that can turn a house into a home. Our best purchase was the dinner table that is still admired and envied. When Angela Mackail married McInnes, she brought with her the oak table, designed no doubt by Philip Webb, which had been the first dinner table of her Burne-Jones grandparents. We were permitted to have it copied by Morris and Co. and, with its two extra leaves, the cost was £10. Our dinner service, leadless glaze, was a mistake : it chipped far too easily and was all gone in a few years. On the other hand our dessert service, almost the cheapest to be had at Goode's in South Audley Street, is still in perfect condition, with only one dish cracked. We were not well endowed with carpets, but a Soumak rug given us by Thackeray cousins seemed too good for the floor : in our dining room at Stanford Dingley it hung on a wall. In Emery Walker's drawing room at Yattendon I had fallen in love with the Morris Little Chintz, and I still regret that in neither of our first homes could we have it because it cost 4/6 a yard. When we had to furnish a new home in 1919, it was temporarily unprocurable : we had to go elsewhere for a pretty stuff which cost 15/- and was fading within a month or so. At what cost young people curtain their windows to-day I cannot tell.

So in September 1914 we left Bradfield for Godalming. I had been there almost ten years and had I hope learned a good deal. The College and the Berkshire country retain a sure place in my affections : I had learnt to walk and not forgotten how to cycle, while in recent years my range had been extended by the kindness and the keenness of a neighbour, Mrs Mansel-Jones, who lived at the attractive, rambling house, opposite the College gate, which has now for many years been the residence of the headmaster. She often took Vince and me on what he called a Widow's Cruise to parts of the Downs beyond the reach of our legs. One particular supper picnic remains fresh in memory. When the time came for return the car declined to start, because the body was teed up on a slight ridge and the tyres could not bite. The widow flung down a fine rug which the wheels at once tore into strips ; but it was no good, and we walked down in the gathering dusk to the village of Compton in search of horses and ropes. There we found a farm where we were much impressed by the courtesy and personality of the farmer. We got home to a champagne supper at midnight, when the faithful butler betrayed the anxiety he had felt by refusing to speak to his mistress. In 1923 I had the good fortune to cross Sicily, from Palermo to Agrigento, in the company of Kenneth Grahame, author of *The Wind in the Willows*. Learning that his home was at Blewbury I asked if he had ever known Farmer Stevens. He replied that he knew him well, and told me of his funeral : the coffin had been carried on a farm wagon which was afterwards burnt and the horse which drew it killed. A good piece of folklore to have survived to our age. Another drive that lives in memory was on St. Luke's Day in 1911, when a wonderful summer was followed by a wonderful autumn and the beechwoods had a brilliance I have never seen surpassed.

CHAPTER V

CHARTERHOUSE I

IT was a strange time to begin life at Charterhouse, with no certainty that I should be there more than a few weeks. In point of fact I stayed there for thirty-two years. Had Haig Brown's long career been ten years longer, I have no doubt he would have invited the son of his old friend to join his staff in some capacity or other. Under his successor I had no particular wish to go to Charterhouse. I had noted the retirement of T. E. Page in 1910 and never dreamed of aspiring to succeed him ; but to do so now at the invitation of a great headmaster was a very different thing. For Dr Page had become a legendary figure as a teacher of the Classics and had taught the Sixth Form for thirty-seven years, from 1873 to 1910. He and his friend John Sargeaunt at West-minster must, outside the universities, have been the two most notable classical teachers of their age. Though at the end he was old and tired, to have succeeded him directly would have been overwhelming. But once more I was fortunate in coming in after four years of a not very prosperous interregnum. Our first meeting in Brooke Hall—the name at Charterhouse for both the Common Room and its members—was a surprise to both. I had always known of ' Page's white trousers ', but never knew that they were the St. Kilda tweed which I had somehow seen and liked and adopted two or three years earlier. He cocked his eye at me and said, ' Where did you get that ? ' It was not to be found in the shops and I cannot remember how I acquired it, but somehow we had heard of it long before. Ten or twelve years later an old acquaintance of Stowe Hill days visited M., wearing a coat and skirt of the same. She said she had a roll of it and was prepared to sell me some, enough for coat and knickerbockers, and an overcoat for the small Robin. Page always wore it for trousers, even with his black coat in London. It was rumoured that he kept a roll of it at his tailor's in Godalming ; and that was true. After his death in April 1936 I tried to buy some of it, but the executors would not give permission. That was not the end. When in 1954, shortly before his death, Wilson Harris published his excellent autobiography,

Life So Far, he raised some questions about the stuff which I thought
I could answer, though in fact I could not. I had interesting correspondence with him, which unfortunately I have not preserved,
and learnt that when the population was removed from St. Kilda,
' placed far amid the melancholy main ', Page traced the family who
had woven it, with the aid of the Scottish Office, to somewhere in
the Shetlands (if I remember right) and continued to wear it as
long as he lived. But the cloth in later years had not the same
strength and durability as of old. After my correspondence with
Wilson Harris I fetched out a waistcoat forty years old, and after
the necessary reshaping have worn it for the last three winters. It
is as good as ever.

It is a pity that so little is recorded of so eminent a scholar, who
was also a great personality and a great orator. There were really
two Pages, the scholar who lived in an uncomfortable and eccentric
home at Godalming and the man who had his own distinguished
circle at the Reform Club. Latterly at Godalming his only close
friends were the Headmaster and Mrs Fletcher, who alone knew
a great talker at his best. In his London club he was almost a
monarch. When Mr Asquith was given a dinner on his translation
from the Commons to the Lords, the chosen orator was the old
retired schoolmaster, and his speech was a masterpiece. I succeeded
in wheedling a printed copy of it from him and his only remark was,
' I couldn't eat a bit of dinner '. Only twice did I hear him speak.
Once was as a guest at the Headmasters' Conference dinner in the
hall of Magdalen College, Oxford, when he totally eclipsed the
other speakers with his impressive appearance and magnificent
voice and the roll of true oratory. In the ample days before 1914
a certain number of assistant masters were given the privilege of
attending the Conference, and I twice did so with Vince, at Eton
and at Magdalen. I may say that neither of us had the smallest
desire to be a headmaster. The other time was when, late in life,
he was persuaded to dine as Guest of Brooke Hall. Then his speech
was most disappointingly unlike his best. It appeared that he had
had an attack of giddiness in the afternoon and really ought to have
stayed at home : ' I'd prepared you a nice little speech, please,
and I couldn't remember a word of it '. That was a sad pity, for
few of that generation could ever have heard him. Of the scanty
records of a great personality the best is to be found in Sir Frank
Fletcher's *After Many Days*, with a few pages in the reminiscences
of Wilson Harris and Frank Swinnerton. An admirable story from
the latter will appear elsewhere.

Some years after his retirement he was invited to stand for Parliament, as a Member for Cambridge University, and that he would have welcomed : ' I think I could have made them listen to me '. But the invitation came too late, when many were already pledged to the support of a lesser man. He outlived retirement for a full quarter of a century, in the terribly exacting post of Editor in Chief (one of three) of the Loeb Library, with an office at Heinemann's in Great Russell Street. It must have been an exhausting job, to be master of any author, Latin or Greek, of any period, and to make sure that the translator was correct. His comment on some American scholars was characteristically dry : ' You try to save them from their mistakes, please, and they repay you with insult '. The parenthetic ' please ' is a traditional part of all Page stories, but I am bound to say I can't ever remember hearing him use it. But then I did not know him very well.

I suppose it may be said that Charterhouse was the right school for me, provided I could make good there. How Carthusian my family was I really did not know till I read an article by my friend R. L. Arrowsmith, after my retirement in 1946, on *A Great Carthusian Family*. I knew that I was the third generation in Brooke Hall, a succession in itself unique, and that not only my father and two of his brothers had been educated at Charterhouse and an uncle on my mother's side as well : but I did not know that one of my grandfathers and three great-uncles had been Carthusians. And that is only the beginning ! Robert Watkinson too, Usher (i.e. second master) from 1812 to 1826, was not only a close friend of my grandfather, the Rev. Andrew Irvine, but a connexion by marriage of my mother's family as well. From him, or his wife, came much of our family plate. In later days my wife, with five nephews and five great-nephews at Godalming, became almost as Carthusian as myself.

My father had never intended to be a schoolmaster. But he had been a very good head of his house, Gownboys, and as such was Orator, the boy appointed to deliver a Latin speech on Founder's Day, 12 December 1854—more than a hundred years ago. On such occasions the Orator passed round his cap, and this time he received in it no less than £195 towards his expenses at Oxford, the largest sum ever contributed till then. While still at Christ Church he was invited to return as Master in Gownboys. What that involved I do not know, but it certainly was not a lucrative post, for a copy survives of a paper in which he requests the Governors to raise his pay from £40 per annum. Of course he received a salary as a member of Brooke Hall as well. He intended to seek ordination in 1864, but stayed one more term in order to help Haig Brown to settle in as headmaster. They remained lifelong friends.

Certainly if I had had the pick of any scholastic post anywhere, the Sixth Form at Charterhouse would have been my choice—if any competent authority thought me fit for it.

In the autumn of 1914 military service naturally was the vital issue. As I have said, officers of the O.T.C. were ordered to stay for the present with their units. The Charterhouse C.O. had written to me some months earlier, saying that he much needed the services of another officer ; and all the more so when in August his two Territorials had been called up and he had 150 recruits in the Corps. My first parade at Charterhouse was with a squad of more than sixty, their first drill. Though still a pretty crude Second Lieutenant I was soon in command of a Company. There was no regular calling-up, but all the officers signed a War Office letter declaring their willingness to serve wherever required. Asquith and Kitchener most sensibly left the responsibility to headmasters to say whom they would release and whom they wished to keep ; and also insisted that the work of the O.T.C. should not be left wholly to men too old for active service. That Fletcher wished to keep me was only natural : it would have been very difficult to restore my predecessor to the post from which he had just been shifted. So I remained at Charterhouse with a clear conscience, if not always with a quiet mind. It was not till the spring of 1918 that the War Office asked if any more of us could be spared, and then I was rejected as too old : no officer over thirty-five was being taken at that stage.

Equipment in those early days of the war was ludicrously short. Our large contingent was left with ten service rifles and seventy D.P.s, and the majority were armed with poles. It needs some keenness to take field operations seriously when you have only a pole to present at the enemy, not even to use as a quarter-staff. Our C.O. was a lover of ceremonial, and the drill for cheering an inspecting General could not fail to provoke hilarity, when straw hats raised aloft on poles ' at the word Hip-hip ' went bowling all over the parade ground before a brisk wind. We only put on uniform once a week. I may say that I was greatly impressed with the efficiency of senior N.C.O.s : and in the conditions of 1914 there could be no lack of keenness in the rank and file.

My service in the O.T.C. brought me under the command of Major (later Lt.-Col.) Smart, almost as legendary a figure as Dr Page. Many a time I was urged to collect and write down the ' Colonel stories ' and I heartily wish I had done so, for few of them remain in memory, even of those that I invented myself. It is not true that when he had to ring up the War Office he got into uniform first. It is not true that when starting for a motor tour in France he began driving on the right of the road as soon as he left Godalming, ' for pwactice '. It is not true (though I have been assured it was) that having appointed to meet Mrs Smart outside Boot's, he was later found waiting patiently outside Holden's (now Lotus and Delta). Nor is it true that when asked the French for whitebait, he declared it was *bête noire*. Nor yet do I believe, though I had it from Sergt.-Major Locke, that, instructing a class how to cross an unbridged river, he said they should take off their equipment and swim over. ' But, sir, what becomes of the equipment ? ' ' You swim back and fetch it.' Yet nothing that has been invented of him surpasses the truth. I have been assured on the most respectable and veracious authority that in pre-Charterhouse days at Eastbourne he told a cadet that to stand at ease he must carry his left foot twelve paces to the right, and that in forming fours he should take a pace to the rear with the left foot and a pace to the front with the right. And it is true that after having his hair cut one day he was observed soon afterwards to re-enter the saloon and sit down in the vacant chair. That story was famous some forty-five years ago : it was recalled to me by the driver of the taxi which carried me to the Colonel's funeral in May 1955. In this matter I would not have my own veracity impugned.

Gilbert Murray has told of a walk he once took with von Wilamowitz-Moellendorff, when the great scholar strode ahead till he suddenly turned and asked, ' *Was ist ein Spoonerismus* ? ' One answer might be, ' The same as a Colonelismus '—though that would not be good German. For spoonerisms as commonly told are almost all spurious : the true spoonerism is not a transposition of letters but the substitution of one word or name for another. Julian Huxley on the radio and Sir Ernest Barker in *Age and Youth* have made that clear. The instances I give here are genuine. He once complained to me of a boy in my house whom he found unsatisfactory, but with his native kindliness wanted him to have warning that trouble was coming : ' Have a word with him before you speak to him '. On a hot afternoon in Camp, undecided whether the troops should fall out for a time or just sit down where

F

they were, he made a third choice and asked me to ' go and tell the Company to fall down '. And once we were waiting for the preliminaries of Night Operations when there approached from a neighbouring encampment the perfect exemplar of a stage scoutmaster and curate. We were all a little inclined to giggle before the Colonel helped by asking, 'Are you in tents, sir, or under canvas ? ' It was at the same Camp that, to pull the marching together as we returned from the morning's work, he exhorted the contingent, ' Now, Charterhouse, get to pieces '. He also reminded an assembly of N.C.O.s that lady friends were not admitted till after 3 a.m.

One famous story has found its way into the public prints. Starting back from operations on Puttenham Common, the marching seemed to the C.O. to be ' idle ' (as they say, or used to say, in the Guards). He gave the order to mark time and then the warning : ' If you can't march better than that, you'll have to mark time all the way back to Charterhouse '. But of the most celebrated utterance attributed to him, the wartime question, ' Was it you or your brother who was killed ? ' I have never been certain, for the same story is told of an absent-minded headmaster elsewhere. It is alleged to have been made to one whose reply was, ' Neither, sir : I never had a brother '. I hope this version is true, but cannot vouch for it.

It is from Camp that many of the best memories of him come, and I remember a highly critical subaltern remarking that one had no notion of his capacity till one had seen him at Camp. There was none in 1915 and when it was revived the next year there were few who had been ' in tents or under canvas ' before. So he lectured on the subject, and called it the Public Scamp. His power of discipline was admirable, and he really, I think, believed that to slope arms smartly was the finest thing in the world : and our splendid Sergt.-Major Locke no doubt shared his view. And that the Corps knew they were smarter than the rest was a thing which did not help to make them popular. That insignificant book, *The Charterhouse We Knew*, speaks of the great fight with Eton and Harrow. That fortunately did not occur, but it came near enough for the Brigadier, Robeson of Eton, to call the officers from Mess and to sound the fall-in. In *After Many Days* Sir Frank Fletcher records (under a wrong date) that the Headmasters of Eton and Harrow, enquiring into the facts, received the same answer : ' They are so beastly good '. There should have been four more words—' and they know it '. Further, we alone marched on parade to tuck of drum, an instrument which Harrow had sworn to loot.

And while every other unit, I should suppose, in the British Army marched onto parade in fours and formed close column of platoons, Charterhouse alone were liable to march in close column and wheel into position, a difficult and complex movement. The Camp of 1917 was certainly a nerve-trying one, for it began with the longest spell of rain I can recall. Charterhouse were lucky, for we settled in during a lull of two or three hours. Harrow were not, for they had gone down on the previous day with no regular Sergeant-Major nor one single cadet who had been in Camp before. No wonder they were edgy. That was the only Camp which it was difficult for an officer to enjoy, and for the troops, who went sick in considerable numbers, it must have been very trying indeed.

I attended a musketry course at Bisley in January 1916, which no doubt made me a much more useful officer. I was called away for two nights by the death of my father-in-law, knocked down by an engine on the private siding at his works ; but I worked very hard and took a D. Certificate (Distinguished) and was musketry officer in the Corps for the rest of my time. And it brought me some pleasant, and I hope useful, quasi-military holidays. In the Mess at Tidworth I saw a notice asking for instructors in musketry and other subjects for various battalions on the conscientiously fortified East Coast, and one of the adjutants whose name appeared was Stanley Hall, with whom fourteen years before I had made my first visit to Italy. I applied to be posted to his battalion at Lowestoft, went there several times, made some most pleasant acquaintances, and found in Hall, by this time an architect of some standing, a very delightful friend. No doubt I was of some use at Lowestoft : a spare officer might mean a bit of leave for someone, and I certainly knew more about musketry than those I was required to instruct. But I received much more than I gave, with good quarters, with pay and allowances, and the life-giving East Coast air.

Musketry, by the way, nearly led to my premature resignation of my commission. I had been a captain for a good many years when the War Office announced that I must revert to lieutenant, as not efficient in musketry. To the War Office musketry meant Hythe, and the excellent wartime course run by Territorials at Bisley did not count. My commanding officer, Colonel Jameson, represented that it would mean the loss of what he called a valuable officer, and the War Office consented to pass it as ' a special case '. I remained in the Corps till, I think, 1925, when my retirement, already contemplated, was precipitated by the desire of the War Office to promote me major. That involved learning to ride a horse, which at the age of forty-four was judged to be unwise. Four or five years earlier I had asked for riding lessons, but my C.O. was against it : he said, no doubt wisely, that I should never get my muscles to respond. So the last time I ever bestrode a horse, or crawling pony, was on the ascent to Delphi in 1911.

Colonel Smart resigned his command in 1919 on becoming a housemaster. He never did better service than when he recommended H. P. Jameson as his successor : both had commanded the Corps at Eastbourne College. A shrewd judge of boys and a successful housemaster, he was helped by a good and charming wife. In his first year his house won the football cup, and his voice was heard shouting, ' Well played, Charterhouse ' : an ephemeral publication of the time congratulated him on his strict impartiality. Sometimes no doubt—at least I hope there is no doubt—a sly humour emerges, as when a Robinite, apologising for a late return from a match at Lancing, explained that the engine was missing and was asked ' Did you come without it ? ' And recently a friend recalled a memory of forty and more years ago when, during a French lesson, the Colonel asked how many of the division had ever been in Paris. Kenneth Jardine, who told me the story, put up his hand. ' Very good, my friend : take 50 marks.' Clamour naturally followed : ' Sir, is that fair ? ' ' No, perhaps not. All take 50 marks.'

He lived to be past eighty, very lame with arthritis, but true to form in mind and tongue. In perhaps the last of his notable sayings he deplored the ravages of the Black Watch beetle in Compton church. ' Colonel stories ' are no doubt retailed in most countries of the world. Once in an Alpine hut one of his daughters heard them being told on the other side of the partition. There is a parallel to that which I have always enjoyed, the story of a subaltern in the Boer war, a Bradfieldian, lost on patrol and crawling cautiously towards a laager, not knowing whether it contained Boer or Briton. His anxiety was only relieved when he heard a voice imitating his own housemaster, Andrew Low.

For our first Charterhouse home we rented a house called Sandrock, immediately opposite the water tower at the top of Frith Hill. During the first months of the war someone, generally a member of Brooke Hall, guarded this all the time, but at the beginning of December the guard was withdrawn. A little later, on the night before Founder's Day, 12 December, I woke at 1 a.m. to find my wife insensible on the floor. That morning for the long

Founder's Day service attendance at chapel was very thin and in the course of it thirty-six boys went out, and at one time six masters were engaged simultaneously in carrying out those who had collapsed. But it was not enemy action. The first autumn of the war was abnormally wet and, as our neighbour, the architect Thackeray Turner, had warned the water authorities might happen at such a time, the sewage had contaminated the water supply. Fortunately there were no serious cases and the three central, or ' Block ' houses, which had their own source of supply, were untouched. But for years to come we were condemned to drink chemicals. Our first home was shadowed by the loss of two children and, truth to tell, for the stay-at-home the first war was harder to endure than the second : the organization and rationing were far less adequate. It was a new start in life when in 1919 we were able to buy a house to which we gave the good family name of Lord's Meade. It was an attractive house, and nearer to the school. It had been built in 1914 by the School Secretary, who had bought it off the peg. Visiting a relative in the neighbouring village of Dunsfold, he had seen and liked a house designed by the excellent local builder, and simply ordered a replica. This had one disadvantage, that the front door did not face the road, and visitors at first were liable to appear at the drawing-room window. We lived there for eight years, and it was the birthplace of Robin, Janet and Murray. We also bought the freehold of the land and made some modest additions to the house and certainly added to the value of the property. When I became a housemaster in 1927, we sold it to my colleague J. C. Thomson, who enlarged and altered it, and now it holds more beautiful and precious things than any house of the size known to me.

When we came to Charterhouse, Frank Fletcher had been headmaster for three years, and the school had begun to recover a reputation which under the previous regime had not been high. It was a period of transition, delayed by the war. Since Fletcher came two eminent Victorians had retired, Girdlestone after forty-five years' service and Moss after thirty-nine : it was Moss whose place, though not his work, I had inherited. But among my colleagues there were still two men who had been on the staff before I was born. One of them, A. H. Tod, was the ' character ' of the place, and both as a colleague and in retirement after 1920 I found him and his dry wit a delight. The senior master, due to retire at Christmas 1914, though he stayed on till 1919, was C. H. Parry, a Wykehamist and a College man. Apart from Frank Fletcher, I owe more to him than anyone. He was an enthusiast, an inexhaustible talker and walker, and later a somewhat intolerant young newcomer spoke of him to me as ' the quintessential bore '. That was grossly unfair. He might be, I admit, a bad man to meet if one had an engagement elsewhere, but at the right time and place, on a long walk or cycle ride, he was magnificent company, pouring out the riches of a memory that went back to the Winchester of the sixties. I learnt more of the Surrey country, and indeed of Oxfordshire and the Cotswolds, in his company than in any other. These two men, I should have said, had nothing in common but their loyalty to Fletcher and to Charterhouse, and how it came about that they should spend a holiday together at Leipsig I do not know. But I am glad they did. For Parry undertook the education of an unmusical Tod and induced him to listen to an opera, *Die Hugenotten* of Meyerbeer. Parry coached him assiduously, but one thing even he could not explain—why the Huguenots should wear kilts. It so happened that an English lady was sitting next to Tod, and at the end of the first act she turned quietly to him and said, ' Your friend seems not to have noticed that the bill has been changed. This is *Lucia von Lammermoor* '. Tod's comment was characteristic: ' We nearly had to come home by different trains '.

But the most prominent member of Brooke Hall till he retired in 1921 was no doubt Frank Dames-Longworth. He was a purely natural scholar, for he rarely read a book, and had a truly remarkable gift for writing Latin verse. Tod, perhaps slightly romanticising his friend, declared that after an excellent dinner he could turn out a first-class copy by prayer-time, which was nine o'clock. For a good many years the *Saturday Westminster* ran a competition in Greek and Latin Verse, weekly for a long time and then more rarely, till it died out in the twenties. The competition was a thing that could have existed only in England, and the standard in its early years was exceedingly high. Longworth told me he had never sent in a copy without gaining at least an hon. mention. He was less addicted to Greek, but once gave me a version of a long piece of Matthew Arnold with which he said he had won the Elder Prize at school : if so, it was a wonderfully mature performance. He was, as I have said, by no means a man of books, but he did possess some, and when he retired they lay in piles on his study floor and anyone was invited to buy what he would—a shilling for a large book, sixpence for a small. He had three times won the Amateur Championship of Rackets, and it was to his coaching, and to his generous hospitality to our pairs in London, that the frequent success of

Charterhouse at Queen's Club was due, eight times between 1888 and 1914—and then never again till 1956. He was a man with much of Irish charm and a good deal of Irish unreasonableness—not always an easy colleague, especially to headmasters. But he was an inspiring teacher, and the only one whose services are recorded by a tablet in the sunless classroom which his enthusiasm warmed for so many years.

But of all my colleagues the one I remember with most affection was Reggie Bridge. I don't quite know what we had in common, except that the things I found amusing he seemed to find amusing too. He professed no interest in games. Shooting and fishing in the holidays were his recreation, and he acquired his first pair of white flannel trousers for a voyage to Africa, when he travelled from Cape to Cairo, in a sabbatical year, after retiring from his house, Girdlestoneites, in 1930. He was never ill except for one attack of a complaint which led me to tell him that we should have to call him Pontius Sublicius: and he seemed marked for a happy and mellow old age when he died of heart failure in January 1937, after an attack of rheumatic fever. Of the colleagues of my later years I liked none better than Walter Sellar and his delightful wife, a niece of my old friend Warde Fowler. It would be impertinent to praise the humour of the author of *1066 and All That*. But there must be volumes of fun that never reached print. When he approached with a particularly grave face one always had hopes. ' Have you heard of the journalist who complained that he couldn't get his stuff in because of Reuter's cramp ? ' ' I've been looking over a paper on Othello, and one boy says that Othello complained that Desdemona played the trumpet in bed '. ' Do you know the alternative reading in the Ancient Mariner ?

All in a hot and copper sky
The bloody sun at noon
Right up above the mast did stand,
So did the bloody moon.'

I do not know if his comment on the Health Service is in print, ' weeping and nationalising of teeth' : if not, it is time that it was.

In 1914 the Director of Music was Edward Rendall, elder brother of Monty, and first cousin of Gerald, the headmaster who appointed him. As a musician he was the enthusiastic amateur, and as an amateur not in the first class. Neither was he an organiser. At Dulwich he had taught mathematics, and he knew most of what could be known of the Indian Mutiny. But he deserves to be remembered as the creator of the Charterhouse Masque. This was composed for the tercentenary of the school in 1911: I cannot speak with precision, but must be content to say that he composed most of the dialogue and nearly all the music, and to me it is rather sad that almost all his work has been improved away. But the first scene, the expulsion of the monks, remains untouched, and it is always the best. As with Dr Sweeting at Winchester seventeen years earlier, a new age began with the coming of Dr Thatcher (later Sir Reginald), our first trained professional director. He had been D.A.Q.M.G. on Lord Plumer's staff in the war, which suggests, what is true, that his organization was admirable. His stay was too short, only eight years, because with his rather delicate health the doctors would not let him do London work at such a distance from town. But in later days he always maintained that his Charterhouse years were the happiest of his life, and we may be proud that it was so. He carried our music far up towards the high level it maintains under John Wilson to-day. And if in forty-two years of school life I have seen many changes, I have seen nothing in which the difference is more marked than in the importance given to music, and in the standard of performance. That of course applies not to Charterhouse or to Bradfield alone : it would be true of any school.

There are two classes of schools, those, like the Bradfield of my day, where the masters have all their meals together and not unnaturally sometimes get on each other's nerves, and those where they live separately and rarely meet, except probably for a few minutes daily in a crowded and smoky common room. Charterhouse was a happy compromise ; for there was a most pleasant institution of a Brooke Hall dinner, cheap and good, on two evenings a week. When I went to Charterhouse, Brooke Hall was still a room which should have been a part of Gownboys and, as the table could only seat sixteen, a junior man who had put his name down to dine was liable to find it crossed off the list. This lasted till July 1916, and from the autumn of that year we occupied the new Brooke Hall, with a dining-room which for a special occasion could take the whole staff. We were wonderfully fortunate to possess this building, built with entrance arch, sergeant's lodge, cycle shed, kitchen, dining-room and common room out of a legacy of £5,000 left to Charterhouse by one Henry Silver, who died in 1910. He made his bequest in memory of the time when he was one of three Carthusians at the Punch Table ; and the other two, his colleagues, were William Makepeace Thackeray, who died in 1863, and John Leech, who died in 1865. The plans had come before the Governing

Body in the summer of 1914, and that autumn, in a country quite unfamiliar with war, where one of the chief fears was unemployment, the slogan (a detestable word which had not then come into vogue) was *Business as usual*. In consequence, it was positively virtuous to proceed with the building, and later on, when it became rather indecent, it could hardly be left unfinished. So that invaluable range of buildings was completed at a cost of £5,000. If not built then, it could not have been built at all ; and its only defect was some unseasoned wood in the panelling of the dining-room.

There is a lamentable school of thought which holds that a headmaster should be an official, an administrator, not a teacher. I am thankful that neither Fletcher not his three successors would have anything to do with such a heresy. I was always astonished that Fletcher could find time for so many hours with the Sixth, and in particular to take half the composition. And if he often had to miss an hour, I was only too glad to take an extra one. For if I were asked what part of my Charterhouse life I enjoyed most, there could be no doubt about the answer—my hours with the Sixth. I had some other work as well, Middle or Under School, enough to remind me that there could be such a thing as drudgery. But in my later years my only outside work was English with a division of non-classical specialists and with no kind of examination in view : that I enjoyed only less than the Sixth. Divinity I was not required to teach, except twice for quite brief periods. Of that I was glad because it spared me a Sunday lesson. But teaching is the best way to learn, and I often have cause to regret my loose and unscholarly knowledge of things I ought to know better. It would have been good for me to sit under my headmaster.

In the autumn of 1915 I became still more closely associated with him when, his house tutor having taken a commission, he asked me temporarily to fill his place. A year later, just before Oration Quarter (as we call it) began, I had a letter from Mrs Fletcher at Woolacombe asking me to receive the parents and new boys, as the headmaster had a chill and could not return till after the week-end. The next letter postponed his return for a week : from the next, announcing his old enemy pneumonia, it seemed unlikely that he would return at all. Eventually, after a long convalescence, he came back in December, but not to resume work, though the moral weight of his presence was worth much. Nor did he resume his teaching till the summer. So for the moment I was a full-time housemaster, with an increased share of the work of the Sixth, while the work of the O.T.C. was also much heavier than two years earlier. It is the only time in my life when I have been thoroughly overworked. For the first time I learnt the useful lesson, how much the government of a house is in the hands of the monitors. The monitors of that year were a capable if not very harmonious set, but fortunately the house had a particularly able head in David Jenkins (now Lord Justice) : he kept me in my place and taught me a great deal. Thirty years later I visited an exhibition at the Victoria and Albert Museum of the Old Colonial Architecture of America, which led me to become a member of the Georgian Group, one of the numerous offspring of the National Trust. I found that one of the Saunderite monitors of 1916 was Chairman and another Hon. Treasurer.

The position of house tutor at that time was a new one, and he was more of a guest than a man in authority, a visitor who was not quite a part of the house. It was a good many years before the smaller houses had one. But it was good for the house and good for the young master. In Saunderites it was essential. If a headmaster is to be a housemaster too, there is much routine work which he ought to be spared. It was a step forward when in 1924 Mr and Mrs Fletcher withdrew to the newly-acquired Northbrook, and retrograde when as a measure of wartime economy Robert Birley returned to Saunderites. Now, in the autumn of 1957, a new headmaster's house has arisen in the Saunderite garden, and Mr Young has ceased to be housemaster of Saunderites. A very good measure.

Till 1919 the work of the school could not fail to be affected by the war and by inadequate temporary masters, and the standard of taste in art and literature was pretty low. And here I was able to make what I think was a useful contribution to civilisation. The school was amply provided with prizes in the humanities, but no one was required to compete for them : candidates were few and, I am told, divided up the field so as not to impede each other. Fletcher had not yet dealt with the matter and in 1915 asked my advice about the problem, and what is more took it. Since that year all members of the Sixth of all denominations have been obliged to sit for one or other of the chief prizes, choosing which they preferred. The system answered well and the winner's work was always good. I can only remember one occasion when a major prize (the Elwyn, for History) was not awarded. Once a Science Specialist won the Thackeray, for English Literature, and in the thirties twice in succession a Classical boy won the chief Science prize. These two were the brothers C. W. and E. V. Wright, successively head of the school, and geologists who reported to the highest geological authority on the chalk cuttings when the Guild-ford by-pass was under construction.

Charterhouse was still a markedly Classical school, and the few historians long remained members of the Classical side and did much of the work of the form. It was not till 1925 that they became a separate unit under a fine teacher, a wartime acquisition, George Green, who stayed on for the rest of his active career instead of returning to rebuild his practice as a coach at Cambridge. He contributed much to our intellectual life and in all the performances I have seen of the Masque of Charterhouse, George Green as John Wesley revisiting the scenes of his youth was the most impressive figure. And when the Shakespeare Society was formed, he set the standard for us all. His Lear, who reduced Cordelia to tears, is an abiding memory.

I had long hoped to found such a society, but felt I must wait till the departure of a colleague gave me a free hand. For an informal one had already existed, a truly dreadful affair. A different collec-tion of readers were invited every time and the parts allotted in the room at the time of the reading ; and the standard of literature in the early twenties was very low indeed. A limited membership (twelve boys and four masters, together with the headmaster), an obligation to attend, and an early allotment of parts, seemed to me indispensable. At first we were shy of ladies, but when Mrs Fletcher began to read the whole standard was raised. The excel-lence of her reading in every sort of part was an inspiration. She made *Antony and Cleopatra* our show piece. In later years Mrs Walter Sellar, with her lovely voice, became our leading lady. I always claim to have done two useful things—the founding of the Shakespeare Society and the Art Lectures, both of them on a Bradfield model. The Bradfield ' Shaker ' was more prim, sitting round the headmaster's dinner table and nibbling thin bread-and-butter during the interval. At Charterhouse we usually met at the headmaster's, but sometimes elsewhere, sat in armchairs and adjourned to another room for refreshments. Last winter I had regretfully to decline an invitation to be a guest at the 250th reading.

To come to the Art Lectures, once more I am deeply grateful to my headmaster for his reception of the idea. The first course was given in 1919 by our neighbour Arthur Clutton-Brock, art critic of *The Times,* and they have gone on ever since. I ran them for the first fifteen years, and of course made mistakes till I learned never to accept a recommendation of any lecturer whom I did not know or had not heard personally. It was a good many years before a fair proportion of the lectures came to be home-made. A certain lecturer had given an excellent course, but by the time I asked him again he had become an eminent person, and with eminence had come arrogance : his lectures, thrown at us without preparation, were such that afterwards my colleague J. C. Thomson asked if I would like him to try his hand. We have never had a better lecturer, and I rejoice to learn that Charterhouse has induced him to emerge from his retirement once more this year. In 1934 I was ready to try myself, with a course on *Cities of Italy* which was repeated in 1938. At first visitors were admitted at a modest charge of ten shillings for the course, and when first Dr Thatcher lectured on music, so many came that the expenses of the course were covered. But the lectures came in time to draw such a large voluntary attendance from the school, in addition to those for whom it counted as a school hour, that neighbours ceased to be invited.

In 1914 the Classical Sixth would not have been called specialists ; they were doing the normal thing. There was a considerable Army Class, but at the moment only two biologists and six other scientists, and four boys called Sixth Modern, doing I know not what. Turning over old school lists one day, when having missed my bus I had an hour to spare, I found the name Mathematical Specialists for the first time in 1918, numbering seven. In 1921 Mathematics and Science accounted for twenty-six, and Army Class had sunk to five. Not to labour the matter, the last list I looked at was 1954, when Sixth and Under Sixth Classical numbered twenty-six, History fifty-one, Modern Languages thirty-nine, Mathematics, twenty-six, Science (Chemistry and Physics) forty-one, Biology thirty-six, Geography eighteen. So the process of evolution is pretty complete : the only further stage could be the elimination of the Classics—*quod di avertant.*

Under Frank Fletcher, a great teacher as well as a great scholar, despite the broadening which took many able boys elsewhere, the Classics enjoyed a golden age. In my early years the scholars nearly all went to Oxford, but in December, 1916, the quarter when Fletcher was away, two boys entered for Trinity College, Cambridge, and to my astonishment both got Major Scholarships. In 1919 that enlivening pair E. Holroyd Pearce (now Lord Justice) and R. C. Robertson-Glasgow proceeded scholars to Corpus, Oxford, a coveted college which has too seldom opened its doors to us ; but it was at the end of 1919 that the Sixth ' burst into sudden blaze '. In that year six Carthusians were elected in the December group at Oxford, which meant that of the first eighteen scholarships awarded that year one third went to Carthusians. I kept no record of these things till 1928, when the Master of Magdalene, A. B. Ramsay, examined at Charterhouse for the first time. He afterwards told Dr Alington at Eton that he had found the standard of work very high and was asked in return why then they didn't get scholarships. At his request I looked up the facts and reported that since 1914 we had won forty-seven awards at Oxford and twenty at Cambridge, and from that time I kept a record : the number of awards when I left in 1946 was more than 180. Cambridge took a progressively large share, where King's, Magdalene, and sometimes Trinity showed themselves very partial to our candidates. No pupil of Fletcher's from either Rugby or Marlborough or Charterhouse had yet won the Oxford blue riband of the Ireland, though David Jenkins had been *proxime accessit*, nor I believe the corresponding First Craven at Cambridge. I like to recall a telephone conversation in December, 1924, when I heard an unusually excited voice : ' I say, Webster's got the Ireland '. Part of my reply was, ' Thank God he went to Christ Church and not to Balliol '. And the answer, ' That's because you said he wasn't good enough '. To some extent I will plead guilty ; I had always over-estimated the difficulty of access to Balliol, which took a number of Carthusians in later years, and I certainly did regard myself as a recruiting agent for my own college, which as a matter of fact during a brilliant period quite eclipsed Balliol in the highest classical field. Denys Page, now Regius Professor of Greek at Cambridge, taught there with J. G. Barrington-Ward for twelve years, and in those years the Ireland fell to a Christ Church man six times. Professor Webster's subsequent career has shown that his Ireland was no fluke. Some years later Hugh Trevor-Roper did the same and Hugh Stubbs came very near it, and both these two won the only less honour of the Hertford, for which Webster in his day had been *proxime*. And at Cambridge Patrick Wilkinson and John Chidell won the First Craven in successive years. Just after the war Peter Green did the same. But it is not so much the brilliant few who live in memory as the high average level maintained year after year in those good days. Twice an examiner told me he wasn't sure he didn't prefer our boys to Wykehamists : ' they were so lively '. But I must say a word for the good fellows who sat in the back row, with no pretence to being scholars, but often putting the scholars to the blush by sheer good sense. One such for a good many years ran a little ' Horace Club ' in a Yorkshire village and used to consult me about what he and his friends should read. I like to recall one sitting with a seraphic smile on his face, to whom I said, ' You look as if you were reading Pickwick '. And he was !

The last form of the old quality departed in 1940. The wartime loss of standard was lamentable but inevitable. The keen critical mind of Fletcher had gone from us in 1935 and his successor, Robert Birley, a brilliant teacher of History, ancient or modern, had, alas, no Greek. So after being for twenty-one years very much a second string, I had to be provided with an assistant. But before long Cecil Harrison was engulfed in the war and, when he returned, soon left again for a headmastership.

I began as a second-rate scholar and ended as one : but I also began and ended as an enthusiast. The one real qualification I could claim as a teacher was the power of enjoyment, to which I might add the hatred of slovenliness, and that when I saw occasion for a joke it seemed best to let it come. It has always been a satisfaction to me when a jest has lived in other memories besides my own, or indeed when I had forgotten it. I remember once going into the office and being received with acclamation by the two secretaries. It appeared that they had just heard from the headmaster of a comment passed many months earlier, when, seeing a boy beating at a bumble-bee with an atlas in what seemed to me an undignified manner, I had reminded him that this was the Sixth Form, not Remove B. Only a year or two ago a letter from a Carthusian of that period contained the postscript, ' I shall never forget Remove B '.

I remember once at Oxford listening to an argument between two clever young men—too clever for me—one of whom advanced the proposition that the brilliant is always the obvious. I would rather put it that the effective (in humour) is always the spontaneous. Thus watching a batsman of great possibilities but uncertain temperament lashing the air in a match on Green, when a lady asked why, if he played so well at the nets, he played so badly here, the natural reply seemed to be that it was the difference between a net batsman and a gross batsman. And once when, as I was reading the notices in Brooke Hall, a scientific colleague coming in asked me what was the meaning of ' Consule Planco ', I had the support of the other two men in the room, both classics and now both headmasters, in my suggestion that it meant ' Look at the notice-board '. Only once can I recall an effective answer that was premeditated. The name Herbatius Borda had struck me as having a good Roman ring, and once when someone asked me who was the chief Roman authority on gardening, the answer doubtless should have been Columella, but Herbatius Borda seemed a better one.

When I first met the Sixth, they seemed to me, as at Bradfield ten years earlier, to know very little about English literature, and from the first I made opportunity to read something worthwhile that they might not otherwise meet and that really profited by a little explanation—such as *Absalom and Achitophel*, or *The Rape of the Lock*, or the two poems of Goldsmith which I still read every year, or some of the brilliant dramatic monologues of Browning. Through all my thirty-two years the hour's school on Tuesday afternoon after Corps parade was sacred to English. We could not read much, but it was possible to whet the appetite.

Every four or five years I felt moved to read *In Memoriam*, which really repays experienced guidance, and I used to give a small prize for the best essay on it—always the charming Riccardi edition while it was procurable, and later the Nonesuch. I am thankful never to have lost my taste for Tennyson and to have found so many to share it. The present generation will hardly comprehend how low his reputation had once sunk among the ignorant and tone-deaf—and not only them. I remember that in 1916 a boy of real poetic gifts lent me a book in which the name of Tennyson was once mentioned : he had been unable to pass it without a marginal comment, ' Vile impostor '. But this was an extreme instance.

But I am not sure that I enjoyed anything more than introducing my form to William Morris, always by means of Arthur Clutton-Brock's masterly little volume in the Home University Library, which appeared in 1914 just before I had the good fortune to make the acquaintance of its author, for ten years our neighbour at Godalming. I had read Mackail's fine *Life* of Morris first in 1909, and when I became a friend of his friend Emery Walker, Morris grew to fascinate me more than any other man of his century. But I was never in the least attracted by his political opinions. In that same year, 1909, I had first met him as a poet too, when at the instance of a boy whom I had not regarded as a lover of poetry, I read *The Life and Death of Jason*, Morris's first long poem and first popular success. Forty-two years later I read it for the fourth time in a Yorkshire inn, where I found my landlady deep in it when she was professedly making my bed. It was a pleasure to send her a copy. With all its wonderful wealth and variety English poetry is not rich in narrative verse, and here Morris seems to me to stand next to his master, Chaucer. But I admit that I find *Sigurd the*

Volsung, by which Morris would have wished to be judged, heavy going. I heard recently with much satisfaction that my third Head Monitor, Hilary Wayment, now Director of the *Institut Britannique* in the University of Paris, was planning a course of lectures on Morris in that city.

One of the advantages of taking a Sixth Form is that one need not be too strictly bound by a time-table. If occasionally it seemed good to lay by Demosthenes or Tacitus for an hour while I read the trial of Mr. Pickwick, or the dinner-party at Mr Dilly's, or Cobden's Over, or the description of the gorge of the Adonis from *The Golden Bough*, I am sure it was quite as good education. I remember that at the Jubilee Dinner of the Classical Association an eminent speaker recalled his first introduction to the *Shropshire Lad* on a last morning of term when we had nothing worse to do.

I declined at all times to think much about examinations, and hated the idea of any special preparation for scholarship-hunting. Perhaps that is why so many got them : they generally went up fresh. But once I did have to face the question of examinations, when in 1926 I persuaded the headmaster to let go the very useless Higher Certificate and have an examination with subjects and examiners of our own choice, like Goddard at Winchester. This was a real step forward, but it would take time to explain why.

There was a time in our Lord's Meade days when it seemed that birds were to become a major interest in life. In spite of walks with Anthony Collett of *The Times*, I had left Bradfield in total ignorance, but suddenly awoke to the new interest in 1918. In the spring of that year I doubt if I knew twenty birds : in the autumn after a visit to Aberdovey I knew eighty. It was a most thrilling moment when first from a road above it I looked down on the estuary of the Dovey and saw curlews stalking on the shore and a cormorant sitting with wings outspread like a monster of heraldry. Nests and eggs were never an attraction to me, and even more than the sight of the bird to me was its song. Only once have I been on a bird-watching holiday, to Blakeney in the April of 1922, where I found myself in wonderful company. For a real master of the subject was staying, with E. F. Benson, in our lodgings and, when Benson left, most kindly invited my companion and me to go out with him. We were just too early for the arrival of the terns, but witnessed the landfall of the yellow wagtails, and among them all the blue-headed wagtails, four of them, that I can ever expect to see. There are three reasons why, though birds have always remained a lively interest and I listen for the earliest chiffchaff and willow wren as eagerly as anyone, they have never become a study or a hobby. First, the untimely death of one of my preceptors, then the disappearance of the other, and lastly the intrusion into my life of the game of golf. One cannot stop on the links to look at crossbills, even if one knows they are there.

In the early 1920s birds and flowers brought me in touch with a remarkable man. He bore the good Surrey name of Denyer—a small gipsy-like figure with a grizzling beard, generally to be seen on a bicycle and always wearing a bowler hat, and binoculars on his chest. He had, I believe, a small cycle-repairing shop in the village of Shackleford, having thrown up his job on the Southern Railway because it interfered with his studies : he preferred near-starvation. Then O. H. Latter, the biologist, induced him to come and look after the Natural History department in the Charterhouse Museum, where he introduced the admirable practice, now so wide-spread, of bringing in wild flowers at their annual appearance and exhibiting them in specimen glasses. He was most secretive and would never reveal his discoveries to anyone he suspected of being a collector ; but when he was sure that I only wished to see and hear, and not to rob, he often took me on expeditions, and I learnt more, and more quickly, from him than from anyone else. But it did not last long : he was too much of a wanderer for any regular employment, and only tended the Museum for a year or two. His knowledge of nature seemed universal, and it was a disappointment to Latter that he could get nothing recorded on paper. I remember asking him about some bird in Aristophanes and was naturally astonished when he knew not only the bird but the passage in the play. That Aristophanes had written a play called *The Birds* was enough for him : he had acquired Hookham Frere's translation of it. A good many years later a colleague told me that a woman in Shackleford had a Latin dictionary and hoped to get half-a-crown for it. I went to her cottage and found it was Denyer's widow, who produced an excellent copy of Lewis and Short. I always collected good second-hand lexicons for new arrivals in the Sixth and gladly gave her a pound. He had also left a good microscope, but I do not know what became of that.

So I never became a practised bird-watcher, though I continued to use my eyes and my ears. And when, alas, in 1949 I left my binoculars somewhere on Brignal Banks by the Tees, I felt it was too late and too costly to replace them.

Our years in Lord's Meade covered the period during which the Memorial Chapel was conceived and brought into being. Of its final completion thirty years later I shall speak hereafter. I was, naturally, on none of the committees of the Charterhouse War Memorial, but I was so closely in touch with Frank Fletcher that I know as well as any that it was his faith and courage and tact and patience which gradually won over a majority of Carthusian opinion to accept and finally support the plan. The scheme passed through various perils and vicissitudes before Sir Giles Gilbert Scott (as he is now) was finally asked to design the chapel. After the war a great deal of building was needed to make good our Victorian deficiencies, and when the Foundation Stone was laid on 17 June, 1922, we had no need of any contractor : our own building staff did the work under our own able Clerk of the Works, Mr Boxall ; only a foreman and two masons had to be brought in from outside, and the Bargate stone was quarried two hundred yards away. The chapel was consecrated exactly five years later, on 17 June 1927. It had been a great experience to see it rising day by day, and I only wish I had studied the builder's craft with more intelligence.

The death of my mother in the spring of 1926 brought a great change in our lives, for that summer meant our last visit to the house at Eynsham which, as I have said, holds the happiest memories of any of my eight homes. Sometimes with M. and sometimes alone, I paid farewell visits to many of the places that I loved best. In point of fact, on my cycle or in a car, I have seen some of them many times since ; but in that year I thought of it all as a farewell. Eynsham lies on the Witney and Cheltenham road, six miles west of Oxford, and the west and south sides of Oxford are, in spite of the Chilterns and much besides, more interesting than the east and north. The station is on the Fairford line, and Fairford is a natural entry to the Colne valley and the Cotswolds ; and intervening stations are convenient for the Vale of White Horse, a region of beautiful villages with beautiful names—Compton Beauchamp and Kingston Lisle and Charney Bassett and Stanford-in-the-Vale. And north of the Cheltenham road lay the Windrush valley, from Minster Lovel to Burford. At Burford, by the way, we had twenty years earlier been sorely tempted by a house, the Lady Ham, of which the tenant was the young Compton Mackenzie : it will be familiar to readers of his autobiographic *Guy and Pauline*. But in those motorless, almost busless days, Eynsham was far the better place of habitation. It is not one of the beautiful villages and its chief attraction was its nearness to the river, and I would always claim that the river has far more charm above Oxford than below. Days in a boat became an essential part of a summer holiday, occasionally down past Godstow, but more commonly up to Bablock Hythe (with a notably good cake for tea), and on to the mediaeval New Bridge, with its charmingly named inn, *The Rose Revived*. By this time the river had so diminished that it really was ' this far-off lonely mother of the Thames '. No doubt it was the river, and the views from Beacon Hill and Cumnor Hurst, that have made *The Scholar Gipsy* and *Thyrsis* without question my favourite poems, more often in my pocket than any other. And later, after 1909, it became for me the country of William Morris, with Kelmscott, and the noble barn of Great Coxwell, and Little Coxwell church where the Master found the Fifteenth Century brasses to William Morys and Johane his wife, and Buscot, with Burne-Jones's master-piece, *the Briar Rose*, to which I was never denied admission. I well remember my first discovery of it, nearly fifty years ago. I went into a well-kept church with a good east window by Burne-Jones, and noticing handsomely bound books in a front pew looked in one for the squire's name. The name I read was Alexander Henderson, and it flashed across my mind that Sir Alexander (later Lord Faringdon) was the fortunate owner of those lovely pictures. I sought out the Georgian mansion which houses them, where, though none of the family were at home, no difficulty was made about entry, and after the *Briar Rose* I was invited to see Rossettis and Rembrandts as well.

I am thankful that the loss of the Eynsham home did not mean the loss of all this.

CHAPTER VI

CHARTERHOUSE II

TOWARDS the end of 1926, in my thirty-seventh quarter at Charterhouse, the Headmaster invited me to become house-master of Pageites in the following autumn. I asked, on sentimental grounds, if I might wait for Gownboys, my father's house, and was very properly refused. If I have generally been fortunate in life, I was more than ever so in Pageites. It was architecturally a very poor thing, enlarged by Page out of a small house built by a Godalming solicitor, with a minimum of amenity. Page only occupied it for five years before crossing the road to a larger house, Hodgsonites. Recently a second living room had been built, so that the boys no longer worked and played and fed all in one room. But the new one had not yet been properly furnished, and before going in I equipped it with oak ' horseboxes ' on the Winchester model. The Governing Body undertook to repay me at the price of deal on my departure, presumably fifteen years later. This scarcely sounds generous, but in point of fact they treated me with great generosity. M. had flatly, and rightly, refused to go into the house unless the servants were given decent quarters. The architect had drawn up his plans, though he hardly hoped to have them accepted without modification. But luck or Providence helped. The Finance Committee made their inspection on the best possible day, one of wet February gloom, with the lights on every-where : after which they went away and passed the plans without demur. And as the provision of servants' bedrooms involved a new front to the private side, it gave us a new dining-room, two excellent bedrooms or nurseries, and a proper pantry and bathroom. The existing bathroom would have been deprecated in a minor French hotel. The work was pushed through during the summer, just in time for our entry, and the outgoing housemaster, A. F. Radcliffe, showed a patience for which I must always be grateful to him. At the latter end I believe he could only get in and out of his house on a plank.

If we had a setback in the matter of our first cook, we had a great blessing in our first and last butler. About that time there was a theory at Charterhouse that ex-petty–officers of the Royal Navy made the best house butlers, and we duly applied for one. When he presented himself he proved very cheerful and pleased-to-meet-you, but asked if he could do the job while continuing to reside at Portsmouth. At that point Boxall, clerk of the works, suggested his brother-in-law, one Henry Edgeler, born and bred at Charterhouse and now, after service as bombing-sergeant in the Queen's, assistant to the Art Master in his studio. The help of this admirable friend and servant was above price, during our sixteen years and half my successor's time—in fact till his sudden and unexpected death. Had our naval P.O. put in as many hours' work while returning to Portsmouth at night, he would have got home after midnight and left about 4 a.m. Edgeler was almost the last of his kind : it would be scarcely possible to find, or to pay, a butler of that stamp in these days. Further, we inherited in Miss Hutton the ideal matron, who stayed with us till her marriage in 1938.

So we entered our new home, still in the hands of workmen, in September 1927, with our family of three—Robin, just short of seven, Janet five and Murray three. The family was completed in the following June by the arrival of Betty Chambers, the only nursery governess known to me who rose to the rank of Lt.-Colonel in the forces. One of the maids bore the name of Dorothy House, of a family well known in Farncombe. No one could have prophesied that thirty years later she would still be with us—cook, house-keeper and devoted sick-nurse.

An increased income led to the inevitable car, driven with untiring enthusiasm by M. and Betty Chambers, and unenthusiastically by me. Besides my irrational want of sympathy with engines, I had a genuine dread of becoming one of those who can hardly leave their door without the aid of petrol and who think nothing of lunching or dining fifty miles from home. That life of rush-about is abhorrent to me. Even in old age I generally find that public transport will get me quite easily where I want to go, and a railway journey is a positive pleasure.

We went into Pageites in a period of transition. Till quite recently, when a man became a housemaster his salary had been reduced to £150 a year, and for the rest of his living he had been a hotel-keeper. Henceforth he was an adequately paid servant of the school and his tenure of the house was limited to fifteen years. Girdlestone, who retired in 1912, had held his house since 1869—42 years. I have only once heard Lady Fletcher make any claim of service done to the school, but she did tell me recently that she was responsible for the abandonment of the hotel-keeping system. Instead of this, each housemaster was now receiving an experimental allowance for running his house, and if he made a profit was allowed to bank it in a House Improvement Fund, which could be used for any purpose sanctioned by the Governing Body. No housemaster could make a profit for himself, though with care he could probably save something out of his salary : that was a different matter. My salary for my first five years had been no more than £300, and the first rise had only come with a new scale after the war, which more than doubled it. Against the coming day of family school bills I did a good deal to protect myself by insurance.

At first there was no limit to the House Improvement Fund, but a few years later the amount was limited to £100 a year : then, with finances less easy, it was closed altogether. But by that time I had done all that I hoped to do except to provide a decent porch for the boys' entrance. In our first year inexperience led to a loss, but after that, with low prices and M.'s admirable management, we made a considerable profit. After a few years I asked permission to panel the Dining Hall and refurnish it in oak. But I was told No : I must first be repaid in full for my furnishing of New Long Room. That did not mean a long postponement, and with the new panelling and Morris curtains (my favourite Medway), it became a room in which anyone could take pleasure. It was the good Edgeler's pride to keep it in spotless condition. The architect was our nephew Christopher Green, head of the school in 1919, who had entered Charterhouse with me—whence no doubt my nickname of Uncle. Next he converted the hideous den occupied by the head monitor, which with its linoleum walls, oak desk with strip-light, and steel chair, was so successful that he proceeded similarly to recondition the rest of the studies. The pictures which some boys put on the walls might ruin any room, and I was not prepared for that. During my Oxford years I had subscribed for a series of a hundred excellent reproductions of Great Masters, published by Heinemann : I never spent £5 to better purpose, and had already used them in classrooms and elsewhere for most of thirty years. I had frames made with removable backs : the occupants of the studies could choose their own pictures and change them whenever they liked. I bequeathed the set to our successor when we left. Lastly came Monitors' Hall, a less easy room to convert. But with such improvement as was possible, and with curtains of Eyebright, it certainly looked a great deal better than ever before.—I had better explain that the two ranges of printed cottons produced by

Morris & Co., of blessed memory, were named from wild flowers and from the rivers of England.

Two gifts came to the house in our time that remain as abiding treasures, the Garnett dish and the Price bowl, both the work of the famous craftsman Omar Ramsden, who died in 1939. The former was given in memory of thirteen members of the Garnett family, and had thirteen garnets set in the rim. At Christmas 1938, a young Pageite, Tony Price, was killed tobogganing five years after leaving school. His father offered to give some athletic cup in his memory, but I suggested that we would rather have a cup that was not competitive or athletic, but just a thing of beauty, and that it should be a family memorial, for himself, his brother, and two sons. The idea was accepted : the piece was made by Omar Ramsden and sent to the father. We met by appointment in April at the final of the Arthur Dunn Cup and the gift was duly handed over to me. That match was played in a scarifying wind : the old man caught a chill and was dead of pneumonia within a week. But a lovely piece of silver stood on the top table in Dining Hall to recall the memory of a good Carthusian family.

But more important than the furnishing of a school house are the boys who inhabit it, and here our fortune was good fortune indeed. Yet I can only remember two cases in which I went out of my way to secure a boy who might not otherwise have come. Once, having a casual vacancy, I turned over some entry forms in the office and saw one marked ' Refer to Richard Goolden '. I did so, and asked if he would advise me to take a boy named Michael Melford. The reply was in the affirmative, and anyone who knows the Austin Melfords will heartily agree. The other time, I wrote to a schoolmaster and asked if a boy named Tanner who was entered for the house was coming. He replied that he understood that the boy was likely to go to Marlborough, but was a remarkable soccer player, the best he had ever had in the school. I wrote to the father and asked if, that being so, it wasn't a pity to send him to a school that played the other game, and fortunately he agreed. Denys Tanner captained Charterhouse in the first year of the war and Oxford after it, and played for England and in a winning Pegasus team at Wembley. He was also a very good head of the house, living harmoniously with some intellectuals extremely unlike himself.

The house had a kindly and humane tradition : it did not pride itself on being tough. Indeed some thought it a little wanting in energy, though I certainly did not find it so. It also had a good classical record, which is no doubt why my headmaster wanted me to take it. All houses have their ups and downs, and Pageites was on the up grade for a good many years, culminating in 1939 when all seven monitors were also School Monitors—seven out of about twenty. When we went in there were only four who had been judged ripe for authority, and only two who could read from St. Paul or a Gospel at prayers ; for one of the four had a monstrous stammer and a second asked, for technical reasons, to be limited to the Old Testament. After 1939 I was conscious of a decided loss of quality, not wholly due, I think, to the war. In our earlier years there was more stability, less change : in the first eight years we had only seven head monitors.

The great Pageite family were the Garnetts : for fifty years the house can seldom have been without a member of the clan, especially if all first cousins were counted—Admiral Given and four Eccles brothers, of whom two were noted cricketers and rackets players. The most distinguished of them, and the only scholar, came in our second year and in July 1933 celebrated his last Saturday at school by coming out first (equal) in the final examination and scoring his thousandth run of the season for the school, a feat not performed before or since. He scored five centuries that season and had a devastating habit of getting them before lunch, and, one year or another, made his hundred against every school we played except Winchester : then he failed by no wide margin, for he was caught on the boundary with his score at 96. No house can ever have had a better head, and he is now Master of Marlborough. His brother, W. J., had left young for life in Canada, but returned as the first Carthusian Rhodes scholar, a privilege very rarely granted to one who has had an English schooling.

The success of the house in the humanities was remarkable. The Thackeray Prize for English Literature fell to a Pageite six times in eleven years, and for the Talbot, mentioned earlier as the chief Leaving Scholarship, a Pageite was first, or equal first, five times between 1930 and 1938. And in the first four years of my successor's time, from '44 to '47, four of our younger scholars came out first in their turn.

We left behind us, quite unwittingly, a remarkable brood of University politicians. If Dick Taverne had become President of the Union at Oxford in 1950, as was to be expected of one who had held the three preliminary offices, there would have been three Pageite Presidents of the Union in successive years, with a Verite to follow. I cannot find that any other Carthusian has held that office except Sir George Tomlinson in 1901. In one year a Pageite was President of the Union, another was producing for the O.U.D.S., and a third captain of a notable football XI.

In my experience a house which works well generally plays well too, and in the years 1930-40 Pageites had as many captains as in the previous ten years they had colours. The game in which Pageites had of late been most conspicuous was rackets, and that period came to an end early in our time—rather to my relief. For in my first quarter the rackets bill of the pair, one of whom was also the school's first string, came to more than the book bill of the whole house. That problem solved itself, for Brian Eccles had no successor and henceforth it was at fives that a Pageite pair was most prominent, winning the House Cup over and over again. To my great disappointment we never won the Cricket Cup, played at that period as a league of all the eleven houses, but three times in succession only lost it on the result of the final round. At football, the time when we did win under the captaincy of Tanner, it was done very thoroughly, for no house scored a goal against us while we collected twelve.

Our time at Pageites was divided into two exact halves, eight years under Frank Fletcher and eight under Robert Birley. To the earlier period belongs a piece of work to which I look back with much satisfaction, my edition of a selection of Cicero's letters, ' those models ', as Gibbon called them, ' of every form of correspondence,' and one of the most fascinating bodies of writing that has come down to us from the ancient world. I could never have have been happy through fifteen or sixteen weeks of holiday, particularly at the seaside, without some regular work, and preferably not simple reading. So for eight years I was intermittently occupied with ' Tully's Epistles ', doing at a leisurely pace what a strenuous worker could have done in eight months. I remember that the final proof reached me during my first visit to Ipswich, where I kept my fifty-second birthday, a long golden week-end which introduced me to Butley and Lavenham, Kersey and Long Melford and other delectable places in the company of Alice Tanqueray. I so much enjoyed the work that I thought little of the remuneration, but as the book has sold steadily for 24 years, I am not sure that £50 was a very liberal sum and think the Cambridge University Press must have done pretty well out of it. Twice in early years Mr C. E. Carrington wrote from the Press to say how warmly the book had been commended by the chairman of some examining board.

A year earlier the Sixth had taken possession of a newly built room, close to the south-west corner of Library : it was the third that I had occupied, and certainly the most pleasant. I had put it to the headmaster that, as it was something more than a classroom, a place where school authorities met, it deserved something better than the dreary desks and benches that had hitherto seemed good enough. It was a day of easy money and a well-peopled workshop, and I think Fletcher was rather pleased that something should be asked for purposes other than scientific. Christopher Green was commissioned to design oak desks and chairs, with recesses for lexicons and other books and, as we had ' first refusal ' at two big bookshops, our provision of lexicons was soon complete. The chairs proved too expensive to be made at once, so Sussex chairs, specially strengthened, were made at High Wycombe by Morris & Co. They were supposed to last ten years but have already served for twenty-five, and I can only remember one that collapsed and left a head of the school seated on the floor. In 1934, when the room was still fresh and clean and well-kept, it received its best adornment. We had been ' doing ' William Morris and, as always happened at such times, a large parcel of textiles had been sent down at my request by that ever-to-be-regretted firm. One day the then captain of cricket, P. L. Richards, a good scholar whose family profession claimed him and precluded a certain scholarship and a more than probable football blue, suggested that we might well have some Morris curtains for the room, and he was sure the form would subscribe. I conferred with the headmaster and was told to find out if there was any money in a certain fund ' for the benefit of the scholars ', which proved to have an adequate balance. But our architect was for something more modern and recommended a short-lived firm in Berners Street—killed like Morris & Co. by the war—which sold textiles designed by well-known painters, Duncan Grant and others. Curtains of a really noble beauty in crimson and black were chosen : one looked forward to the short afternoons when one could turn on the lights and draw them. Unfortunately when they had to be lined for purposes of black-out, the very long curtains became too heavy and liable to tear, and their life did not exceed a dozen years. But with the clean furniture, the curtains and the pictures, the room was one it was a pleasure to inhabit. The walls were free for the formation of a picture gallery, which grew from two Medici prints to thirteen, derived from various sources and ranging from Leonardo da Vinci to Charles Furse. And very useful they were. Everyone was expected to have an adequate knowledge of them and occasionally that knowledge was tested on paper. Two attributions deserve record. Attention had no doubt been called to a likeness between Whistler's Carlyle and Dr Page—still sometimes passing the door on his way to Library but never induced to come inside—and also between Velasquez' portentous figure of Alessandro del Borro and the late G. K. Chesterton. The latter once appeared in a list as Lord Chesterfield, the other as ' Dr Page, after Raphael ' : at least the critic realized that Whistler was not a Pre-Raphaelite. I can testify to the sincerity of the attributions.

In 1934 the family received an addition when Patricia Lloyd, hitherto a frequent visitor, decided to make her home with us. Her father, Jack Lloyd, had been killed in France in 1915, and her mother, the lovely Nora Lawrence, had died in 1927. She remained with us till her very happy marriage in 1936, and she is one of the many whose debt to her aunt must be past calculating.

The summer of 1935 brought the retirement of Frank Fletcher, the man to whom I have owed most in life. He had been at Charterhouse for twenty-four years, and Master of Marlborough for eight years before that. There, at the age of thirty-three, he had been the first layman to be appointed headmaster of one of our great boarding schools, and long before his retirement was regarded as the head of his profession. He was a great scholar as well as administrator. It seemed to me that the secret of his power was humility, and the serenity that goes with it, and the refusal to be hurried. He did nothing until it had to be done : it simmered long and peacefully in his mind, and when the time came he was ready. He and Mrs Fletcher had received a fresh lease of life when in 1924 they withdrew to the newly acquired Northbrook : otherwise health never too secure might have deprived the school of their service much earlier. Anyone who wishes to feel the quality of his mind would do well to read the volume of addresses, *Brethren and Companions*, seen through the press by his colleague L. J. Allen in 1936, while he himself was in Australia. It is hard to imagine better school sermons : not a word wasted, so steeped in the language of Bible and Prayer Book that ancient and modern become one, never long and never obscure, not beyond the comprehension of the simplest and yet the most scholarly would admire them most. I have no doubt that his years at Charterhouse were very happy, and they certainly ended happily when he was able to announce that his successor would be Robert Birley. His first year of retirement must have been happy too, with his visit to Australia, and the writing of his volume of reminiscences, *After Many Days*, and his well-earned knighthood.

Birley was only thirty-two when he came to us, but youth in a headmaster is no drawback when coupled with tact and unpretentiousness and personal charm. We were able to help him at the outset by making him and his family free of Pageites for a week or so before his own quarters were ready—though I was away myself (as so often) at the Three Choirs Festival. He was a delightful man to work with, and I have known no one with so many surprising and fascinating byways of knowledge. Once, reading the last chapter of Job as a lesson in Chapel, I omitted the ridiculous names of his daughters. The same evening came a letter of mock rebuke, quoting doggerel Latin verses—I forget from what source— in which all three names were used. I know no other man at all likely to have met, and been able to quote, the name of Keren-Happuch in a Latin pentameter. And there are not many men who could lecture acceptably on the Elephant in Art. He is one of those to whom experience tends to come in odd ways. He does not look at all like a footballer, but it has never surprised me that in the railway station at Turin he should be greeted as the Captain of Bolton Wanderers.

To me that year, 1936, was not one of the most prosperous. In Anglesey the previous summer I had first known the pains of lumbago and all through 1936 I was conscious of the threat, but persevered with cricket, though I never bowled a ball that didn't hurt. But a much more severe attack in the autumn, with other signs of deterioration, led to my first X-ray, the discovery of a dangerous tooth, not easy to remove, and some months of severe dieting followed. It justified a brief and enjoyable convalescence at Bath in the following January, and by the spring I was back in normal health.

In one pleasant task I was involved under both headmasters, the creation of a new Hymn Book. By degrees a certain number of hymns and a certain number of tunes had accumulated, requiring a modest supplement, but with whom the idea of an entirely new book originated I cannot say. It was very good fortune which brought us a new chairman and a fresh mind half way through our task : fortunate too that when the time came to look for a publisher, the authorities at the Oxford University Press thought so well of the work that they offered to make it their own with the title of *The Clarendon Hymn Book*. The musical director was Thomas Fielden, his second string John Wilson, while the gifted V. S. H. Russell represented verse and music alike. My contribution was the suggestion that we should include biographical notes on authors and composers, and when I made it I did not foresee that I should be commanded to write them myself. Under the guidance and correction of John Wilson I found it an interesting and decidedly worth-while job.

By the time the book was ready I had become more closely associated with John Wilson when, in a good hour, he was assigned to Pageites as their first house tutor. We had yet to discover him in the Studbook as a cousin of M. So for some years from 1937 the success of Pageites in the house-singing competition became habitual : his gift for choir-training gave us an unfair advantage.

Our last four years in Pageites were years of war. Trenches had been dug for the whole school in one place or another, and we had the advantage of being within a few yards of ours on the field known as Doddites. Digging them was doubtless good exercise, to squat in them on a winter's night a very different matter, and fortunately we never did so. I cannot remember that we entered them more than three times : once on the first morning of the war, once on a June night, balmy and delectable, in 1940, and once early in the morning a few days later. Wisdom prevailed : it was decided that the probability of pneumonia was worse than the possibility of a bomb. For a few miserable nights in the autumn of that year the house tried to sleep on palliasses downstairs, but a more harmonious community than at that time it was would have found it a strain, and we never had cause to regret a return to our beds. Four times that autumn bombs fell, nearer and nearer—one indeed within a few feet of Saunderites—after which Birley procured the removal of a provocative searchlight on Northbrook, and we were left in peace.

I have no doubt that that term, Oration Quarter, 1940, was the most trying of the 126 terms of my professional career, for, together with the nightly anxiety and interference with sleep, a thyroid had brought me so low that by the end of the year I had difficulty in getting out of a bath. The doctor's iodine did no good and it required an ultimatum from M. before he sent me in the following March to Sir Maurice Cassidy—almost my only visit to London in five years—who ordered an operation without loss of time. And no time was lost. The surgeon, Hugo Romanis, himself a Pageite and son of a Pageite housemaster, lived close by, and a bed was secured at Mount Alvernia, the Franciscan nursing home in Guildford. The nursing of the nuns was no doubt amateurish, and if one rang the bell one never knew who would appear, but their happy friendly ways were more endearing than professional competence could have been. I had less pain than when my tonsils were removed seventeen years earlier, and after an operation on Saturday morning was astonished to have the stitches out less than 48 hours later. After a few days I was assisted into the doctor's car and taken up to Stoneycrest, a nursing home at Hindhead. The weather was so vile that I was only too happy to be indoors and in bed and thoroughly enjoyed a whole month of idleness such as I could never remember before. Janet's attempt to interest me in crosswords was superfluous : I was quite content to read and sleep, and the only thing I lacked was music. Later, with a doubtless illegal donation of petrol coupons, we were able to go down to Coat, near Martock, to the cottage most kindly lent us by my headmaster. It was characteristic of Robert Birley that, in that land of magnificent churches, I should find a list awaiting me of those most worth visiting that were within easy reach.

I was able to resume work with the loss of little more than a month divided between the two terms. Cassidy had told me plainly that without the operation I had not long to live : after it I was able to return to cricket in 1942. During my absence my colleague J. C. Thomson, owner of Lordsmeade, took charge of the house, as he did in time of need of several others. He also had two periods as acting headmaster in the absence of Birley : a more efficient man or one more unostentatiously public-spirited I have not known.

Physically I was completely restored to health by the end of the summer, but I forgot the warning of a wise man that a part of convalescence would be depression ; and that in August and September must have been a trial to more than myself. I have always known and feared depression, though it has generally passed off in two or three days : in 1941 I had reason to dread it for months. But the operation had given me a new start in life.

The Governing Body had done much to prepare for the war. I do not mean merely the provision of trenches and black-out curtains and the apparatus of rationing : they had laid their plans to save £10,000 in 1940, and as a matter of fact saved more than that. The school being not quite full, one house was closed : the headmaster returned from Northbrook, which was profitably let, to Saunderites, where the housemaster was due to retire : and £100 were lopped off the salaries of housemasters. This was perfectly fair, because a recent legal decision had saved them a good deal in income tax.

Having been through both wars at Charterhouse, I am conscious that the experience of the one was not the same as the experience of the other. First, the roll of honour. When I was new to the place, the long lists of names read out week after week in Chapel were with few exceptions only names to me : the much shorter lists of the second war were full of those whom I could call friends It is a strange fact but true, that only one boy who was in the Sixth during my early years did not survive the war : in the second, because the pick of the school served in the R.A.F., it was the pick of the school who did not return. They are too many to name, so I will name none. Secondly, the life of Brooke Hall. The first war brought us three men capable of giving years of good service to the school, but far too many of the *passés* and the incompetent : in the second the general capacity of the temporary masters was much higher. Further there were a number of men in my own position, who could prolong their service or having recently retired could return to their posts.

The catering and rationing after 1939 were far better than twenty-five years earlier : on the other hand the finding of domestic staff was much more difficult. I had been accustomed to refer to the Pageite staff as the eleven, and sometimes there was a twelfth man. When we left, M. had had some slight experience of what housemasters' wives have to endure to-day : one wonders admiringly how they do endure it. At worst we had the firm nucleus of Edgeler, and the cook who coming to us in 1933 gave twenty-four years of service to Pageites, and her sister who is with us still, and a matron, Miss Hutton's successor, ready at all times to do the work of three.

The effect on the work of the Sixth was much more marked in the latter war than in the former. In 1914 Charterhouse was still a classical school and the upper forms were as full as usual, and if the humanities were rather at a discount, there was nothing like the slump both in numbers and in quality from which we suffered in my last years. Further the average age of the school was never so high as between 1914 and 1918. The War Office asked that no boys should be superannuated, or they would have to go in the ranks; and it was the policy of those days that they should enter a Cadet Battalion straight from school at eighteen and a half : only the Guards took cadets at eighteen. After 1940, my last good Sixth, there were still some excellent scholars, but they were few ; and even a depleted form contained some who could never have found a place in an old-time Sixth. And it was always uncertain when a boy would leave school for the services.

When the war came we had made no provision for retirement because, while we had the responsibility of one house, we did not want the responsibility of another. I had always hoped that in the end we might occupy a house built for us, perhaps in the Cotswold country, perhaps in Suffolk, by the family firm, Curtis Green & Partners. I was due to retire in July, 1942, but it was clear that I should be wanted as a teacher till the war was over. So once more we were fortunate when we were able to secure our present home at Chiddingfold, which M. could occupy while I remained in a lodging or guesthouse at Godalming. We were even more fortunate than we knew : for an identical offer for the house had been accepted and then withdrawn when it was found that house and furniture did not match. And even a few months later such a house would have cost us much more. We occupied it, partly furnished, for the Easter holidays of 1942, and had hoped to complete the migration in August. But that was not to be. I had a letter from the headmaster telling me, without giving reasons, that it would be a help to him if I would stay on another year in Pageites—and I could hardly say no. A year later came a delightful letter of thanks, explaining that, if I had refused, the Governing Body would have closed the house. And clearly, had they decided to do so, it would have been to their advantage that there should be a housemaster already due for retirement. But now confidence was returning and entries more numerous. To have closed the house would have been a tragedy indeed, for none had had so much care and money spent on its improvement. In our last year we had the support of a notable head monitor in John Powell-Jones, who was also head of the school : yet it was a relief when the Summer Quarter ended and the time came to make way for a younger man.

Mr Boxall, clerk of the works, did everything to make our migration easy. He took to pieces and reconstructed in our new home the bookcases he had built for me in 1927, moved our household goods and even some of the family in the Charterhouse lorry : he even brought our store of coal : he even, after a time, found us a fridge. And as our move took place during a heatwave, such help is very grateful in memory. My department was the hanging of pictures and arranging of books, and with a library of perhaps 2,500 volumes that was not the lightest task. Once order was established the house became a place of delight, though also a place of peril to head and foot. I would rather have had a modern house built to our needs, but if one is to have a sixteenth century cottage with discreet additions, one could hardly have a pleasanter one. It was of course claimed, from its name, to have been a residence of Kate Greenaway. That is not true, though she often stayed nearby at Witley, and a house on the Green at Chiddingfold appears as an illustration in one of her books ; and an old inhabitant remembers her, looking very like one of her own pictures. The garden, rather more I believe than half an acre, was not unmanageably large, though a reluctant and incompetent gardener did not take kindly to the clay after the clean dry Greensand of Godalming. It did not take long for M. to make it a place of beauty.

The family had entered Pageites still requiring a nursery : they left it ripe for the services, though it was only Janet who wore uniform in the war. After a very fortunate three years at Oxford, she had interesting and responsible work in North Africa. Robin, as a medical student at Guy's after two years at King's, Cambridge, was ' reserved ', though when qualified he served as M.O., in North Africa and Palestine, till tuberculosis brought him home— to make an excellent recovery. Murray fell a victim to polio on the very day, I believe, when his papers were to have gone in for the Navy. He too made a fortunate recovery, and if his years as a scholar of Magdalene fell in wartime, yet there was plenty of life in Cambridge : the universities were far from empty as they had been in the former war. After taking his degree he spent some months driving a lorry in Germany, before proceeding to Ely on his way to ordination. The times have been few when all the family could be together at Greenaway.

I thoroughly enjoyed my last three years of professional life and, with freedom from the responsibilities of a boarding house and with a depleted Sixth, they were the easiest years I can remember. After the spaciousness of the private side of Pageites, I could not know how happy I should be in one small bed-sitting-room at a house nearby, and that it would be nothing of a trial to turn out for my meals. These I had—and very good they were— at the Red House, a guesthouse now, but built originally by Lutyens, before the days of his celebrity, for a retiring housemaster of Gownboys. In its early days, because it was not exactly like the dismal buildings that surrounded it, it had been known as the Jam Factory. We knew it best when it was the home of Arthur Clutton-Brock. Later, for a time Dick Sheppard lived there, in the interval between St. Martin's and Canterbury, and though we saw all too little of him it was enough to know him as a winner of hearts. Chiddingfold was not more than eight miles distant, and I went

H

home to M., by bus or bike, twice a week and with luck could spend
three nights there, though often I had to return to Charterhouse
for some engagement on a Sunday evening.

Life, truth to tell, was singularly uneventful, not least because,
after Somerset, the Cotswolds and Dartmoor all in 1941, we went
away so little in the holidays. But one brief holiday in the spring
of 1944 is very much alive in memory, when I took my bicycle
to rediscover the Bradfield country once so familiar to me. I
lodged at what had in my time been the blacksmith's cottage, and
the blacksmith had been a well-known character, distinguished
both as a craftsman and as a poacher of trout. Most of the country
was just as I had seen it thirty years before, except for much-
improved roads. All the traffic seemed to be in the air, with gliders
rehearsing for D-Day less than two months ahead. The woods
were white with anemones and ' the cherry hung with snow ',
but it was too early for the hyacinths. Only three places seemed
changed, but those markedly so. I had been warned that I should
not be allowed to cross Bucklebury Common ; but it seemed well
to try : I could hardly be arrested, I could only be turned back.
As it was, I only remember seeing one man, an American sentry
reading a newspaper in his box. I said good morning to him and
rode on through acres of transport wheel to wheel on both sides
of the road, and completed my favourite round of Cold Ash, and
back by the well-loved Yattendon. Another day I rode to the
Mapledurham which I had known since, I think, 1893—if that was
the year of the first great epidemic of influenza. There again, in
that peaceful spot, I found transport lined up along both banks of
the river and a bridge across it, I suppose for the first time in history.
I could not go into that country without visiting the pasque flower
(*Anemone Pulsatilla*) on the downs beyond Aldworth, as we had
done annually for some years till 1939. But the Army had done a
good deal to keep me out. When I entered Unhill Wood I first
met a keeper, who told me I shouldn't get far ; then a red flag :
then a sentry, who told me I couldn't go beyond the edge of the
wood, because there was a minefield. Barbed wire confirmed his
statement, and just as I turned back mortar practice began in the
valley between me and the Fair Mile opposite. I had chosen
Jude the Obscure for my pocket, because sometimes on a bright
April day one may see such a distant view of ' Christminster ' as
Jude once saw. I may say that I found the book at once less
impressive and less depressing than I had many years earlier. To
tell the truth my early taste for Thomas Hardy has not remained
strong. But all this has little to do with Charterhouse.

One major pleasure which came to an end with my retirement was music with Arthur Trew. It must have been about 1920 that I formed the habit of going to sing with him every Sunday morning, and with his patience in teaching me we built up an enormous repertoire. In 1922 we first ventured on a recital, and then for twenty-one years from 1926, except for one year when I was in hospital, it was an annual event. Lecture Theatre was a delightful room to sing in, and we employed a method of our own. There were no lights except on the piano, and the words of the songs, or translations, or notes on them were thrown on the screen. I always stood by the piano and did the turning over. There I could have no misgivings about the words, and the darkness gave a delightful sense of freedom. Whatever the qualms of anticipation, when the time came, vocally mellowed always by two glasses of port, I thoroughly enjoyed the performance and the years of co-operation had produced a real ensemble. After the last recital in 1946 Robert Birley, in some farewell words, said that Trew must surely be one of the best accompanists in the country. I was at all times conscious that the inspiration came from him, with the confidence it begot. During the war a correspondent in India wrote that he hoped I hadn't forgotten to say that all the merit was Trew's, ' because I always did '. If I did so, it was because it was the truth. Since 1946 I have seldom been able to revive the partnership with an ever-busy man.

When I retired in 1946 I had worked with the Sixth for thirty-two years and enjoyed every one of them. The great merit of the able Carthusian was that he was so seldom bookish and sophisticated. Of the alleged division between those who played games well and those who didn't I scarcely ever saw a trace. One year the Classical Sixth played the rest of the school at cricket and did not have the worst of a close drawn game. Another time the History Sixth issued a similar challenge at football, but unfortunately a date could not be found. I never regarded myself simply as an instructor in Latin and Greek. One annual pleasure the war cut off : in the Christmas holidays I always introduced a few boys to the National Gallery and to *zabaione* at a Soho restaurant afterwards, or possibly to lunch at the Arts Club, which I had joined in 1931. And if the Charterhouse I left was not the same as the Charterhouse I came to, I certainly do not think it had changed for the worse. As the High Master of St. Paul's wrote recently, ' An organism which does not change dies ; and the reason for the vitality of the Public Schools is that they have changed steadily to meet new needs and new conditions.'

Even 1946 was not the end. In April 1949 I left York after a delightful Historical Association tour and, thinking that Fountains should follow Rievaulx, had gone on to Ripon. There I found a letter asking me to take over my friend Arrowsmith's work for the Quarter, as he was about to undergo the same severe operation for arthritis which four months earlier had done such wonders for M. I accepted gladly and never enjoyed a term more. I was excused early school at 7.30, and leaving home at 8.30 was able to reach Charterhouse by well-linked bus, train and bus in forty minutes, and in that lovely summer the weather was such that I only once put on a raincoat. I had always coveted the experience of taking Special Remove, where the junior scholars spent their first summer, and I also had the delight of rediscovering Horace with a promising Under Sixth. But that was eight years ago, and I can hardly hope to teach at Charterhouse again.

CHAPTER VII

GAMES

1. Lawn Tennis, 1905—1914

I HAVE written already of the lawn tennis of my Oxford days, but not of my comparatively mature experience in open tournaments. It was not till I was earning my living that I could afford three or four weeks of continuous play. My first open tournament had been at my native Colchester in 1901. Many years later the referee, H. S. Scrivener (whose son by his second marriage was head monitor of Pageites in 1937) told me that he remembered the secretary saying to him, ' There's an awfully nice boy and girl entered who can't play at all : what *are* we to give them ? ' The conclusion was a handicap of 30, with which my sister and I reached the final, where we met a distinctly good pair who had been ' let in ' at 15·3. But it was good enough for a start. I played at Colchester more often than anywhere else, almost every year till 1912.

The Colchester tournament was one of the earliest to be founded and came into existence because one of my father's curates, R. H. Gee, had been at New College with Scrivener and played with him in the Oxford Six : he induced his friend to come and found an Essex Championship. Gee was a man who would have gone far in his profession, a really notable preacher. He left Colchester for St. Anne's, Soho, where he died prematurely of typhoid fever.

In those days tournaments were few and entries small and, with plenty of courts available on the Cambridge Road ground, three days were ample for carrying it through, given good weather. Entries were most impressive. It was there I first saw the Dohertys, the Allen twins and Roper Barrett, with Miss Douglass and some of the best Wimbledon ladies. Later, when building encroached on a field that had been the town's cricket and football ground, with larger entries and fewer courts, and with tournaments by this time so multiplied that it was impossible to give Colchester a whole week, anyone who did well might have a pretty severe task on the final day.

Barrett came habitually to defend the championship of his native county, and I played him four times. At our first meeting I got within two points of a set, but he never allowed me to get as far as that again. When we played together in the doubles we had rather too easy a time, but whatever the opposition it was an education to be his partner. There came a time when we were officially the Essex first pair, but it was very seldom that we were both free on the day required. He was a busy London solicitor and always asserted the fact that he had done a morning's work in the City by coming down to Wimbledon, at least in the old Worple Road days, correctly dressed in morning coat and silk hat.

In 1922 F. R. Burrow, the best referee of his time at Wimbledon and elsewhere, published a book, *My Tournaments*, in which he wrote, if I remember right, that the heaviest day's play he could remember was that of Harold Sloman (afterwards headmaster of Tonbridge) and myself at Colchester in the heatwave of 1909. But so far as I am concerned, the year should have been 1911, when the heat I believe was the greatest yet recorded. It was the only year in which I might possibly have won the Essex Cup, for Barrett under doctor's orders had not entered. But I was beaten after 5—5 in the final set by A. L. Bentley, the winner, a man well behind me in handicap, though I had defeated him in a previous encounter at Folkestone. When Saturday came, that was the only match I had lost, and in two of the five events I had not even reached the semi-final. In the Handicap Singles I could scratch, and that left me with six matches to play in the intense heat—five sets before lunch and ten after. I ended by losing both Open Doubles, men's and mixed, after winning the first eight games in one and the first six in the other.

Every year from 1905 to 1912 I prepared for my brief season of tournaments by a visit, sometimes repeated later, to the Goldbergs at the Red House, Newdigate, in Surrey. I have said that I went there first after our Wimbledon venture in 1904, and so long as Fritz Goldberg and I played in August tournaments, we prepared ourselves for them by singles which each of us was desperately keen to win. To begin with I was a poor singles player and it was several years before I beat him for the first time : then I seemed established as the better man of the two. He was always a worrier, in life and on the courts, but in 1911, which I take to have been my best year, he was not free for any tournaments and, delivered from all responsibility, played better than ever before and defeated me every time. He and his elder brother, Carthusians both, fell in the war of 1914, and I gave the lamp over the pulpit in Charterhouse Chapel in their memory.

In 1905 I made a bigger advance than in any previous year and met in the Essex team the partner whom I think I appreciated more than any except Roper Barrett. His name was Thurgood and he lived at Wanstead. We did so well that year against Middlesex, and against Staffordshire in the County semi-finals at Edgbaston, that I persuaded him to enter for an open tournament, and at Chichester we took a set off the Allens, a considerable feat in those days, and won the handicap from 1/6. His work gave him little freedom and it was not often that he could play, but we always did well for the county and I admired both his skill and his temperament. But of course county matches were few, even if we were free for them.

I never went where cups were cheap and only once won an Open Singles. The Scottish Championships had from their inception been played at Moffat in early August, and after 1904 I was regularly invited there by my kind hosts of Moffat House. But the tounament acquired such a reputation for bad weather that the championships were transferred to Bridge-of-Allan at a different date. The good people of Moffat were so disappointed that a year later they put up new cups for a South of Scotland championship and (in splendid weather) Mrs Larcombe and I were the first to have our names inscribed on them. The next year was my last, and if I lost the cup I was well content with a score of 2—6, 7—9 against the captain of the Australian Davis Cup team.

But without doubt my most distinguished tournament was at West Worthing in 1908. The Goldbergs had taken lodgings at Littlehampton for a mixed party of golfers and tennis players (and musicians), and I was summoned by telegram to join it and play with Fritz. In that we did no good, for he was generally a Jonah and we drew the Allens, and he E. R. Allen in the singles. The twins were still a brilliant pair and their mutual recriminations, vastly amusing to the gallery, never disturbed their play. In doubles the one was as good as the other, but in singles C.G. did not count. They always spent most of the summer term at Cambridge, and if the undergraduates gained little in moral stature from the association, their tennis gained a great deal. None of them, not even Wilding, had a chance against E.R. in a single. At Worthing I played the two most remarkable singles of my career. In the handicap I was reduced for the first time almost to scratch, 1/6 in fact, and there were two dark horses, or ' let ins ', obviously destined to meet in the final. One was T. E. Haydon, afterwards a County

Court Judge at Leicester, a good player who had not been seen in a tournament for some years and so was given the very liberal handicap of 4/6. The other was a young player in his first tournament who, given a handicap of 15·5, showed a range of really beautiful strokes : win or lose, he was never likely to see such a handicap again. We met in the semi-final : he began with decorous caution, the balls went into the net, and I won the first set. Then he began to play his proper strokes and I won three games of the next thirteen : set-all and 4—1 to him. And then, if you please, he reverted to caution and I pulled up to 5—4, 40—30. Then, too late, he began to hit again, and I had the vantage point six times, and he twice, before I could finish the match. It so chanced that I never met F. R. Price again till some forty-five years later I looked into a tent at Cranleigh and asked the spruce gray-haired referee if he remembered that match—which he did. I had beaten Haydon easily enough in the Open semi-final, but to give him 3/6 seemed a different matter. Yet in fact I only lost two games, playing with an accuracy that surprised me. I had outgrown an early belief that it was impossible to play in the morning. It was the last time I played from in front of scratch. The next week, at Folkestone, I was at scratch for the first time, still under Burrow : then at Chichester under Evelegh, a less subtle handicapper, I found myself owing 15, a position conducive to pride but hardly to success.

But more important was the game I did not win, the final of the Open Singles. E. R. Allen, fat and self-indulgent and relying on brilliance of stroke to make all his matches short—he had only lost ten games on his way to the final—had no use for third sets, much less fifth. Burrow had told me that, as my only possible chance, he was going to make the final best-of-five. That did not seem to have made much difference when the score was 6—1, 6—3, 5—3, 40—15, but somehow I saved those two points and took five of the next six games for the set at 8—6. Then we went on and on till 9—9 : then he won the last two games, in both of which I had led at 40—15. Had I got those two points he must have retired. The twins had still the doubles to play and C.G. shepherded his brother off the court, indignantly proclaiming in his high-pitched voice, ' We scratch, we scratch.' Afterwards I found him fussing round his brother as he sat with his feet in a basin of water, and was told that we had played like two old women. In due course they proceeded to their doubles final and won as easily as usual. Burrow, referring in his book to that game, wrote that it taught him a lesson—never to put C.G. on a court within sight of one where E.R. was playing an important match. I have a snapshot that illustrates the point ; it represents our game, but two courts away is C.G. with his back to his own Mixed Double, watching his brother. They were a queer couple but genuinely devoted, especially C.G. to his more brilliant twin. They never faced the highest opposition at Wimbledon or Eastbourne, nor did they go where it was negligible. But in what I will call upper middle class tennis they were almost unbeatable as a pair. Yet they did not always win. I remember meeting them somewhere coming off the ground, C.G. carrying a piece of paper which he flapped at me :   ' Ten and six between us, and they call us pot-hunters '.   A half-guinea order was the usual prize in those days for one who reached a semi-final.

Another tournament of which I have pleasant memories is Torquay, but I only went there once after Oxford days. I recall the delightful hospitality of Harold Michelmore at Newton Abbot, an evergreen player who won the championship of his county for twenty consecutive years. ' Khaki ' Roberts, Q.C., in his book of reminiscences, *Without my Wig*, calls him and E. R. Allen the two best players who never appeared at Wimbledon. He died only in this present year of 1957. Folkestone I enjoyed because I liked the place, and Charles Jelf allowed me to sleep in the unoccupied Little Grange, while the Radnor Club gave me its hospitality for my meals. At Southampton I played only twice, 1910 and '11, but I never had more good matches anywhere. My partner was G. A. (afterwards Sir George) Thomas, a firstrate player, but more eminent in chess and in badminton. Once we won the final and once lost it. But Southampton I associate with my best lady partner and with my most protracted match. In the summer of 1956 I fell into conversation on the Green at Chiddingfold with a man who had got out of his car to give his dog a run, and it went on so long and interestingly that I finally asked him his name. The reply was ' Kingscote '. The year 1910 must have been almost the first season of that beautiful player, who had reached Davis Cup stature by 1914, though he had to wait till 1919 actually to play. His partner was a very good local girl, about as much below my partner's form as I was below Kingscote's. Mine was Mrs Hudleston, whom as Miss M. A. Ferguson I had first known at Moffat as Champion of Scotland. Except that Kingscote generally won his nasty kicking service, it looked as if some games would never end ; and what I remember it by is this. My partner Thomas umpired the first set and then was called away to play a match of his own : he did so, then changed, ate his luncheon and came back to see how we were getting on. The next year I came up against Kingscote twice, winning a Mixed Double and losing the final of the Men's.

But my favourite tournament was Chichester, with which I finished every season from 1905 to 1911. Priory Park, with its Gothic refectory for a changing-room and the Cathedral spire soaring in the distance, was the pleasantest of all tournament grounds known to me, though it certainly had not the best courts. I stayed always in the North House Hotel, only a few yards away, with a great mulberry tree in the garden. After a time we formed an Old Oxonian table there, to which came generally two or three men hardly to be met at other tournaments. We always hoped that one of the company would be Jack Ganzoni, now more generally known as Lord Belstead, though to a few of us he is still Zooks. He had been my contemporary at Christ Church, and we once won the Handicap Doubles together at Folkestone. Where Zooks was there was always hilarity, and he was with us in 1911, the year after the Crippen murder. He was not one to waste a moment of his holiday, and when knocked out of the tournament promptly left for Dieppe. There he found in his hotel a public man, not here to be named, whom he disliked ; and next morning came a telegram : ' —— in hotel send reliable Crippen '. With the meeting of 1911 really ended my claims to be taken seriously as a player, and if it brought one major achievement it was otherwise disastrous. Only once before had I failed anywhere to last into the final day, that is, to reach at least one semi-final : this time I did not even survive to the Friday. And yet I nearly brought off a surprising defeat of M. J. G. Ritchie, who with Wilding had won the doubles at Wimbledon twice in the previous three years. I threw the ball higher than most in serving and therefore was more liable to be troubled by the morning sun, and had one long game with deuce after deuce gone the right way I might have done it. 4—3 is so very different from 3—4 ! In that astonishing summer the courts were burnt bare and I, accustomed to playing on indifferent courts, probably watched the ball more closely than one who, used to perfect surfaces, sometimes put his racket where the ball ought to be instead of where it was. That was what Ritchie's comments after the match came to.

If I was to abandon tournaments, 1912 was a good year to do so, the most dreadful summer I can remember, far worse than 1956. My seven years had been intensely enjoyable and not expensive,

for it was only at Chichester that I had to pay a modest hotel bill.
I generally found committees friendly and amenable, and emerged
without any of those useless cups which cumber the sideboards
and mantelpieces of some who care for such trophies. Sometimes
I procured orders on booksellers, twice at least on Bluett & Sons ;
Folkestone brought me a good eiderdown, Southampton the armchair in which I have written much of this. ' Perfectly illegal '
as Burrow said ; but he did not denounce me or compromise my
amateur status. The only cup that remained in my possession was
the Palmer Cup of the Reading Club. After many years I handed
it over to a craftsman, once a schoolmaster, then a farmer, and
always an artist, who exchanged it for an equivalent weight of
rolled plate and hammered it into a lovely bowl which on this very
day of writing I have lent to a ' Treasure Show '. As to the tools
of my job, I used Ayres's rackets because I disliked the domination
of Slazenger's. I have little doubt, though I don't know it for a
fact, that some eminent players received their rackets free of charge.
I was just eminent enough to be given my SND at a discount.
As the price of the best rackets in those blessed days was 30/-, my
two new rackets every spring cost me £2. 5s. 0d. Whether it was
good for one to be a prominent player I am not so sure. Doubtless
it ministered to self-complacency, but as I have said it was immensely enjoyable. And eight years later, in the spring of 1919,
it was pleasant to find myself not forgotten, when an article in
The Times, no doubt written by Burrow, on University Lawn
Tennis, 1900-1914, gave four Oxford names, and the other three
had played in the Davis Cup.

2. AFTER 1918

At Charterhouse good lawn tennis was easier to come by than
at Bradfield, where it had involved much cycling or dependence
upon a neighbour's car. The time was still far distant when the
school was to have good courts and some encouragement to play ;
and the few who showed promise owed much to the coaching of
that clever player C. O. Tuckey. He was senior mathematical
master, and he and Mrs Tuckey, old foes of my tournament days,
were only too ready to play. They were a formidable pair whom
for more reasons than one people were anxious to defeat. Mrs
Tuckey liked, very reasonably, to play with three men, for she had
won the Mixed Doubles at Wimbledon, and also the Ladies' Doubles
while that championship was still played at Buxton. So every

Friday for a good many summers I partnered F. S. Porter against them. Porter was the man to whose place I had succeeded with the Sixth, and it was good for both of us to form an alliance on the tennis lawn. At first we owed them half-fifteen and then, when we had quite taken their measure—Mrs Tuckey after all was not a man—the whole fifteen. The Broadwater Club too, till it closed some years later, had a very good team, and Brooke Hall also played a few matches. In such club games, Porter and I went through eight seasons with only two defeats. He was a brilliant and unorthodox player, difficult to play either with or against, but experience made us into a genuine pair and I enjoyed our partnership greatly. I had never meant to return to tournaments, but in 1923 we went *en famille* to Bembridge in the Isle of Wight and, fearing boredom, I entered for the tournaments at Ventnor and Sandown ; with my colleague Tuckey at the one and my old partner Sir George Thomas at the other. At Sandown I hoped to partner the great Miss Ryan, then certainly the best Mixed Doubles player in the world and repeatedly a winner at Wimbledon, but she had made arrangements with another partner and I had to play against her in the final, which was rather a different matter. I had met her once eleven years earlier, when she was Champion of California, but two years before her first doubles victory at Wimbledon. (After the war she won no less than seventeen times !) And that was a truly remarkable match, for my partner and I recovered from 0—5, 0—40 in the final set to 5—5 and deuce. But we couldn't win those last two points. I enjoyed these tournaments so much—not least because they synchronized with the re-discovery of *Pickwick*, never read since I was fifteen—that next year I induced Porter to play at Cranleigh, where we won the Open Doubles (and almost won the Handicap) and in the final met a now rather elderly Ritchie. My last tournament was at Cranleigh in 1927, once more paired with Thomas, then living at Godalming. But we played deplorably and lost to a most commonplace pair. For the sake of a game I had entered for the Singles, though I had hardly played one since 1913, in which I was soundly beaten by a player far below me in handicap, in a gale of wind which blew down the stop-netting three times in the course of the match. I thought that at the age of forty-six there were more enjoyable pastimes than this, and as Porter had developed an unsound ankle I almost gave up playing : and the next year began our holiday tenancy of Trewyn at Rhosneigr, which meant much golf and no tennis. I played my last game in my fiftieth year and gave it up with little regret.

The fact is, when life grew more normal after the war, I found that my heart was in cricket, not lawn tennis. One day in the summer of 1956 I was talking at Witley station to a man whose face seemed not wholly unknown ; and he gave his name as General Martin. I immediately claimed him as an unconscious benefactor. That needs explanation. In 1920 the Club at Busbridge, just south of Godalming, asked for three or four players from Charterhouse to help in their post-war revival, and my colleague P. C. Fletcher invited me to be one. The Busbridge ground was a truly delightful one, sometimes used by touring sides for their opening game before their first three-day match at Worcester. I remember a large picture in *The Times*, with the South Africans in the field and the small Robin and Murray Irvine occupying a seat as the only visible spectators. But my first appearance for Busbridge was not there, but at Charterhouse, against that historic club the Charterhouse Maniacs, on the ground known as Wilderness, where I was to play for more than twenty years. One Wentworth Martin had made a great many runs when I was put on to bowl, and the batsman, instead of having a look at the new bowler, decided to hit him off at once, and from the first ball was well caught on the boundary. Three more wickets gave me an analysis of 4 for 20. In the return match at Busbridge I took 6 for 18, and when Brooke Hall played their annual game with Maniacs in July I had 6 for 22—in all sixteen wickets for 60 runs. And against Cranleigh I did my only hat-trick. The fact is, the fast wickets of the Godalming greensand suited me better than the slower ones of Berkshire, and I was a far better bowler at the age of fifty than at thirty. The next year the Busbridge Club was reconstituted for the employees of the estate and I did not play there again for many years.

It is a common weakness of men who are mainly concerned with the things of the mind to take themselves very seriously as cricketers. Frank Swinnerton has a delightful story of a group of intellectuals talking in the Reform Club of their exalted experiences at cricket, and then T. E. Page having the last word : ' I had Julius Caesar to bowl to me at the nets '. It was a plain statement of fact : the Surrey professional of that name was the first coach at Charterhouse, and his handsome portrait hangs in the Elevens Room of the pavilion. And I like to think that when first I played for Godalming in 1921, another Julius Caesar was my captain.

So if my best memories of cricket are vainglorious, I cannot help it. Fifty years ago, when I was once concerned in raising an Old

Wykehamist side, a friend declined a pressing invitation and said that he had given up playing because he found he thought too much of his own success or failure. I could never view the game with such detachment : with persistent failure I could not have enjoyed it. Yet I envy those who by keen and efficient fielding can justify their place in the side though they may rarely get runs or wickets.

In the early twenties Brooke Hall began to run a regular side, and I naturally was in it. But there were plenty of players and in 1926 I seemed in some danger of superannuation, not always being selected against the strongest sides. In 1928 I was out of health and did not play at all. In 1929 I played only once, but in 1930, to quote a postcard to my sister which has survived, ' I did an astonishing come-back . . . They were short, so I agreed to play, and Stoughton (Guildford Barracks) used to be my lucky ground. I went in at 103 for 6, and of 55 runs added before the innings closed I took 48 not out. There was a very good moment when I caught a full toss just nicely and saw the ball disappear over the trees and then heard it meet an upper window in the barracks—a locked room too, and they had to get another ball. Then —— being away, I was invited to bowl, and went right through an innings of 130 for 39 runs and 7 wickets. I am unashamedly pleased, and now they expect me to resume my place in the side '. After that I continued as an opening bowler till the side ceased temporarily to exist in 1940. I may say that the grand old bat of 1930 was one I had bought in 1907, after my cricket bag had been stolen at a railway station. Two bats served me for 37 years of cricket. But my boots did better than that. When my uncle Herbert Bullock died in 1907 I was offered his cricket boots if they fitted me, which they did, perfectly. He had a weak heart and cannot have used them for many years, and I am quite ready to believe that they date from the eighties of last century, or even earlier. In 1940 they needed some minor repair, and John Larkin, the Charterhouse captain of that year, told me that the bootmaker had shown them to him as a model pair of boots. When I gave away my gear in 1943 I felt I could not part with them. I also kept one cricket-ball, and love the feel of it in the hand when it emerges from a very untidy drawer.

In 1933 I had a fresh lease of life when, instead of off-breaks, I slightly altered my action and went for top-spin. Another postcard to my sister records the result. 'At Cranleigh I hit the stumps five times, and when the last wicket made a stand (two gentlemen

named Squelch and Germany), I came on again and got Mr
Germany with the second ball : 6 for 29 in a total of 140 '.

In the spring of this year I was asked by my Franciscan friend
from Cerne Abbas, Father Denis, if it was true that at cricket I
prayed to the Midonna as my patron saint : he had heard a story
to that effect from my former colleague, the headmaster of
Sherborne. I too had heard the story in a speech by Robert Birley
at my farewell dinner in Brooke Hall, in July 1946. As neither
headmaster gave it correctly, I propose to give it here. The bowler
was W. W. Timms, with his curious spinners, the batsman Quentin
Stanham, later captain of the XI and a notable hitter. He hit the
most enormous skyer I have ever seen and it was plain that I, at
mid-on, was fated to receive it. I loathe skyers, which generally
spin like mad and tear their way through the hands, and in despera-
tion I shouted ' O Lord '. Then when at last the ball descended,
an easy catch, not spinning at all, I said I had been wrong : I
should have addressed myself to the Midonna. Stanham has since
assured me that he had started for the third run before he knew
that he was out.

Besides Brooke Hall and Godalming, I had some most enjoyable
cricket with Jack Squire's Invalids, one of whose matches—or
rather a selection of incidents from three—is immortalized in
McDonell's *England, their England*. Squire never regarded me as
a bowler, but took me seriously as a batsman, and it is true that I
never in any of his matches came out for less than 24. I recall
particularly a partnership with the hard-hitting Clifford Bax in the
once lovely park at Aldermaston, where I had played much good
tennis in earlier days. It is now delivered up to Atomry, a fate few
could have foreseen in 1927. But best of all were three matches at
my favourite Busbridge in Dick Sheppard's annual game against
Archie McDonell's XI. This was the only cricket in which I have
played under a captain who controlled his side with a megaphone
from a chair in the outfield. In the last match, I recall that I was the
only bowler on our side to take a wicket who had not previously
bowled for England against Australia : the rest were shared between
Nigel Haig and Greville Stevens. The explanation is simple. I
was put on first and had first go at a journalist who was completely
out of practice, because—such can be the pedantry of cricket—it
was necessary to ' take the shine off the ball ' before a first class
spin-bowler could operate, even in a friendly one-day game. Much
more important, I also made top score and was not out. I treasure
dear Dick Sheppard's comment on an intensely keen bowler who

would have bowled all day if allowed, that he was so kind-hearted that he hated it when he got a wicket.

My thyroid in 1941 might well have brought an end to cricket, and indeed to everything else, but the operation was so successful that the next year I was able to return to bowling at the nets, where I was needed as a coach in the absence of younger men. So in July 1943, in my last week as a housemaster and within two months of my sixty-second birthday, I found myself filling a gap in the Maniac side against Godalming : I had not played for that historic club for more than twenty years. For the last time I quote a postcard written to my sister. ' I am lame to-day after another remarkable rejuvenation yesterday. I played for Maniacs against Godalming, bowled through an innings of 112, except for four overs rest, and took nine wickets for 30. They had two năsty făst bowlers and when I went in we had lost 7 wickets for 21. Though much alarmed, it was 90 before I got out for 23, and we only lost by 5 runs '. I was lame for a fortnight and thought that was the right moment to retire. The next year, to keep out of temptation, I gave my gear to the village club.

One of my many regrets in life is that in the golden age of English cricket, 1900-1914, having given my heart to lawn tennis, I never made any attempt to watch a first class match. It was August 1920 before I found out my mistake. It was the year when the endless run of *The Beggar's Opera* had begun at Hammersmith, and I went up to a matinée on a morning too splendid for my usual haunt, the National Gallery, and went to Lord's instead. I found it so fascinating that though I duly repaired to the Lyric Theatre I came out after the first act and returned to Lord's. How many times I saw *The Beggar's Opera* afterwards I cannot say, but never on a fine summer afternoon. In the next year the discovery of the delightful ground at Horsham made me a follower of Sussex during the brilliant period of Gilligan and Tate, of Bowley and Duleepsinhji. In 1934 I did the obvious thing and became a member at the Oval. But nowhere is cricket to be watched more enjoyably than on Green at Charterhouse. Between 1940 and 1946 Green on a Saturday afternoon must have been as sane and whole-some a place as could be found anywhere, and I am truly thankful for all that it has given me.

As I have said, if a schoolmaster enjoys games and wants to play them, it is only too easy for him to do so, and I think I probably played more after the age of forty than before. At Bradfield in early days I had played a good deal of bad golf, but had long given it up. Now, spending Christmas and Easter at Will Green's delightful home at Farnham, I found myself called upon to play once or twice a year, and no one can expect to hit the ball in those circumstances. I thought I might dislike it less if I practised, and with a vast football field adjoining Lord's Meade it was very easy to do so. I also joined the West Surrey G.C. at Enton and took lessons from Howlett, the pro. In those days the club for some reason admitted Charterhouse masters for a subscription of two guineas. I suppose every beginner's ambition is to get his handicap down to single figures, and ultimately I did so when I took to the far more enjoyable course at Hindhead. But I was soon back at my proper handicap of 12. The worst of this fascinating but exhausting game is that one wants to play it every day, and that could only be possible in our holiday resort of Rhosneigr, or when my good friend Leonard Bennett took me as his guest to such delectable links as Hunstanton or Turnberry or Newcastle, County Down—the only time I have crossed the Irish Channel. The memories of golf at Rhosneigr are particularly happy, especially while that delightful man Sir Henry Maddocks, K.C., spent his holidays there—the only man I have known who could be genuinely pleased when his opponent holed an indecently long putt. Later, I had internecine combats with a Scotch doctor from Sheffield, each desperately keen to beat the other : we ended with honours pretty well divided. In the middle thirties a new pro came to Hindhead, one of the large tribe of Bradbeer, and to eliminate some bad habits I applied for a course of lessons and, to force myself to take them, paid for the course in advance. But he was so much in demand, and I so much occupied elsewhere, that a lesson a month might be all I could get. My keenness was not what it had been, and when I found that he wanted me, apparently, to begin again at the beginning, I wearied of the task and gave it up. It meant that I walked and cycled, and even motored, the more, and that was all to the good. I have found no other game so absorbing as golf.

Till I went to Charterhouse I had never seen the admirable game of Eton fives. I sometimes played in the Winchester courts at Bradfield, but never cared much for the game. But to the strange Eton court with its step and its box I took very readily. For many years every Friday, except in the summer, as many pairs of masters as cared to put down their names played a corresponding number of pairs of boys. As no running is involved, it is possible, given a good eye, to be an efficient player when youth is long past, and I played regularly till my illness in the autumn of 1940. And I will claim a record that is without doubt unique, to be the only player who has never lost a match when playing for Old Salopians against Old Carthusians, or for Old Carthusians against Old Salopians, *without being a member of either club.* The fact is, holiday games were generally played in the Hodgsonite courts immediately opposite Pageites, and if, as sometimes happened, a team was a man short, I was generally at hand to take his place. This happened in two successive years, and for Shrewsbury I found myself paired with A. T. Barber, a cricketer who captained both Oxford and Yorkshire, and probably the best fives player I ever was in court with except T. R. Garnett and perhaps Tony Wreford-Brown. He won our match, not I !

CHAPTER VIII

HOBBIES AND TASTES

I DO not quite know what is to go into this chapter : it seems to me that a good deal of the ground has been covered already. But of one thing there is no doubt : nothing has been said of the Chinese porcelain which has for so many years been one of my chief sources of pleasure.

My mother's drawing-room contained a number of pleasant pieces of china, and her pantry some really fine services which only appeared on state occasions. My father had an eye for such things and liked discussing them with his friends, but I don't suppose he ever spent ten shillings on a piece in his life. Anyhow, I must have inherited an eye for them. I bought my first piece in my first term at Oxford, and if it was bogus (as it was) it none the less served its purpose. My first genuine piece was one of those barrel-shaped mugs, with crisscross strap handles, made for export in eighteenth century China and fifty or sixty years ago so strangely called Lowestoft. It had a small chip in the rim and two rivets in the handles, and how many times I stared at it in the window of Ogden's little shop, near Worcester College, before I could commit the audacity of buying it for a guinea, I cannot pretend to say. It is before me as I write and still gives me pleasure, when almost all my other early acquisitions have gone elsewhere. From that day to this my eye has lingered for a moment on the window of every antique shop that I have passed. If at first I was ready, in defiance of advice, to buy much-damaged pieces for a shilling or two, one can *learn* as much from a cracked plate as from a perfect one : and later I was generally lucky in passing them on to someone else. For many years now blue and white has been my chief love, and I well remember the first good pieces that I bought, for £1 each, at Henty's in Winchester High Street : two chrysanthemum plates that after fifty-four years still give me much satisfaction.

About the turn of the century my father came across a Charter-house contemporary whom he had not met for many years—one Henry Johns Fielding, a rather eccentric old bachelor who lived in Hereford Square, in a house crammed with china and antiques of all kinds. He claimed to possess 250 Bartolozzi prints and once greeted a visitor with the question, ' Did you say you wouldn't come to a house where there weren't fifty teapots ? ' He proved very hospitable, and I stayed there several times. The last occasion was my match at Queen's Club in July 1904, and next morning he took me to visit his favourite dealer, W. E. Pimm, at 150 Brompton Road. An introduction from Fielding constituted me a friend and ensured special prices, and for some years a visit to Pimm's was a necessary part of every visit to London.

Pimm was an interesting and many-sided man. His ambition in youth had been to paint, and his father, holding the view not too common in parents that a man is likely to do best what he wants to do, did not claim him for the family business. Painting did not in fact provide a livelihood, even when eked out with coaching in mathematics, so he used another skill and became a skating pro at Prince's ; then, having a flair for antiques, he opened his modest shop in Brompton Road. Meantime he played the piano, taught boxing in the East End, and shot for England year after year on the miniature range. Favouring small profits and quick returns, by about 1910 he had achieved a competency and went back to his painting. No longer a dealer, he still bought a good thing when he saw it and would sell it to a friend, though not to a stranger. The first time I went to his studio in Chelsea I carried away a large turquoise vase which I enjoyed for more than forty years and then sold to Bluett & Sons for £20, twice what it had cost me. But my next piece had a more complicated history. It was an exquisite vase of *rouge de fer*, 18 inches high, which George Salting saw in an exhibition and offered £25 for it. He was told it was not for sale : otherwise its home would have been in the V. and A. It was however for sale to me. Pimm told me I could have it any time for £15 and that it would not be sold to anyone else. It was two years before I felt I could afford it. In 1943 Bluett, who had always admired it, bought it for £20, but afterwards wrote that he and the expert of the British Museum had decided that it was certainly a nineteenth century piece and not Ch'ien Lung (d. 1795), and asked to have another piece instead. I told him to send it to a forthcoming Red Cross sale and recorded a modest bid for it, and as it could not be catalogued as Ch'ien Lung, it returned to its former owner, who was extremely glad to have it back. When a thing is of exquisite quality, it would seem to matter very little whether it was made slightly before or slightly after the year 1800.

Pimm was a very good friend to me and contributed much to my education, in which connexion he called me the most inveterate self-improver he had known. He it was who first introduced me to restaurants in Soho where it was never necessary to pay more than half-a-crown for a good meal, and guided me in unfamiliar museums and to the once famous Caledonian market. It must be all of forty-five years since I saw him : but I heard that he had moved to the charming village of Alfriston, near Lewes, and staying there in 1946 I learnt that in 1940 he had been persuaded to go to America. I procured his address and had a long letter from him, in which I was pleased to find that he still used the word *squog*, old Fielding's term for a desirable antique.

Unconsciously, through a concatenation of events, Pimm influenced the destinies of my family. He early advised me to insure my china, took me to 7 Waterloo Place and introduced me to the branch manager, Digby Haworth-Booth, father of the famous gardener. On the wall hung a photograph of a beautiful house with a pool in the foreground, and I asked where it was. He told me it was his home at Balcombe, and he hoped that if I were ever in that part of Sussex I would pay him a visit. That opportunity did not occur till 1927, when we were at Horsham, on an occasion elsewhere referred to, within cycling distance of Balcombe. Haworth-Booth told us that if we were at Horsham we ought to meet his friend Layton, of the Manor House, from which school one of his sons had just been elected into College at Eton. Moreover, when we had left, he rang up his friend, and on arriving at our hotel we found Mr Layton waiting in the hall. When we had seen the school and its grounds, the destiny of Robin and Murray was soon settled : and that is how they came to go to the Manor House and not Horris Hill.

I have already noted briefly my discovery of Mr Bluett's little shop in Oxford Street in the late summer of 1907. My season of tournaments was just over, and I had come up from Chichester with an order on Mappin and Webb in my pocket. The little window contained a choice display of blue and white, and I went in. I found a most courteous Mr Bluett—courtesy is endemic in that family—who told me he had only just opened his shop, presumably the day before, since this was a Tuesday. I told him I had money to spend but had got to spend it at Mappin and Webb's. He replied that he knew a member of that firm, and perhaps something might be arranged. So I departed eastward with a note from Bluett, and after a satisfactory transaction could return home with a blue and white pot which after fifty years still remains a favourite both with me and my family. Next day at Eynsham our architect carried off some inferior pieces on which I was glad to improve, and I was able to send a telegram to Bluett for my first piece of coloured Ming—one which eleven years later I sold to Bluett *fils* for twice what I paid for it. It certainly was a step upward from Pimm in Brompton Road to Bluett in Oxford Street : he sold nothing but Chinese, and his prices were most reasonable. Sometimes the two came into competition. I remember an agitated day on which I hurried to and fro from one shop to the other, trying to decide between two *flambé* pots both of which seemed irresistible. Need I say that in the end I acquired both ? One of them I sold a few years later to a friend because he liked it so much ; and after thirty-five years the good fellow sent it back to me because there was no one in his family who would appreciate it when he was gone. The other stayed with me till 1943, when I left a big house for a small one and it was one of the things that changed hands, on terms favourable to both parties.

It surprises me that my first good bit of Ming should have come from Bluett *père*, for his very conventional taste seldom went further back than early K'ang Hsi—say the reign of Charles II. In the spring of 1913 I consulted him about some cheap rough—but to me still delightful—plates that I had just bought in Holland. He pooh-poohed them ; but his son quietly put in a word for them as certainly Ming, and more than forty years later introduced me to the Secretary of the Oriental Ceramic Society as the man who first interested him in Ming blue and white. That may not have been such nonsense as it sounds : for Mr Edgar Bluett certainly was not brought up among the early wares which have given a worldwide reputation to 48, Davies Street. I asked him recently if it was true that I was his father's first customer. He said no, but he thought I was the second. So I am always treated with undue deference by the brothers in Davies Street ; but they have risen far above my level and have bought more pieces from me than I from them.

I first discovered the charm of Ming blue and white when I was given a card for an exhibition at the Burlington Fine Arts Club in Savile Row in the summer of 1909. It was confirmed by the Bloxam Collection at the V. and A. The Rev. J. F. Bloxam was a London clergyman who began collecting Ming when it was little known or valued, and in 1916 deposited his collection on loan at the Museum. For me, every visit to the V. and A. began and ended before those cases in the Loan Court. By the time of the owner's death, in April 1928, the number of pieces had risen to 321. I at once wrote to the Director, Sir Eric Maclagan, to enquire about the fate of the collection and received a non-committal official reply, but I was ill that summer and heard nothing of the sale till it was long over. Nor did I see Bluett till the following January, when I found that a large part of the collection had passed through his hands. Just two pieces were still in the shop, and by good fortune they were those small deep bowls, with a bird on a rock inside them, which I had always coveted. I have seven such bowls now, and few things give me more pleasure.

One day in the early twenties I took a niece to the British Museum and introduced her to the Franks Collection. On coming away, I stopped before the window of a small shop in Museum Street to examine her on what she had learnt. At the back of the shop I could see a dish with a design of flying cranes, and once seen at close quarters acquisition became inevitable : it still remains my favourite piece, and also Janet's. And now for thirty years and more I have bought as many things from Mr Norton as from all other sources put together.

One other good source of supply I must mention—Franks, an Oriental importer in Camomile Street, E.C. To do business with such was regarded by West End dealers as black market (a term we had not yet learnt to know) and required an introduction, which was given me, I think, by Emery Walker and Clutton-Brock. The first piece I bought there, in 1915, is still among my favourites— a flattish ' ginger jar ' in underglaze blue and overglaze green and red, and I remember the man saying ' it will be a long time before you find the pair to it '. That is true : I have seen none like it in more than forty years. Of course an Oriental importer has mainly modern stuff, and from Franks we were passed on to Priest, Marian & Co., a few doors away, and from one or other we acquired the excellent cheap Chinese tea services and bowls that must be the envy of anyone setting up house to-day. But 1939 put an end to all that.

My collection is modest enough and I calculate that it cannot have cost me more than about £500, which spread over more than half a century is hardly criminal extravagance. Only four pieces, all acquired since 1946, have cost more than £20, and there is scarcely one that has ceased to interest me. I seem to possess about 120 pieces, nearly half of them Ming blue and white. And though I have no proper register, I can recall the history and provenance of almost all that I possess. I have been fortunate in disposing of early indiscretions and only about half-a-dozen pieces survive from Oxford days. Of Oxford shops the best was Godfrey's in St.

Giles's, but that excellent dealer had retired by 1939. Not knowing that he had gone to New Zealand, I looked into the shop one day in wartime and found a stranger in possession. I asked the usual question : ' Have you any blue and white ? ' ' Wait a moment ' was the reply : the proprietor finished his conversation with someone else, then went into the back of the shop and returned with a bottle of whisky. I offer no explanation.

My net has been fairly wide-spread, but it is quite unusual to see good blue and white outside England except in Holland, the chief importer of such wares in the seventeenth and eighteenth centuries. Still, Florence, Venice, Milan, Bruges and Tours have all contributed to my store ; from Tours in 1921 came what is perhaps my finest dish and my only Persian plate at a cost of less than £3. In England the good thing may turn up anywhere : my best pair of Ming plates I found at Ripon in 1949 : they cost me £4. 15s. 0d., and when I saw an identical pair at the Berkeley Gallery they were priced at £24. Fortunately it is generally the simpler things which attract me most. When the Bennett Collection was on show at Gorer's in Bond Street in the summer of 1909, I was permitted to dandle a lordly K'ang Hsi magnificence, one of a pair of vases of which the price was £8,000. With that plutocratic house my only commercial transaction was remarkable enough to be worth recording. In her house at Woolacombe Mrs Fletcher had a beautiful eastern carpet—Kizil Irmak I was afterwards told by an expert that it should be called—which she knew I admired. Some years later she asked if I would like to buy it : she was letting the house and preferred that we should have the trampling of it rather than strangers. She had it valued, and the estimate, in those days of moderation, was £30. I told her I would buy it if she could get that amount for a piece of *famille verte* which I handed over to her. It was a thing with a history. Many years before, on a visit to our friends the Wratislaws at Colchester—a unique household which deserves a chapter to itself—I noticed an unfamiliar pot and asked about it. I was told that it had been brought out of a cupboard to take the place of a cup that had been broken : ' it was nothing ', and had been given to them, or to their aunt, many years before by a woman who came round with a vegetable cart and had bought it at a rummage sale. I assured them that it was the most valuable bit in the room, and when I departed it was presented to me, ' for being so clever '. Gorer had been lost in the *Lusitania*, and old Mr Hartley (father of Sir Harold), whose clerk Gorer had been in early days in the Welcome Club at Earl's Court, was presiding over the gradual dissolution of the house. His reply when Mrs Fletcher asked what he could offer for it was, ' Would you accept £30 ? '

I write elsewhere of my interest in fine printing. Some years ago Robin met a keen-witted Carthusian who said he was never sure whether I was a book-lover or a speculator. I would claim to be the first, and the second only so far that I felt justified in spending a good deal of money on fine books because I was sure they would not lose their value. They have not gained in value in recent years, because no man could earn his living by a private press to-day, and with the supply the interest in them seems to have declined. The time for speculation in the noblest of books, the Ashendene folios, was immediately after their appearance. StJohn Hornby once laughingly said to me that the thing to do was to order two copies and sell one to pay for the other. That could certainly have been done.

I hope I have not thought too commercially of either my books or my china. If I have often sold a piece of the latter, it was generally in order to buy a better one, or something else we could not easily afford, such as a Persian rug. With limited means, or a scrupulous conscience, that is the better way.

Of books as things to read, as the principal food of the mind, as the best of recreation, as the stock in trade of my profession, I have said nothing ; and there is so much to say that it is a temptation to leave it at that. But I can hardly do so : books after all have counted for more in my life than anything else. My early youth was nourished on Henty, and Henty overlapped with Conan Doyle : it was good fortune at that stage to look forward to *Rodney Stone* and *Brigadier Gerard* month by month in the *Strand Magazine :* and only this year I have re-discovered *Rodney Stone* as an excellent story. The first great writer to capture me was Tennyson, the next Kipling : I must once have been nearer to having his stories by heart than any others at any time. There followed my long allegiance to Stevenson, a taste now selective and critical, but by no means dead. After all, has *Treasure Island* any rival in its own kind ? Since Oxford and its philosophy I have seldom known what it is to be bored by a book : if I found it boring, that seemed to me a sufficient reason for not continuing to read it : and a votary of Aeschylus and Thucydides, or of Virgil, learns early to distinguish between the difficult and the tedious. There are not many books with which a mistaken sense of obligation has led me to persevere to the end, unless I really enjoyed them. So reading has been with

me for the most part a series of discoveries and re-discoveries ;
and some of the best things did not come to me early. Scott I did
not discover till 1910 ; Miss Austen in the same year, little suspect-
ing that there would come a day when I should have read all her
books aloud six times or more. *Pickwick* only arrived when I was
past forty, Trollope still later. That is less surprising : he was long
in eclipse, and in my first year at Bradfield I heard without emotion
that his books had been thrown out of the school library as dead.

I have always preferred the broad highroad and have seldom
been lured into the byways of eccentricity : that no doubt is the
reward of being deeply rooted in the Classics. Pimm was right to
a certain extent about the persistent self-improver. I distrust the
dilettante reader, and have honestly tried to temper inclination
with education and to read what seemed to me really worth reading.
For many years I have set apart the precious time between waking
and getting up for the Scriptures (or their equivalent) and the poets
—both so easily taken as read and crowded out. In general I have
preferred long books and pocket editions, adding on a holiday least
to the weight of the luggage which whenever possible I like to carry
for myself. So a long India-paper volume of Dickens or Thackeray,
and a pocket Virgil, have been my most faithful companions abroad.
The biographies that are really my best-enjoyed reading belong
to the home fireside : and we live in an age of notable biographies.
Virgil I suppose is my poet before all others, and there can hardly
have been one of my forty-two years of teaching when I did not
attempt to understand and help others to appreciate this most
subtle and inexhaustible of poets.

For a choice of three Desert Island books the Bible and
Shakespeare would obviously come first : the choice may be
conventional but is only common sense. As for the third, I really
cannot say. Possibly I might put five names in a hat and leave it to
Chance or Providence : Boswell, *Pickwick*, and three poets, Virgil,
Milton and Wordsworth. But if that were forbidden, I think
perhaps it might be the last. In Desert Island conditions I do not
think I could ever exhaust *The Prelude*, and I might achieve a
second reading of *The Excursion*. Fortunately the question is not
likely to arise.

This chapter cannot end without some reference to architecture.
After six years in College at Winchester, with St. Cross on one hand
and the Cathedral on the other, I went up to Oxford crassly
ignorant of the subject and came down four years later almost as

ill-informed. When in the autumn of 1904 I paid a visit to my friend Barrett at Norwich, we looked in at the west door of the Cathedral and agreed to take it as seen. It was Vince who helped to open my eyes, one more part of my debt to him. Now there are few of our greater churches that I have not seen—though I can get not less enjoyment from little ones. My delight in Georgian building is a later growth. In the years when we had a nursery and someone to take charge of its inhabitants, M. and I made a practice of spending a week-end every winter at some Cathedral city, or at Windsor, and those days are very good in memory. I have kept a living interest in them by a simple and inexpensive device : I am a ' friend ' of fourteen of our cathedrals, or of great churches like Beverley and Tewkesbury. The annual reports, some of them of much historic and even literary merit, serve to keep interest alive, and as membership nowhere costs more than ten shillings and usually five, the whole thing does not amount to £5 a year. I remember long ago a discussion with our friend Dorothy Swayne, who contended that it was better to identify oneself with one or two causes and give a good deal to them, rather than to dissipate one's efforts by giving a very little to many. I heartily disagree : my choice is *multa*, not *multum*, to reverse a favourite phrase of Monty Rendall's. Of course the five-shilling ' friend ' should be ready to respond to the special appeals that must inevitably come at times, but that is another matter.

It surprises me that the ' friends ' of our great churches are not infinitely more numerous : so little is asked in return for so much. And it is the same with greater societies. In this present year the National Trust, for which every one of us ought to give thanks daily, needs 40,000 new members to offset the rise in costs. The National Art Collections Fund has never reached a membership of 10,000 since 1938 : *Les amis du Louvre* number 24,000. I joined the N.A.C.F. as long ago as 1909, when it numbered little more than a thousand members, in recognition of the anonymous generosity which sent £40,000 to save Holbein's *Duchess of Milan* for the nation, on the very last day before the option expired. Till 1939, whenever I went to the National Gallery, I visited the lady last thing before coming away, partly for the incomparable charm of the picture, partly to give thanks for a still unknown woman's generosity. One thing is known : she gave one-third of her fortune.

To a lover of the arts and the country it seems only natural to support societies of this kind so far as one can : every one of them would be more effective with a larger membership, and none of them asks for more than an annual guinea. They are only expensive if the opportunities they offer of seeing good things are too much of a temptation. I belong to more than it is reasonable to detail here, and my only regret is that I can so seldom attend their meetings. Of our local West Surrey Society I have been on the Committee for thirty-six years.

I am not sure that propaganda and recruiting and begging are a hobby or taste, but rather a duty, and one of the duties that I have not shirked. When in 1944 the Council of the Classical Association did me the honour of electing me a Vice-President, it was not for an eminence in scholarship which I do not possess, but as an assiduous recruiter of new members, especially among Carthusians. How great was the honour neither I nor, I suspect, the Council realized, for after a time the Secretary wrote that he had been looking up the records and could not find that any schoolmaster had been a Vice-President except Dr Warre of Eton. Another schoolmaster, a Carthusian, was elected at the same time, and two years later Sir Frank Fletcher was President, the first schoolmaster to hold that very distinguished position. For several years a Carthusian, T. B. L. Webster, was Chairman of Council, and another, J. S. Shields, Hon. Treasurer, and I was very glad to be their humble servant.

CHAPTER IX

HOLIDAYS

I WENT abroad for the first time at the age of twenty, in April 1902. My companions were my Winchester friend Joseph Clay and his future brother-in-law, Stanley Hall, both scholars of New College : we were all in our second year and had just taken Mods. It was much less common for the young to cross the Channel in those days, and the cult of winter sports had barely begun ; but in the thirties, with the grim clouds looming in the distance, I gave the younger generation every encouragement to go while they could, and they must have seen more of Europe before they were twenty than I had in my thirtieth year. In 1902 there was certainly nothing in life that I coveted so much as a first sight of Italy, and that might well have been my most memorable visit. Now I think of it as the least memorable, because my *cicerone*, Clay, held a Victorian view of foreign travel which involved evening dress and boiled shirts and the sort of hotel which invited their use. It is the only time I have been to Italy with registered luggage instead of what I could, however laboriously, carry for myself. Also, though educated after a fashion in pictures, I had as yet little eye for sculpture and less for architecture, and for the wild flowers which would now be to me a chief source of joy, none at all. I like the Spanish proverb which I doubtless misquote from Dr Johnson, that he who would bring back the riches of the Indies must carry the riches of the Indies with him. Mentally, I am far better equipped to enjoy Italy now than then.

My second visit, in 1905, under the erratic but inspiring guidance of Monty Rendall, is far more vivid in memory. But it was an experience for the young, for we seldom knew when we should eat or where we should sleep. We slept first at Viareggio, a watering-place where no party of Britons was expected to arrive after midnight at the end of March. How that happened is worth recalling. We were due at Pisa at midnight and just at that hour ran into a station where a gleam of water caught the eye. That was enough for Monty, who sprang up with a cry of 'Arno, Arno ', and the six of us dragged down our luggage and left the train, which proceeded on its way. Officials were too sleepy or too supine to inspect our tickets, and it was only during a search for our Pisan hotel, the Nettuno, that we learnt where we were. We reached Pisa towards midday. Monty had been many times to Italy and should have known that, in those days, if a train was due at midnight, it most certainly would not arrive at that hour : also that one does not see the river on arriving at Pisa.

The most memorable part of the holiday was our tramp to La Verna, as a start to several days walking in the Casentino ; but the weather defeated even Monty. When Firth's book, *Rendall of Winchester*, was in the process of gestation, I sent him an account of that expedition, and borrow from it here.

Bibbiena was our starting-point. Monty, as sometimes happened, stood in need of a shave, and the discovery that the barber also dealt in *antichità* prolonged the session to an hour and a half— though it was obviously going to rain. So it was 5.30 before we passed the gate, just as the floods descended, with seven miles to go to La Verna and 3,000 feet to ascend. We had strangely resolved to carry no rain-coats, only pyjamas and a toothbrush, and were wet through in the first mile. The party consisted of two hares who could go Monty's pace and two tortoises who could not. But halfway up the hill the tortoises found the hares standing over an exhausted form in a barn. So the slowcoaches were the first to reach the monastery on its crag, where their polite noises failed to win the attention of the monks. Soon the united party were raising such a barbarous din that the good fathers were reluctant to admit us. But Monty, bareheaded in the rain, holding a long staff cut on the journey and explaining that we were *pellegrini inglesi* come to do honour to St. Francis—which in his own case was doubtless true—won us entry, and soon we were supping off cold tunny and a thin red wine, wearing our pyjamas and the Franciscan cloaks which our hosts took off for our comfort. They were particularly attentive to one who is now Archdeacon of Basingstoke,* who in his fancy dress might have been the model for Donatello's *St. George*.

I cannot say that we slept well or comfortably, or that our half-dried clothes were good to put on, or that our breakfast was appetizing or the weather encouraging : hence the decision to return to Florence. It was Palm Sunday, and the rain did not deter the peasantry from climbing the mountain to keep the day in the holy place. The good fathers asked us to delay our inspection of the church, which contains perhaps the noblest of all Della

---

* Archdeacon Chute has died since this was written.

Robbias, till the *funzione* was ended : but as it took a long time and the weather looked momentarily less unpropitious for a start, after a time we were invited to proceed. Till Easter the altar-pieces might not be unveiled, but—believe it or not—we were encouraged to stand on the altars and hold the curtains above our heads : only very genuinely holy men, I feel, could have been so obliging.

So after more cold tunny we started back for Bibbiena. When we reached the foot of the cliff it was discovered that Monty, who had previously hit his head a fearful crack against a stone arch, had left his camera behind. We prepared to decide by tossing who should fetch it, till we found that ' St. George ' had already started on the climb. So early in the afternoon we were back at the barber's. The time for the train drew near, and we left Monty kneeling between two mountains of textiles, the sheep and the goats, the good pieces on his right hand and the faded or damaged on his left. On that particular day the little station was crowded, and at the last moment Monty appeared, under a trailing mass of drapery, shouldered his way through the throng and entered the carriage. Then came the discovery : he had brought the goats and left the sheep behind. So at Arezzo another train had nearly to be missed while a telegram was despatched *al barbiere chi anchè vende antichità, Bibbiena.* At Venice and Lugano he was cheated by rogues, but the barber of Bibbiena was an honest man, and when Monty returned the next year he was welcomed with a kiss on both cheeks. And the curtains were still hanging at Butley Priory when he died forty-five years later.

On these two journeys I was *in statu pupillari :* afterwards till 1939 I was always in charge of those who knew nothing of Italy, and had to do the staff work, the talking and the paying. I became reasonably competent in the language, if not grammatical, and later on even had one pupil in Italian at Charterhouse. So it was a disappointment, and an unwelcome symptom of old age, to find that in 1953 all power to speak the language or to understand it when spoken had departed : I found myself wholly dependent on Robin.

It is a common belief that an Italian spring always enjoys lovely weather, but that is not so. Just as our planned walk in the Casentino was ruined in 1905, so, as I have mentioned already, was my first visit to Rome, with Vince, in 1907. Every day but two was wet, insomuch that we escaped to Naples in search of the sun, and found it ; but when we returned to Rome, we returned also to rain. Again it was a matter of inadequate education : not knowing the fascination of the early churches, we spent far too much time in minor picture and sculpture galleries, and though the weather generally cleared before evening, it was too late to escape into the Campagna or the Alban Hills—an absolute necessity if one is to avoid mental indigestion. The finest day was given to the Forum and the Palatine, with a delightful lunch on the Aventine in between, under conduct of an old Wesleyan minister who knew every stone almost as well as Signor Boni himself. Apart from this bright day our chief success was the little German restaurant where a good lunch, with excellent Munich beer, cost one *lira* and a half, or one-and-threepence. By the way, till 1939 I regarded it almost as a point of honour not to exceed £30 in a three weeks' holiday, travel included : and our money, till after 1918, we carried in good gold sovereigns.

So from this rain-ruined holiday came a distaste for Rome of which I did not learn the error for thirty-two years. Then in a lucky moment I was offered, at the age of 57, an emergency vacancy in a team of ' young teachers ' organized and run by the British School and guided by Russell Meiggs (then of Keble, now of Balliol) and Professor Ronald Syme. It was a truly glorious time in glorious weather, with Rome seen as she ought to be seen, and excellent drives in our own coach to Ostia and Veii and Cerveteri, and an unforgettable day's walking on the Alban Hills. Naples too was included, with Herculaneum as well as Pompeii.

The tour was not without its anxieties, for it began in the week when Mussolini marched into Albania, and for twenty-four hours, as we learned afterwards, it was touch and go whether we should not be sent home   It was also a time of stringent A.R.P. exercises, with streets darker than I ever saw them in London : for a meeting in a large hotel dining-room we were allowed one candle at the maximum distance from the street windows. It was a strange experience to return from the British School, after a lecture by Mrs Strong—to whom my niece Joan Yeo had once been secretary—with taxis crawling in a ghostly procession under the dimmest of blue lights. There was a daylight ' air-raid ' also, which caught many of us in the Vatican at an hour when luncheon was becoming an imperative need. My power of sightseeing was exhausted, when I luckily found an unfastened door and sat in a delightful garden reading Virgil till the All Clear went. Another novel experience is good in memory too, though it was pretty exhausting at the time. Someone gave me a ticket for St. Peter's on Easter Day, the first Easter of the present Pope, Pius XII. How early we had to arrive I cannot remember, but I was given the tip to buy a campstool in the Piazza, and I was very thankful for it. But when the time came for the Papal procession and I mounted the stool with the aid of a friendly priest, it proved less good to stand than to sit on, and through it I went just as His Holiness came by. As a good Protestant I had never imagined myself, with untold thousands, shouting ' *Viva il Papa Rè* ' in St. Peter's on Easter morning. Besides organized expeditions, we had plenty of time to ourselves, and I was able to revisit the graves of Shelley and Keats, and to assure myself that Velasquez' portrait of Innocent X in the Doria Gallery is as magnificent as I thought it in 1907.

Since 1939 I have only once been to Italy, in September 1953, in the excellent company of Robin and Murray, and with a particularly fortunate first experience of flying. One is left with the feeling that for a short holiday that is the only way to go and return, giving one or two extra days in Italy, if not more : and when you have the rare fortune to cross the Alps on a cloudless day there can be no doubt about it. But Italy in September is a flowerless land, and I cannot set off the peaches against the flowers of spring. It was a well varied tour : a night at the pleasant town of Parma (my third visit), two nights at Ravenna : then good quarters in the *Casa Stefani* at Venice : a coach drive to the hotel recommended by Freya Stark at Asolo, and two nights at Verona. Venice was what I had long known it to be, but Ravenna was a revelation. I had been there fifty-one years before, and remembered a poor shabby town and mosaics that I was too crude really to enjoy. I have never forgotten the story told me by Signor Coscia of his visit to Ravenna with a party of friends, no doubt back in the nineteenth century. They had the services of a guide who was a real scholar and at the end of the day rewarded him with ten *lire*. The old man wept— ' *si mise a piangere* ' : he had never received so much money at one time before. In 1953 there was no evidence of extreme poverty : if there were mercifully few *vespe*, there were as many cycles as elsewhere : the streets were clean and the noble churches well kept. I am sure the mosaics were in far better condition than when my uncomprehending eyes saw them in 1902 ; and their beauty is quite astonishing. Of one thing I am certain : I would rather see Ravenna again than any town in Italy—even Assisi, even Lucca, even Siena, even places I have never seen, such as Urbino and Subiaco. To stay at Browning's, or Pippa's, little town of Asolo also satisfied a fifty-year-old desire ; and the name of Freya Stark, whose good offices I claimed as a friend of Sydney Cockerell,

K

procured us entry to the Villa Maser, at whose door I had knocked in vain in 1905 and 1909. The house is famous for the frescoes of Paolo Veronese ; but when at the third attempt I actually entered it, I found the painter much less enthralling than the architect, Palladio. When we had padded round in the slippers provided to protect the floors, we sat by the roadside and basked contentedly in its mellow beauty till our bus came.

The memory of my visit with Rendall & Co. is very fresh. The owner in those days was one Count Giacomelli, a man who had deservedly known the inside of a jail. We had made no application for a permit to enter—Monty would hardly do that—and were told that the Count was out. The humble henchman was afraid to let us in, but, scenting a tip, he told us that his master, *il padrone*, had gone for a walk and would soon be back : indeed he could soon point to a distant figure on the road below. So we went down to the gate to receive him. On the way, one of the party, a man of an ugliness almost historic, asked to be shown to the *ritirata*. So the party, minus one, met the Count as he returned to his domain, a magnificent stage villain swathed in a black cloak, with a huge black hat, and followed by a hound to match. The conversation was carried on with frigid politeness, and to Monty's disgust the Count declined to speak anything but French. The last word was with him : '*Je ne peux pas être à la disposition des étrangers.*' So the Count proceeded to his house, and as he approached his garden *ritirata*, out came *l'homme laid* : they passed with a solemn raising of hats.

A year later Mr ' Lumley ' succeeded in effecting an entry, but in 1909 I was once more bilked, though armed with a written permit. The Count was again out, and the woman who answered the door declared that she could not leave the preparation of his dinner : so we pursued a hot and dusty walk to Asolo. I am glad that 1953 did not bring a third disappointment, and by that time I was ripe to enjoy Palladio.

I cannot discourse on all my nine journeys to Italy, not even my only visit with M. in 1914, nor the revelation of Sicily with L. H. Bennett in 1923. But of a particularly happy tour in 1931, in the company of Michael Lloyd and my colleague Geoffrey Facer, I wrote a record at the time and propose to give it as an appendix.

I seem to have crossed the Channel outward bound twenty-five times, never for so much as a month. The Hellenic cruise of 1911 was in its consequences the most memorable of all, and I have only less good reason to remember that of 1924, made at the expense of my generous friend Bennett, when I introduced Alice Green to Truman Tanqueray on the first day of the cruise and was informed of their engagement before it was ended. A bare statement is all I can give, that I have been once to Holland, Belgium, the Rhineland and Switzerland, three times in the best of company to that enchanting country Austria (once with Ober-Ammergau included), and seven times to France. And those seven visits I feel to have been all too few : there is far too much of that lovely land that I shall never see. In 1936 I learnt how admirable a conducted tour can be, when I went to Provence with a party of members of the Classical and Historical Associations, under conduct of Professor and Mrs Dobson—he to discourse on things classical, she on matters of history and archaeology. We went by train to Avignon, and then had our own coach.

The holiday of August 1939 must be mentioned for its unlikeness to the rest. Pralognan gave me my first sight of Savoy and of an Alpine flora, and we contrived to enjoy ourselves by dint of not reading newspapers. Then we removed to Menton, on the Lac d'Annecy, on the day when the news became most menacing. After the high mountain air, the day of a long drive to see the Prado pictures at Geneva is an oppressive memory. I am thankful to have seen so many great works of Titian and Velasquez, which I shall never see in their proper habitation, but cannot call it an exhilarating experience. Robin was to have flown out to complete the family party, with our friend Michael Peck, now Archdeacon of Portsmouth, but that fortunately was prevented. Mobilization had been ordered, and reports of the difficulty and discomfort of travel were such that, on the advice of our landlord, we decided to hire a car for the journey to Paris, a distance not less than from London to Edinburgh. We started about four in the afternoon and, while daylight lasted, it proved a most enjoyable drive through lovely country, with such a dinner at Châlon-sur-Saône as I did not meet again for thirteen years. We reached Paris at 3 a.m., slept comfortably in a waiting-room at the Gare du Nord, were first at the barrier when the train came in, and landed in England with no difficulty at all. Difficulties only began when we arrived at our own door and found neither staff nor keys. Our one qualm was the cost, and that was relieved in the following April, when to my astonishment Cook's sent us a refund from French Railways for unused tickets.

First place among my French holidays goes without doubt to the few flawless days in 1952, my first foreign tour in a private car, with

Michael and Priscilla Lloyd and M., the incomparable companion on such an occasion—her last holiday abroad. I wrote an account of it which I hoped the editor of *Blackwood* might accept, but he rejected it as too much of a ' travelogue ', which no doubt it was, though I deprecate the horrible word. But it gave pleasure to some who read it : two of them enjoyed it enough to have some copies typed, and it will appear here as another appendix.

The reasons for putting foreign holidays first are obvious enough : they are a more complete change—in surroundings and diet, and I wish I could say in ideas and language : but there my linguistic incompetence comes in. Hugely as I enjoyed my holidays abroad, I should have enjoyed them still more if I could have talked rationally to a waiter or a railwayman or *hôtelier*, and not been so often put to shame by those who spoke decent English to one who could not converse in French or German even of the worst.

A schoolmaster is privileged to enjoy some fifteen weeks of holiday in the year, and for me, as I have said, that would have been a great deal too much if I had had no work to do. But I early realized that if a Sixth Form master begins to live on his capital he must go downhill, and almost all my work involved preparation, more or less careful, in vacation. But I could never have risen to the virtue of Burge at Winchester, as recorded by Spencer Leeson, who when he had finished a course of lectures destroyed his notes, so that he must tackle the subject afresh next time.

I have never thought of education as only a matter of books : to me it has stood for the enlargement of interests, seeing things and places that are worth seeing. Almost every vacation must have added something to my *choses vues*, and I certainly intended that it should.

I have said something of the region that gave me so much in my most active years—the Berkshire and Oxfordshire and Cotswold country for which my base was Eynsham. There are three other districts which have played a memorable part in my life : the Lakes, Storrington and West Sussex, and Anglesey. And I am tempted to add a fourth, Suffolk, less well known but not less loved.

I first saw the Lake District in April 1910, and my approach to it, with Vince for guide, is so fresh in memory that I have not needed to refer to written records. Starting early from Oxford we reached Barnard Castle in time to visit Greta Bridge that afternoon, spent the night in the hotel where Newman Noggs commended the coffee, and made an early start next morning for Middleton-in-Teesdale, where a carriage was to meet us and take us to breakfast at the High Force Hotel. In expectation of a party, not two only, a wagonette had been sent, and the driver's remark ' I'll yok a less trap ' was my first introduction to the true Northern Doric. I have a notorious habit of meeting or making acquaintances in unlikely places, and as we reached the hotel out walked a grey-bearded figure, a friend of my father, one whom I was to know well in later years, Phelps, afterwards Provost of Oriel. He told us that he took a reading party there every year, and found that the scholars walked better than the athletes : ' the fells are strewn with the bones of Oxford Blues '. We set off over the moors (with my first curlews), via Cauldron Snout, to the wonderful cleft of High Cup Nick, which I saw again forty-two years later in the good company of Katharine Lloyd : then down in the late afternoon to Appleby : then after dinner by train to Keswick and the Royal Oak. Our luggage consisted of a rucksack which we carried by turns. Next morning I was still in bed when Vince came in and ordered me to get up and come to Friar's Crag instantly. I am glad he did, for I have never seen Derwentwater as I saw it that first time, in the still gray morning, with the reflections if anything a little more luminous than the mountains themselves. But that still beauty was ominous. We took a boat across the lake, and had got no further than Catbells when the floods descended, and the walk by Maiden Moor and Scawdel Fell and Lobstone Band and Robinson—those who know the Lakes will welcome the familiar names and those who do not will I hope forgive them—had to be postponed for two years. We descended perforce to the road, and that in drenching rain is *triste* enough : and the downpour continued for twenty-four hours. But the Fish at Buttermere gave us good food and shelter, and though the next morning held no promise of anything better, the clouds suddenly cleared towards midday and we were able to take Great Gable on our way to Wastdale Head. True to form, as we left Keswick, I had recognised a man in the street as an old Cam-bridge opponent at lawn tennis, who was moreover a nephew of my Macaulay godparents and a pupil of Vince in pre-Bradfield days. We fell in with him again at the foot of the Gable and climbed it with him and his friends.

Next morning the weather was good and we left early, because Vince resented the airs of certain loud-voiced climbers and their wet ropes extended on the banisters. So we could take both Scafell and Scafell Pike, and in a fresh snowfield on Mickledore, between the two, we met a solitary walker—a red-haired Wykehamist of my day, known to me only by sight, though afterwards as a

Wellington master I saw him often. We lunched crouching in a sheepfold for shelter, then on by Esk Hause and Rossett Gill to tea at the Dungeon Gill Old Hotel, and down the Langdales in an afternoon of incomparable spring beauty to our lodging a mile or so beyond Grasmere. There our luggage awaited us : railways were to be relied on in those days. My memory of those walks owes nothing to a diary, though something to a map.

To that holiday I owe something besides the discovery of the Lakes : I owe to it the discovery of Sir Walter Scott. For the three days of walking I carried one book, my first Waverley Novel, and in my ignorance took *Quentin Durward* when I meant to take *Guy Mannering*. No one who knew both would make that choice, but it served its purpose and did not last out the three days. I am certainly not omnivorous of Scott : to be at his best he must be in his own country and his own century ; and given those right limits, I will quote the words of a wise man, Frank Fletcher : ' What a lot of pleasure people lose who think they can't read Scott '.

In my Lakeland experience 1910 was good but 1912 far better— that year in which April and early May gave us high summer, before those dreadful months which left the crops unharvested in October. When I say that I bathed in Crummock Water before breakfast every morning I have said enough : it was summer weather all the time with the young beauty of spring. Vince had taken all the rooms in Wood House, on the strath between Butter- mere and Crummock, for a very harmonious party of seven. It included old Andrew Low, the Second Master, who had come to Bradfield simultaneously with Dr Gray in 1880, and generally seemed oppressed with the cares of thirty-two years and more of bachelor schoolmastering. But one mile, or half a mile, from the College gate he became a different man. I was deputed to persuade him to be of the party. His reply was, ' Me dear sir, you couldn't stand me for a moment : I'm alternately a brǎssy gaspot and a leaden dullard '. However, he came, did the High Cup Nick walk —past his own birthplace at Langdon Beck—in a bowler hat, walked his twenty miles a day and drank his quart of beer, and contributed more than anyone except Vince to the enjoyment of the holiday. Afterwards he referred to it as the happiest fortnight of his life, and I don't know that I ever had a happier. We needed it before a disastrous term. The commissariat was safe in Vince's hands, the cooking excellent, as always in Lakeland, with a special cask of Lichfield beer and of Canadian apples. The cost to each of us was six shillings a day.

The tour began on the day which brought news of the loss of the *Titanic*, when most of us heard for the first time the expression S.O.S. We were not in Edwardian times inured to horror and disaster, and I have no doubt that day gave a greater shock to the country than any single event since.

That spring I registered a vow to visit the Lakes every year, but like most vows it has not been kept : I have only been there five times. Anglesey has therefore meant more to me than Cumberland : we went there first in 1928, and then most years till 1937—eight times I think in all.

The house had been built by J. W. Marshall, a mathematical master at Charterhouse before he became a farmer in Sussex. He and his wife enjoyed remoteness, and had Rhosneigr for a winter resort, and for the summer a cottage in Finland. They were dear people, but their standard of comfort was not high and Trewyn at Rhosneigr had no amenities and a staircase which cost Murray a broken arm. But its situation, looking away to the Holyhead Mountain, was a delight, and it stood in some acres of uncultivated ground for privacy, while at high tide (when caution was necessary) bathing began within thirty yards. I had never more than tolerated the sea before, complaining that it cut me off from half the land ; but Rhosneigr, given fine weather, I loved as much as the family did, though our employments were seldom the same, except when we assembled on wet days or at prescribed times of rest to share Dr Dolittle, or later Henty. Anglesey, I am told, has the largest flora of any county except Devon and, with the much better educated M. and Janet, it was a wonderful field to explore. Only there have I met elecampane or the giant buttercup, *Ranunculus Lingua*, or seen, near Hell's Mouth, a sheet of orpine (*Sedum Telephium*) stretching for forty or fifty yards, and far warmer and richer in colour than the isolated specimens I have lit on in Surrey. But once it was the other way on. We used to visit a remote spot in the hope of finding a single plant of *Dianthus Deltoides*. Then one day at golf on the West Surrey links my partner remarked that it was nice to see the Maiden Pink coming out, and I learnt for the first time that if I had erred from the straight course at the 18th hole, I might have found not one plant but fifty.

There remains Storrington. We owed the discovery of this friendly little town to a chance meeting in a train, when an Old Wykehamist, one of our Italian party of 1905, recommended the White Horse. The year was 1917 and we wanted a short holiday not far from home. Our next-door neighbour at Sandrock was a very delightful old Haileybury master, the Rev. Augustus De Morgan Hensley—more briefly Uncle Gus—cousin of the potter and novelist. He loved to recall the days some sixty years earlier when he had stroked a Trinity boat ; and on hearing that we were for Storrington, he said we must go and see ' my number six '. His No. 6 proved to be one Canon Palmer, who held a family living at Sullington, a mile or so east of Storrington. We attended divine service on the Sunday, where a magnificent old man gave us unmitigated matins, with sermon, litany and ante-communion. Afterwards we introduced ourselves and were invited to the Rectory, a beautiful old house smelling like Radwinter. The Rector told us he was one of the oldest living Marlburians, and I asked if he knew William Morris. ' What, Crab Morris ? ' was the reply : ' he taught me to net '—which is of course just what Morris would have done. But what other living man would have referred to him as Crab, a name unknown to his daughter and his friends ? The rest of the story is so queer that I leave it for my appendix, *Coincidences.*

I stayed at the White Horse again in 1918, with Christopher Green, still a boy at Charterhouse. But it was in the middle twenties that a visit became an annual event, lasting till 1940. In the thirties, when the delightful West Sussex Golf Club had opened, near Pulborough—with my old Wimbledon opponent George Hillyard as secretary—I several times went down for a few days in April too.

My summer practice became, weather permitting, a routine. The Summer Quarter always left me extremely tired, and when it was over I would ride down on my bicycle, with a rucksack, and return on Saturday evening. It was Goodwood week and the Petworth road intolerable, but the remedy was easy. I pushed my bicycle up Holloway Hill and had a choice of routes with hardly a car upon them. On Saturday I would take train from Steyning to Hove for the first day of Sussex *v.* Middlesex—and in those days I was a Sussex member. Then back in the evening by train to Bramley, and home in time for a bath and supper. Much as I like company, or some company, I like solitude almost equally well, and I found these little holidays infinitely refreshing. When my friends the Miss Hammonds gave up the White Horse and retired to a little Georgian house which they owned, I followed them there, for they continued to take a few guests. We never went *en famille* till 1940, which, alas, proved to be my last visit ; yet the place contained valued relatives of M., and them, while they lived, we often saw. But the family visit was a questionable success. The

Battle of Britain was just beginning, and the ladies and gentlemen of the A.R.P. gathered in the lane which passed the Georgian house, whenever a distant siren went, to the sound of an enormous dinner bell, and dispersed again on the All Clear. Sleep being impossible, it was hardly worth paying for one's keep : we were happier at Pageites.

Most of that dear West Sussex countryside, inland at least, remains unspoilt, and if I had to name the country I love best it would claim a place very near the first.

I have often thought what was my most perfect day, and my mind has always come round to the same one. It was a Sunday late in April 1916, before I had begun the discovery of Sussex. I had no doubt come from Eynsham on my bicycle, with no luggage but what my basket and frame-bag would hold, and spent the night in a small house at Broadway, where I paid 1/6 for my bed. I left on a perfect spring morning, with all the bells of the Bredon villages ' sounding so clear ', and rode to Tewkesbury, my first sight of that noblest of churches, where I arrived in time for a Choral Celebration of great beauty and simplicity, a form of worship of which I had at that time had little experience. I lunched at the old Bell Inn. I had seen a notice that the afternoon service at Gloucester Cathedral was at 3 o'clock and was a festival service for the tercentenary of Shakespeare's death. On that level road I covered the twelve miles in an hour and arrived in time for a noble service with anthems by Handel and Brahms and a good sermon by Bishop Frodsham. The Cathedral, like the Abbey, was new to me. Afterwards I found a lodging over a small confectioner's and finished the day by ascending the hill of Tuffley (a thing I have only done once since) to enjoy a sunset over the Welsh hills that was a worthy conclusion to a perfect day of English spring. I have been to these two great churches many times since and have long been a ' friend ' of both ; but to have seen them for the first time on the same day under such conditions was a privilege indeed, and the memory of that carefree day in a most anxious year remains wonderfully fresh.

CHAPTER X

SOME FRIENDS

A SCHOOLMASTER, unless he is very unfortunate, is making new friends all his life—and I have never considered myself unfortunate. But there are a few friends, sometimes people I very seldom saw, or who are long dead, to whom I feel a special indebtedness. Of Monty Rendall and Campbell McInnes I have said enough, and the first I would refer to now is William Warde Fowler. If I had known him earlier, or had guessed that Cicero's Letters were to become a favourite study, I should have sought out his lectures in my Oxford days. My friend Bridge was his pupil and testified that when Fowler talked of Cicero's Rome ' he knew all the people '. I first made his acquaintance in 1914 when I wrote to him about some plant in Virgil. In replying, he suggested that if ever I were in his part of the world, Kingham in North Oxon, I might perhaps pay him a visit, and that with a home at Eynsham was an easy thing to do. I found a deaf old man living with a deaf old sister and, like many people, I often find the harsh voices of the deaf rather trying ; but this couple had a charm which overcame any difficulties of that kind. Many years later Cyril Bailey wrote that ' to each of us the day on which he came to know Warde Fowler marked an epoch '. My first visit certainly bore fruit. He remarked that in bed that morning he had been reading the Gathering of the Clans in the Seventh Book of the *Aeneid*, a favourite book of mine, and I said I wished he would write something about it. I thought no more of it, but in the following spring I received for my consideration the proofs of a little book to be published by Blackwell, a book that no other man could have written. It was followed later by two more, and established the series of ' little green books ', of which a row of eleven now stand on my shelves. In 1920, reviewing John Sargeaunt's *Trees, Shrubs and Plants of Virgil*, I spoke of the series as the best contribution to Virgilian studies that this country had made for many years. When I myself had the privilege of adding a volume to it three years later, I was amused to find my own laudatory words used by the publisher as an advertisement of my own book.

I visited him a good many times till his death in the spring of 1921 and treasure his memory and his books, including two that were never published, but printed privately for the enjoyment of his friends. One was a brief autobiography written in the last year of his life, and one on Mozart, whom he knew and loved long before the modern cult of that delectable master began. Reggie Bridge, his pupil, told me that when he was ill what he took to bed with him was a score of Mozart's Quartets.

Perhaps he is best remembered for the charm of his writing about birds : here again he was ahead of his time. But the subject of which he was the acknowledged master was the religion of Ancient Rome, though I believe that Virgil and Mozart were the chief loves of his life, with Miss Austen not very far behind. He possessed or acquired few luxuries, but among them were first editions of all her novels.

His deafness was not complete : he still could hear music, and I found him an entirely competent accompanist for my Elizabethan songs ; and he could always hear a bird. Frank Fletcher once spoke of him as a rather inconvenient guest at Marlborough (his old school), because he might walk past the gong as it sounded for dinner to listen to a bird in the garden.

My friendship with Stephen Gwynn was almost wholly epistolary, for in a period of forty-five years I can only remember meeting him nine times. He had been Sixth Form master at Bradfield as long ago as 1889, but disliked the profession and soon gave it up for journalism and letters, and in course of time for the House of Commons. But he always retained his friendship for Low and Steele. In my first weeks at Bradfield he paid a visit to Low, who invited me to meet him at supper. Macmillan had just published his textbook, *Masters of English Literature*, and speaking of it he said that it was impossible to do the Victorians satisfactorily ; they were too near us. I read the book and liked it so much, despite its numerous inaccuracies, most of which I was then too immature to detect, that I was still using it forty years later. Early in 1923 Macmillan announced a new edition. I wrote and said that, having used the book for eighteen years, I hoped I might be allowed a copy. In those days of two maids and a nurse to two parents and a child, one might even enjoy the luxury of the morning's post in bed, and there I opened the new book on a gross misquotation of Wordsworth. Scrutiny showed the new edition to be a mere reprint, with all its imperfections on its head. I wrote to the publisher and, instead of a formal typed reply, received a long letter in an almost illegible hand, saying that my letter had left the writer ' one big blush '.

I then reminded him that we had once met and of what he had said on that occasion about the Victorians, and suggested that he should have another try at them for the next issue of a book that was still widely used. He came down to see me at Lord's Meade, when I found that he had known Frank Fletcher as a schoolboy during a temporary engagement at Rossall : so he was made welcome at Saunderites also. After that we not infrequently had occasion for letters, and in August 1938, when for once we had taken a house at Southwold, I received one in which he told me that Macmillan had asked him to write a new volume of *English Men of Letters* on—whom ? I told him that the name had defied the united efforts of the family to read it, but that we hoped it was Stevenson, surely overdue for a volume in E.M.L. He said, no, it was Sheridan, and he didn't want to supersede an existing volume by Mrs Oliphant ; he had never thought of Stevenson, but liked the idea and Macmillan had accepted it. So the book duly appeared and I found it inscribed to me. No one was better qualified to write it, for he had reviewed R.L.S. while still a living author and had remained faithful to him, though not uncritically, through all the years of depreciation. Later, when after 1939 he had a new impulse to verse, he wrote that he had become poet laureate to one of the Sunday papers—I forget which—and often sent me his verses for criticism. I may say that I believe his volume of poems published in 1923 to be his best work, a view which he held himself. I greatly enjoyed his *Experiences of a Literary Man*, an excellent auto-biography which unfortunately stops short with his election to Parliament in 1906. The war found him a Nationalist M.P., and he was one of the two selected to apply for a commission as a token of loyalty, and he served for three years in France with the Connaught Rangers when already past fifty. He was also at the head of a recruiting campaign in Dublin, where my brother held at one time a post in his office.

He turned his hand to many things besides writing : fisherman, yachtsman (in company with his cousin Conor O'Brien), traveller, cricketer, gardener, who in his eighties was still efficient with axe and spade. He had taken two First Classes at Oxford, and the number of Firsts acquired by a very able group of brothers was a family joke. At one time after he left the Army he and his charming daughter were market-gardeners in Ireland, where on one occasion Sheila came in and announced, ' There's a curse on this family, I'm first in digging '. After the Sinn Feiners had blown up his house he lived mainly in England, till he finally withdrew to end his days on his native soil. He died in 1950. Sometime before 1939 he was sharing with the widow of his friend E. V. Lucas a house, Paradise Cottage, off Bucklebury Common, three miles from Bradfield. In the autumn of that year, as a piece of war service, he actually returned to the school which he had left a full half-century earlier. But he had grown rather deaf and spoke in a very low voice, and his gallant effort did not last beyond a term or two.

There are two matters in which I owe him a special debt. One of my most treasured possessions was, and still is, a panel of stained glass given me as a wedding-present by my Dublin friend Geoghegan. He said that the maker was ' a canny young Ulster-woman who works for my Aunt Sally ', alias Miss Sarah Purser, founder of the Dublin school of glaziers. Gwynn on seeing it thought it was the work of Wilhelmina Geddes : Okey Belfour thought the same, and said she was making a window for Laleham church, a memorial to his father. He sent me the artist's address, for she worked part of the year in London, and I went to see her. Providence, or my own incompetence, led me to the wrong studio in a house which contained many, and I found a man working on what seemed to me a very beautiful window. He tolerated my intrusion, and when I asked where I could see any of his work, he said it was mostly in Ireland, but he had been making some windows for the Convent of Notre Dame in Ashdown Park. Now it chanced that M. and I intended to spend our exeat that June (1927) at Horsham, within cycling distance of the Convent. We found an order of nuns who, refugees from Belgium, had been building their convent and its chapel with stone quarried in their own park, and they were extremely interested to learn that we came from Charterhouse, where the chapel, likewise built of home-quarried stone, had been growing up simultaneously with theirs. I have revisited the place several times, and always find the chapel glass as beautiful as any modern glass known to me. Unhappily the artist, Harry Clark, died untimely of tuberculosis before he had done all the work that the nuns had hoped for.

Not long ago Janet asked me about the panel, and I told her it accounted for the blue carpet on the floor. For when we visited the convent we were about to enter on our sixteen-year tenancy of Pageites, and we so liked the blue carpets and linoleum that we furnished our new private side in the same way ; and the dining-room carpet went with us to Chiddingfold. So do things link up with one another.

But to return to Miss Geddes. I found her at work on the Laleham window and wondered why it should have been necessary to give St. Cecilia so ugly a head. Indeed when the window was put in, there was such an outcry from the churchgoers of Laleham that the vicar was moved to offer his resignation ; but a compromise was reached by transferring it to the west end, where no one was obliged to look at it. The artist suffered at times from mental disturbance, and many years later Okey told me, on her authority, that the Saint's head derived from a doctor whom she disliked in a mental home. After her death in 1955 a reference in *The Spectator* to this fine window led me to a pleasant exchange of letters with John Betjeman.

Whatever Gwynn liked he wrote about with zest and charm, and one of his subjects, possibly his best, was wine. Now though I had learnt to enjoy wine when I was ten or eleven years old, I had never kept a cellar nor inhabited a house which offered one. I always had a little light port from Shipston-on-Stour to drink before a concert, when I found it good for both voice and morale, and large stone jars of Marsala from a now extinct firm, William Sykes and Co., at the London Docks. I never possessed a bottle of the sherry that now appears indispensable till I was nearly fifty. Now, as a housemaster, with more scope for hospitality, I wrote to Gwynn for advice about claret, always my favourite wine. He replied that if I would leave it to him he would find me some in Dublin, and I duly received a supply of beautiful wine. I cannot remember the price, only that it was absurdly low. I was fortunate in the friendship of Max Hodsoll, Chairman of Grierson, Oldham and Company, a connoisseur and lover of claret, but it was some years later that, when he was discoursing on his latest wine list, I asked if I was allowed to buy anything from it. ' Why not ? ' was the reply. I had always believed that it was not etiquette for the private customer to buy from the wholesaler. After that the way was clear, and 1939 found me with a stock of the beautiful clarets of 1934 which lasted me till about 1950. On one memorable occasion I had the opportunity of bringing my two friends together. In the summer of 1943 Hodsoll rang me up and asked if I had seen a certain article of Gwynn's in *Blackwood*, which of course I had. On the strength of it he wanted to ask him to lunch at Claridge's, where he kept a private cellar for the entertainment of the eminent in the world of wine. Having secured Gwynn, he invited me to be of the company, the one outsider in a party of experts. I will name them : Colonel Campbell, Chairman of the

Wine and Spirits Trade Association, brother of one V.C. and father of a second ; André Simon, and Ernest Oldmeadow, author of that little masterpiece *Not Claret* and biographer of Cardinal Bourne ; he was also that ' Downman of Dean Street ', whose wine lists are things to preserve as literature. The Colonel was pleased to find that I was a teacher of the classics and told me that when he read his son's citation for valour in North Africa, his first thought was, ' I wish someone would put this into Latin prose '. That wish I was able to satisfy, but not by my own scholarship ; any capacity I ever had for writing Latin, small at best, has long since perished of atrophy. What was needed was supplied by the ever-ready Patrick Wilkinson. When I heard of Hodsoll's death some two years later, I at once wrote to Oldmeadow and said I hoped he would write something about him. He replied that, as it chanced, that luncheon party was the only time he had met Hodsoll except in the way of business, so in the end the task devolved upon me—a notice in *Ridley's*, the oldest of wine journals, of which I had never heard. I was glad to pay tribute to a man whom I admired as much as I liked him.

Another in whose friendship wine played a large part was A. B. Ramsay, Lower Master at Eton and then for twenty-two years Master of Magdalene College, Cambridge. In December 1927, I attended an Old Grange dinner, so far as I know the first of its kind ; and asking who was in the chair was told, the Master of Magdalene. Suddenly it came back to me that when one of us made a particularly ignominious howler, old Hussey might remark that Ramsay would never have done a thing like that—and I am quite prepared to believe it. It so happened that a week or two earlier Magdalene had, for the first time in my day, elected a classical scholar from Charterhouse, my friend R. E. C. Broadbent. On the strength of it I went and introduced myself after dinner and was at once invited to visit him at Cambridge. The meeting was indeed fruitful. We took to each other at once and I invited him to examine at Charterhouse, which he did repeatedly : in fact he almost alternated between Charterhouse and Winchester. More important, there was no year till he retired in 1947 in which a Carthusian name, sometimes more than one, did not appear in the scholarship list at Magdalene. I enjoyed his hospitality more years than not, and dinner at his table included wine from the choicest cellar I have known except Hodsoll's. When at last retirement came, he found a pleasant house at Malvern, with the noblest arbutus I have ever seen beside its gate : and as from 1949

I went to lecture at Malvern every October, I became his guest even more frequently than before, till the final breakdown of his health. He died in the autumn of 1955 : his sister and lifelong companion followed him a year later.

More than once he said to me that he had been a lucky man ; and I think that is true, if a man is lucky who denies himself wife and children. At least the war gave him an extra five years at Magdalene, and when at 75 he withdrew to Malvern he was able to start a third career, and to enjoy it with all his old zest, as a teacher of Latin to the highest class in a private school only a few yards from his gate. And how lucky was that school ! Our generation, as small boys, were taught by scholars, but of how many is that true to-day ? He had stipulated for three things in his retirement : the sea, a chess club, and a school where he might sometimes teach. If Malvern could not give him the sea, it gave him the hills, which in long leisurely walks he came to know from end to end.

There is a story which he told me at my first visit to Magdalene, which certainly suggests a favourite of fortune. On moving to Cambridge he had resolved to sell the family home near Bicester, which contained a picture, clearly a good one, of ' Mr Fermor and Hounds '. (There was also a portrait of Mistress Arabella Fermor, of *The Rape of the Lock*, to whom I paid my humble and grateful respects at every visit to Cambridge and Malvern. After all she gave occasion for the most brilliant poem in the language.) As Mr Fermor's hounds were the ancestors of the Bicester Hunt, he wrote to the Hunt Secretary to see if anyone among their members was interested in it, and he would no doubt have accepted the most modest offer : but none was made. A little before Christmas that year *Country Life* published some pictures of King's College, Cambridge, and sent a copy to the Ram as a representative Kingsman. Turning over the pages, Miss Ramsay remarked on a picture ' very like yours ' : it was in the possession of the dealer Ackerman and the painter was stated to be Ben Marshall. The dealer was requested to visit Croughton, which he did : he certified the picture as a Ben Marshall and offered £750 for it. That evening the Ram went to some public dinner, where he found himself sitting by a stranger and, to make conversation, told him the story of the picture. The man pricked his ears. ' Ben Marshall ? He's all the go now. Lord Woolavington is making a corner in Ben Marshalls.' It seemed best to put a good reserve on the picture and send a marked copy of the catalogue to his lordship, and on the afternoon of the sale came a telegram. ' Picture sold Woolavington

£4,200 '. The whole process was packed into a very few days. I may add that at the Academy in the winter exhibition of 1934 it rightly commanded admiration.

The Ram was a remarkable man. I never saw him with a secretary and never received a typed letter from him : every letter seemed to be answered by return of post in his scrupulously neat and legible hand. He was chairman of endless committees : he was in due course Vice-Chancellor of the University : he was President of the C.U.C.C.—surely an honour that he loved : and he must have been alone among Heads of Houses in taking pupils himself. Yet his Eton pupil, Roger Mynors, could speak of him as a man who had never been *seen* to do an hour's work ; he always appeared to have done it, as indeed he had, and to be at his ease. At the age of eighty he was still showing small boys what scholarship is and, as a friend wrote of him, with a not dissimilar sense of fun. He is the only Vice-Chancellor of my acquaintance who kept a catapult on his desk for the discouragement of intruding cats. Certainly he was a lucky man, and I lucky in his friendship.

Again, I have been singularly fortunate in my friendships among printers. When Emery Walker became tenant of The Grange at Yattendon I had read the *Life of William Morris*, but I had not yet come across his textiles or seen a Kelmscott book. Whether I saw any such books there I cannot remember : probably not. Later, at any rate, at Hammersmith, I saw a complete set ; for it was Walker who taught Morris to print, and he had the first copy of every book issued from the Press. But I certainly had my first sight of my host's own Doves Press books, including the great five-volume Bible and Apocrypha which then meant little to my untutored eyes. It was three or four years later in the house of Schultz Weir, designer of the Chapel of St. Andrew in Westminster Cathedral, that my eyes were opened to its beauty ; and at last in 1943 I came to possess it as the gift of Pageites on my retirement. When we left Bradfield, I thought I had made pleasant acquaintances, whom I hardly expected to see again ; but one day a year or so later I met Walker on the platform of Reading station, and from the genuineness of his welcome felt that this was a friend, not a casual acquaintance. I had plenty of opportunities to learn that it was so. His house in Hammersmith Terrace is the only one from which I have watched the Boat Race—and a sad fiasco it was. The wonderful house in the Cotswolds, Daneway, at Sapperton, which in later years he rented from Lord Bathurst, he lent to us for our

L

Charterhouse exeat in the last summer of his life, when he was too ill to go and enjoy it himself. When in 1933 Sir Emery died, the obituary in *The Times*, written by his friend Cockerell, said of him that ' few who knew him would hesitate to declare that he was the best-loved man of their acquaintance '. Not many I think would dissent from that judgment. To him I owe my friendship with two other men concerned with printing, but with many other matters besides.

One was Sir Sydney Cockerell, whose genius made the Fitzwilliam at Cambridge the wonderful treasure house that it is. When in July 1957, I sent him a greeting for his ninetieth birthday, I really felt the link with the Victorian age, for he was secretary to William Morris at the Kelmscott Press, and Morris died in 1896.* The other was Loyd Haberly. One day in the early thirties I paid a visit to Hammersmith Terrace, where Miss Walker asked me if I had heard of their new poet. She then showed me two or three books, well printed and beautifully bound, including a masque that bore the title of *Daneway*, and all with the imprint of the Seven Acres Press, at Long Crendon, near Thame. The masque was the fruit of a week-end visit in which Sir Emery had given the printer some valuable hints on his craft. I asked where these books could be got and was told that John Wilson at Bumpus's always had some, which proved to be the case. Now it so happened that M. and I were wishing to give an altar book to Charterhouse Chapel, and I asked Wilson to find out if Haberly would like to bind it. A week later he sent on to me a letter written in a curious childlike hand, saying that he would love to do the binding but could not think of naming any price until he knew that the people for whom it was intended were entirely satisfied. I did not know the man and felt happier with ordinary commercial relations, so I asked John Wilson to get it bound as he thought best. Some time later he sent me on another letter, which said : ' How about the people who wanted the altar book ? If they are very hard up, I think I might be able to do it for nothing.' (It was some years later that I learnt that this altruist had never earned enough money to pay income tax.) I could hardly do otherwise than write and thank him, and then one day in early summer I came out of school to find an unknown man on my doorstep, with no hat and an Oxford half-blue tie. It

---

* If Sir Sydney is a link with the past, much more so was his friend Emery Walker. He once told me of his first visit to Hampstead, in company with an old bookseller who said to him, ' I used to come here to see a chap called Keats: did you ever hear of him ? '

was Haberly who, being in the neighbourhood, had come to inspect a recent patron. It was the beginning of a delightful friendship. He stayed with us at Pageites in 1933, when Tommy Garnett was head of the house, and I visited him annually at Long Crendon, putting up at the Spreadeagle in Thame, once a resort of the London intelligentsia, but now, under a former landlord, returned to a decent simplicity.

This remarkable man, poet, printer, engraver, binder and goodness knows what besides—it was as a gardener that he professed to earn his keep—remains almost wholly unknown. So in 1950 I was asked by the editor of the oddly named *Book Handbook*, ' an illustrated quarterly for discriminating book-lovers ', to give some account of him.

His boyhood's home was a farm in Oregon, in the far West, where he had no education till some boys clubbed together to get someone to give them lessons in a barn. The first book he ever read was Johnson's *Rasselas*, because it was the first that came into his hands. (My first, and last, reading of it was at the age of sixty-four.) Born in 1896, he was old enough to be conscripted in 1918 and was actually embarked for the battle-fields of Europe : but the voyage was countermanded, and he never crossed the Atlantic till a scholarship in International Law at Harvard had led to a Rhodes Scholarship at Trinity College, Oxford. It was from Oxford that he went for a week-end to Long Crendon, and prolonged the visit for several years. His hostess was a Mrs Durnford who, her own family being out in the world, was ready to give a home to young artists, and the household already included Agatha Walker, the sculptress whose delightful Beggar's Opera figurines are, I hope, still to be seen in the foyer of the King's Theatre at Hammersmith. Mrs Durnford was herself an exquisite needlewoman.

Here Haberly had every opportunity to develop his powers, which were crude enough at first. He usually rose at 6 and worked at his crafts till lunch time ; and his crafts included the building of the studio or printing-house in which he practised them. Then he put in an afternoon's gardening : then sometimes went for a cross-country run and, if he felt disposed to write, did it in the evening, or if the afflatus lasted, far on into the night. When the family left Oxfordshire for Corfe Mullen in Dorset, the new house was of his design. For his capacity to learn or teach himself art after art I know of only one parallel, and him I have named often enough !

His books, beautiful as they are, remain so little known that they are not even valuable : they never appear in auction rooms or bookseller's catalogues : of ten which I lent last spring for exhibition in Moberly Library at Winchester, none cost more than fifty shillings. Editions when the printer does the whole work of production with his own hands must be extremely small, and with a large percentage of copies destined for America, only a very few were left for his admirers in this country. For types he stuck to Caslon till the last book of his English period, when he used a new type designed by himself and Graily Hewitt and called Paradiso type, because it was based on that used for the first printing of Dante at Foligno. The edition consisted of 150 copies and M. and I took twelve of them, as the perfect small present for the right person. I wish the twelve had been twenty-four.

I last saw him in 1938, in which year he was induced to return to lecture at Harvard. There the war caught him and so far as I know he has never crossed the ocean again. And, alas, he has not maintained the ties with his English friends, even those to whom he owed the most.

The last of my printing friends was C. H. StJohn Hornby, a director of W. H. Smith and Son and creator of the Ashendene Press—a man of fine character and attainments who at Oxford had combined a First Class with a rowing blue. The press had its place in a little printing house in the yard of his home, Shelley House, Chelsea, and to the last Hornby took a hand in the work. Daily when he returned from the office he would change his coat and repair to the printing house to read the proofs of the day's printing ; and he always put in the reds with his own hand. I owed my introduction to him to Monty Rendall, and the Ashendene *Fioretti*, which came out in 1922, was the first fine ' Press book ' that I bought. After that I had a standing order for all his books, and I still think the two folio volumes of Spenser and the quarto *Ecclesiasticus* in its orange-dyed vellum the noblest books that I possess. Some of his books I sold when we moved from a big house to a small one : I wish I had not.

Another printer, Robert Gibbings, I can hardly claim as a friend, though I had the privilege of entertaining him twice when he lectured at Charterhouse on the submarine experiences which are the subject of his book, *Blue Angels and Whales*. As a printer he was wholly the amateur ; but printing, he remarked, is only common sense. Perhaps so, if you start as a ripe artist. He was by profession, as most people know, an engraver, and was engaged to do some work for the Golden Cockerel Press, but was asked to cancel his contract because the owner was in his last illness and the Press about to close. At this point a wealthy friend suggested that he might put up the money if Gibbings would like to carry on the Press. He was so much outside the printing world that he had never even seen a Kelmscott book—and all fine modern printing stems from Morris. But that did not prevent his producing admirable work, and the Golden Cockerel *Four Gospels* contains the finest of all Eric Gill's wood engravings.

Lastly, the Nonesuch Press. I only met Sir Francis Meynell on the cricket field, but I am the grateful possessor of many of his books. As the private press has in these days become almost wholly extinct, I may remark that the Nonesuch was not strictly a ' press ' at all, but a publishing concern, and the books were printed at many different places. The fine Bible, for instance, with Stephen Gooden's famous copperplates was printed at Oxford, the George Herbert—perhaps the masterpiece—at the Chiswick Press, and so on.

So much for the private presses. But there is one more name I should wish to mention—the late John Johnson, Printer to the University of Oxford. I cannot claim him as a friend, for I only met him once, but he did me a kindness worth putting on record. He was also a good friend to my sister and she to him, for from the endless accumulations of Radwinter and Norham Road she made a great many contributions to his museum of common things, ' the things that people throw away '. I was only once shown round the Clarendon Press, and then each of the party was presented with a little illustrated essay on Oxford by Greening Lamborn. It seemed to me so excellent that I wrote to the Printer (that is the correct form of address) asking if I might buy a stock to send to intelligent Carthusians on coming into residence. He replied that they were not for sale, but that I might have as many copies as I liked. So at no cost to myself, I was able for some years, till war came, to send a copy to all freshmen who I thought would care to have it. It is the sort of kindness one is glad to remember, and it was not the only one. In 1943 a young scholar had to go to India instead of Oxford and asked me if I could tell him of a pocketable *Odyssey*. I could not, so I wrote to Dr Johnson for advice ; he replied that he did not know of one that could be procured—so he sent me one of his own.

I don't know that Cockerell was ever a printer and certainly he is, for me and most people, more closely connected with manuscripts. It must have been nearly thirty years ago, on one of my early visits to Magdalene, that in one of the rooms of the Fitzwilliam I noticed a man who somehow radiated personality and authority, and who I instantly knew must be Cockerell—not yet Sir Sydney. He spoke to me, and as I could quote Emery Walker for a sponsor I was at once invited to tea. Though he has never been under my roof, I have many times been under his, and never without pleasure and profit. As I said, I think of him as a man of MSS, not only the ancient treasures which recently, if I remember right, fetched £11,000 at auction, but the almost flawless MS of Freya Stark's then unpublished memoirs, the presses containing the innumerable letters from which sprang those delightful books *Friends of a Lifetime* (1942) and *The Best of Friends* (1956), the scripts for the annual writing competition between Eton and Harrow, and not least the thick volume of letters or envelopes preserved for the interest or merit of the handwriting, in which I was startled and gratified to find one of my own, *vis-à-vis* with the strong bold hand of my admired StJohn Hornby. ' I thought you'd like that ', said my host. I may say that I have never been satisfied with my own handwriting and have only prevented its running to seed by constant care and effort. And the effort is greater now, not so much from the effects of age as from the inferiority of the available pens. I used to be happy enough with either metal or quill ; but I have never learnt to use a fountain pen, and now am not sure I am not as happy with the serviceable biro—despite my prejudice against such things.

It was Cockerell's book which first introduced me to ' the sweet Roman hand '. On the left hand page was a letter in a clumsy schoolboy hand signed ' Cholmondeley ': opposite was one in a beautiful Italic script with the same signature. That apparently was the beginning of it all. Cockerell explained that when already past sixty Lord Cholmondeley had so disliked his own writing that he taught himself the Italic script and founded a new Eton and Harrow match : and now there is a thriving Society for Italic Handwriting, of which a niece of StJohn Hornby, herself a beautiful calligrapher, is secretary.*

One more friendship, out of many, I feel I must put on record. At the Cranleigh lawn tennis tournament of 1924 I found myself sitting next to a very pretty girl whom by good fortune I mistook for someone else. She proved to be the daughter of a schoolmaster,

* **Sir Sydney** has lately given his volumes of MSS. to the **Library** of the Victoria and Albert Museum.

at Malvern College, and on learning my name she asked if I hadn't
sung at a concert there. That I had, before my old friend Shera
left for his professorship at Sheffield. She told me that her father,
who was in holy orders, was taking duty for the Rector of Chiddingfold, and it was to lunch and make music with her parents that I
first visited my present home : previously I had only known it as
a place one passed through on a bicycle on the way to Sussex. I
found the family installed in the temporary rectory which, when
the new one was ready, became the home of Lady Dudley, whom
some will prefer to call Gertie Millar. I found a spare athletic-
looking man, as indeed he must have been, for R. H. Moss had
bowled for Oxford in 1889 and turned out again for Worcestershire
when he was fifty-six. His wife had the remarkable gift of non-stop
talk without being a bore : charm and humour and a pleasant voice
prevented that. Both alike were lovers of music. Twenty years later
his voice still retained its sweetness, a baritone high enough to
serve as a tenor at need. His wife one can only call a genius : not
for nothing was Ruthmos the Greek for rhythm. On leaving Malvern
they retired to the small village of Icomb on the Cotswolds, near
Stow-on-the-Wold, where very appropriately they had a famous
cricketer as squire and churchwarden. I cannot give the facts as
accurately as I could wish, for a letter of enquiry has come back
to me, showing that since her husband's death two years ago,
Mrs Moss is no longer to be found in their home near Bridport.
At Icomb I visited them and attended a choir practice, after which
I can believe anything of her. The choir which she trained there
for a competition open to every parish in England (graded I
presume on a basis of population) was placed first at all three stages,
and I believe that some of its members saw London for the first
time when they sang victoriously in the Albert Hall.

But it was the Three Choirs Festival on which our friendship
really was based. They, or at least she, frequented it even more
regularly than I did : and they first taught me that it need not be
an expensive luxury. Between the wars it was my practice always
to find an inn—though for Hereford it was a delightful farm—a
few miles from the cathedral city, and to get exercise and quiet
nights by going in and out on my bicycle, till after 1937 I decided
that cycling at night was intolerable. It was Mrs Moss who taught
me that there is no need to pay for an expensive seat and sit like
a claustrophobic sardine. Lady Chapel or Choir Aisle, or at
Gloucester the Choir itself, is as good for hearing and never
crowded ; and if a seat now costs three or four shillings, in the

twenties the price was usually one-and-sixpence. An old letter has told me exactly what I enjoyed for seven-and-sixpence at Hereford in 1927, a year which has always been to me the high mark among Festivals. This is the list : the B Minor Mass : the Choral Symphony : César Franck, Symphony : Parry, Three Motets (these are gems) : Vaughan Williams, Pastoral Symphony and The Shepherds of the Delectable Mountains : Elgar, Violin Concerto, 2nd Symphony, Gerontius, and the Music Makers : Holst, Hymn of Jesus, and three short works, two of them new, by Bainton, Brent-Smith and Charles Wood. The wonder is how they got it all in, and what the Trades Union would say about it to-day. It is true, of course, that if the cheapest seats were full and the others empty, it would be impossible to pay the soloists and orchestra, but it need not affect the Charity which lies behind the Festival. That depends not on the sale of tickets but on the collection at the doors, a fact which too many people never discover.

It was Hereford in 1949 which set the seal on my gratitude. In that year I did two rash things : I asked the hospitality committee to recommend a lodging and, for once, committed my suitcase to the van instead of the rack. British Railways left it behind at Reading, and I spent the night without the necessaries of civilization in what proved a deplorable hostelry. On Sunday morning, meeting Mrs Moss in the Cathedral, I told her of my plight. I was at once invited to become their guest, and slept delightfully on a study sofa, with a moonlit garden beside me. (The summer of 1949 was a memorably beautiful one.) At the time of the Festival there are generally a few ecclesiastics whose one desire is to escape it, and here Moss was occupying the house and doing the duty of one such, ' to oblige '. There was already a guest, a good semi-professional soprano, and Mrs Moss had with her a little unpublished Quartet given to her by Brent-Smith. We learnt the piece and the composer was invited to supper to hear it. Moss was already in his eighty-first year, but still a very adequate tenor. Mrs Deas rather lowered the average age of the performers, which even so I should estimate at 65 : and I should certainly not call it a bad quartet.

As life goes on, one does I hope learn not to trust first impressions. I blushed to read a postcard written after my first hearing of The Dream of Gerontius just over fifty years ago : ' I certainly don't want to hear it again '. When I heard it at Cambridge in King's College Chapel, on 23 May this year, it was my twenty-first hearing in twenty years : and my love of it is still growing. At Worcester, Gloucester, or Hereford it is for me the climax of the Festival.

CHAPTER XI

ON THE SHELF

RETIREMENT when it finally came in the summer of 1946 was very unlike what I had anticipated, still more unlike what I had planned if it came at the expected time in 1942, in a world not bedevilled by war. I had even taken out a small insurance policy for a holiday abroad, and had hoped to go with M. to Sicily in April 1943, travel north to be at Gubbio for the festival of the Ceri on 15 May—an event I have for forty years longed to see—and to return via Switzerland, a country I never visited till 1947.

I left Charterhouse with two hopes, to escape the boredom of idleness and to get on with my education : in particular I designed to make up for the neglect of years by reading largely in French and Italian : in point of fact I have read next to nothing of either. Almost my first act was to join the Three Counties Club at Haslemere, in the belief that I should thankfully fill in one of seven blank days by walking over to look at the weekly papers. But as I scarcely ever went there, my two years of membership produced little more than the wearing of a pleasant tie. My next act was to visit Methuen's, to interview Dr Rieu about producing one of their new classical editions. I offered the first two Books of the *Histories of Tacitus*, and the proposal was accepted : but I was told there was no hurry, or the thing would only have to go in the queue. The result was that when after more than four years a letter came to ask how I was getting on, I had not touched the work, though I had read all of Tacitus that survives, a necessary preliminary. I then set to work diligently and enjoyably at this brilliant but difficult author, and the book finally appeared in the autumn of 1952.

The first plain duty of my leisure was to take over the secretaryship of the Parochial Church Council from a hard-worked Clerk in the House of Lords, like myself a Wykehamist and Christ Church man : and in these days the job is by no means a sinecure. I did the work for eight years.

The year 1947 brought a summer of weddings, Janet's at Chiddingfold, admirably organized as always by M., and Robin's in

Guernsey, an island I had not visited since 1906. From that time we have generally been a party of three, the third being the indispensable Dorothy House, on whom our comfort has so long depended. Perhaps I should say four, since Teifi, a white cat of marked character, had already become a member of the household. It occurs to me that I have made no reference to the brute creation, except to a cow which is alleged to have kicked a lady in the chest. I grew up with the common assumption that no house is complete without a dog, but disastrous experience taught us that it is not so, and I think that acceptance of the fact, before we went into Pageites, has made for peace of mind. The name Teifi, I may add, derives not from a Welsh river but from a well-loved Austrian friend, now Christl Lethbridge. It means ' little devil ', a term used with affection rather than abhorrence, which she bore in her early years—and I can very well understand why.

Already, before my retirement, M.'s health had given signs of deterioration. As a housemaster's wife she had shown every gift, an excellent manager, winning the affection of boys and staff, and inexhaustible in her energy and zest. But when we stayed for a short holiday at Alresford in the spring of 1945, she was already walking lame : the arthritis to which she became a martyr was beginning to assert itself. The removal of her tonsils next year was no doubt beneficial, though she was thoroughly unwell for a time and unable to enjoy our little holiday at Burpham, secluded in the Downs near Arundel. From that time she suffered many things from doctors, till at last a nurse convinced her that a big operation was the only alternative to the life of a cripple in constant pain. It was performed by Mr Alexander Law in January 1949, in a nursing home at Lambeth, with magnificent success. She pursued her exercises with the same wholeheartedness as everything else, and directly she left hospital was allowed to cycle and drive her car. She walked lame, as was inevitable, but painlessly. She had long wished to live in a village, and identified herself with its life, a mainstay as always of the good works which were second nature to her.

At the luncheon at the Café Florence which marked our Silver Wedding, attended by nearly all her regiment of bridesmaids, some of them now grandmothers. I attributed to her the gift of glorious absurdity. This I had discovered in very early days, when, in order to prove the gentility of her family, she produced a pedigree to show her descent from Joan of Arc. (I had better explain that the Lloyds claim descent from Edward I through his daughter

Joan of Acres, whose place of burial I was astonished to find at Clare Priory in Suffolk when I paid a memorable visit there with Alice Tanqueray in September 1933.) I quote here a few of the great sayings treasured by the family, and infinitely endearing : the comfort offered to a child whose birthday someone had forgotten, ' She won't forget when she remembers ' : and the exhortation to the family to ' stop thinking about Christmas and come to church ' : or sympathizing with a friend on a slipped disc in her eye : or getting stuck in a crossword because she had decided that the name of an inn was the moo-cow : or passing the house ' where old Mrs —— lives who died the other day ' : or holding out a jam spoon at the breakfast-table with ' If you can't lick it it must be washed ' : or striding up a bare hillside in Scotland ' to find a Gents ' : or after a very small carriage accident in Ireland, insisting on taking the name of the horse. The driver's reply is worth recording too : ' What's the good, lady ?, He'll never win the Derby '. On the same occasion she fell into an Irish bog and emerged with a new species of Veronica. I wish more such things had remained in memory.

At her so-called Ruby Wedding in December 1953, she had seldom looked happier, but little more than a month later came the first stroke. From this she had almost recovered by the middle of June and was just beginning to drive her car again when there came a second, slight in itself, but starting the long and weary period of decline into helplessness. The worst times have their alleviations and all the family are deep in debt to the devotion of Dorothy House, and to the comfort brought since August of this year by Sister Jones, of Aldenham, and by the Elisabeth Zielinski who had already helped Joan Yeo and her family in dark days.

To someone who urged me to write down some of my memories I said that it would be an escape into happier times, and so it has been.

First I suppose it is natural for me to put reading and writing, and I could wish there had been more of both. But my eyesight and my appetite for reading are no longer inexhaustible, while for writing I have not had so much opportunity, except for the endless task of keeping in touch with Carthusians and other friends by letter. While the war lasted my correspondence was enormous : then came a new burst when in the spring of 1947 my friend Leslie Hextall sent me a list of old Sixth-formers who were combining to give me a delightful present. And when in the summer of 1955

I was asked to serve as honorary treasurer for a memorial to Sir Frank Fletcher, I was proud and glad to undertake the task. The money was to be devoted to the completion, after thirty years, of the panelling and organ case in the Memorial Chapel, which would never have been built without the faith and patience of Sir Frank. When the task was accomplished in the spring of this year, I had acknowledged 811 contributions, and a great many had led to an exchange of letters, in some cases with those I had never actually known.

A preference for right accents rather than wrong in forty years of Greek Proses had made me an accurate proof-reader, and towards the end of the war I wrote to Geoffrey Cumberlege, the Carthusian who had succeeded the Wykehamist Sir Humphrey Milford as head of the Oxford University Press, and asked if I could be of any use to him. He replied that he was short of readers and sent me the proofs of *The Genus Gossypium*, a work which proved to be not a treatise on dialectic but a highly technical work on Cotton, so technical that I told Cumberlege that I understood no word in it except the prepositions. I certainly felt that my modest 3/6 an hour was more enjoyably earned when I was sent the World's Classics reprint of Henry James's *Portrait of a Lady*, or John Bailey's *Dr Johnson and his Circle*, a book I had enjoyed many years earlier. In course of time his staff was made up and I became superfluous ; but it was to Cumberlege's recommendation that I owed much the largest and also the most lucrative task of my retirement. I received a letter from Chatham House, telling me of an ambitious series of books projected by U.N.E.S.C.O., *Ways of Life*, representing fifteen or more nations from England to Mexico, from Australia to the Lebanon, and asking if I were prepared to act as General Editor. There were fifteen of them already written and they were to be published in both English and French, eight with an introduction by a learned and distinguished French historian, and seven by the superannuated usher. I never had expected to see myself translated into French ! I accepted the task, though I had no qualification except a preference for decent English and an abhorrence of jargon: I read and did what I could for fourteen of them, but *Canada*, a late arrival, has not yet reached me, though published, with *Switzerland*, in its French version several years ago. The scheme was grandiose and the office in Paris notably inefficient. Many of the books were not worth printing and, naturally enough, no publisher would undertake the lot. I thought the whole scheme was dead, when I had a letter from

Heinemann's telling me that the firm was about to publish the first two volumes, on *Australia* and *South Africa*. When the proofs reached me I found, believe it or not, that Paris had sent the uncorrected typescripts, so that all correction had to be done again in proof, and unpaid this time, since U.N.E.S.C.O. had loyally paid me according to contract before any book found a publisher. Five are now in print—*South Africa, Australia, Norway, Pakistan* and *England*, the last a really excellent book by Professor Smellie of the London School of Economics ; and the publishers tell me they have sold well. I strongly recommended those on Switzerland and New Zealand, and hope that Heinemann may in course of time take my advice. I may add that Headquarters continued to send the uncorrected copies till Mr Alan Hill of Heinemann's went to Paris himself and unearthed the corrected ones from a cupboard.

In 1949 I read typescript and proofs of a volume of Cicero's Letters translated by that fine Carthusian scholar, Patrick Wilkinson, of King's College, Cambridge—a book which ought to have reached thousands of readers as a *Penguin*. But it brought me in touch with its publisher, Geoffrey Bles, yet another Carthusian, who invited me to lunch and afterwards sent me a number of books to read in typescript or proof, or both. I learnt that, as an agent of correction, one can be of service without knowing anything whatever of the subject, for the books he submitted to me included a history of the Chinese Empire translated from the French and an autobiography of a Russian philosopher whom I ought to have heard of, but hadn't. I never saw either of these books after publication : they were by no means in my line. Unfortunately, since the retirement of Bles my connexion with an interesting firm has ceased.

Otherwise I might have hoped to have the correcting of Ben Travers's autobiography, *Vale of Laughter*, before rather than after publication. I have always assumed that authors and publishers *want* their books to be free of mistakes and misprints, which in these days reviewers seldom seem to point out as once they did. At worst, to send in errors one has noticed is a compliment to the author, as presuming that there is a second edition to come. With Ben Travers it was easy, because I knew and liked him as a Pageite parent, and because I wanted to tell him how much I had enjoyed a delightful, happy book. I can only once remember being snubbed, by an eminent historian who replied that he preferred not to verify his quotations, and that one apparent misprint, Pebmerley, was a joke. I refrained from asking whether he thought his words did as well as Keats's or Shelley's, and how we were to know that one particular misprint was supposed to be funny.

The first writer with whom I made friends by correcting his mistakes was Stephen Gwynn, as I have said elsewhere. Another is that delightful writer John Moore, whose *Brensham Village* contains a cricket match that deserves to become a classic : I prefer it to the much-lauded fantasy in *England, their England*. I wrote and asked him if he had yet noticed that the wrong number of wickets fell and that the totals didn't work out right. It so happened that a reprint was imminent, and I offered so many corrections that in due course a copy of the new edition reached me with a charming inscription addressed to the ' part author '. In the spring of this year the same writer asked me if I would read the proofs of his longest and most ambitious novel. It was an after-thought, unfortunately just too late for the first issue of a book which certainly needed vetting.

A publisher who has occasionally asked my help is my friend Basil Blackwell, and this year I was able to dissuade him from publishing a really bad book, already in proof, which could not possibly have been anything but an injurious failure. Business correspondence with Sir Basil is generally spiced with humour. Then not long ago Heinemann sent me an important work, R. T. McKenzie's *British Political Parties*, asking if I would read it as quickly as possible, because a reprint was required at once and too many misprints had been noticed in the first edition : it was really an S.O.S. I am always ready to read a proof and would welcome regular employment as a reader. Cumberlege told me long ago that the best proof-reading is mechanical : so if the book interests one, one has the enjoyment of it : if not, one is not too conscious of boredom.

It has been my lot to see through the press posthumous works of two successive Bishops of Peterborough. The last time I saw Claude Blagden, he told me his memoirs were far advanced, and when all too soon afterwards I read of his death, I wrote to Mrs Blagden and asked if the book had been finished and if I could be of any service in reading the proofs. As it turned out I was able to be quite useful. Further, I chanced to be in the Lakes just at the moment of publication, when I visited her at Grasmere and received a copy from her own hand. *Well Remembered* is a book to be heartily recommended. A very good judge spoke of it to me recently as one of the few autobiographies where the author seemed more interested in other people than in himself. I wish the same could be said of this one. The last work of Spencer Leeson was his *College 1901-1911*, a sequel to my own *College in the Nineties*.

He had finished but not revised it before his last illness, and it was my privilege, jointly with the newly-retired Second Master, R. M. Wright, to see the little book through the press.

The last bit of editing for which I offered myself was to bring out the reminiscences of a man whose memories of Charterhouse go back more than seventy-five years : indeed he was at school before I was born. Mr Veale administered the stationery department for more years than I can reckon, and the excellent tuckshop (a term I abominate, and its only name is Crown) from 1914 to 1946. He chose for his book the title *From a New Angle*, and none could have been fitter, for no one else could have attempted to illustrate this side of school life. The book has recently been published at the expense of that valuable institution, the Carthusian Society, and I am glad to hear that more than half the edition has been sold in a very short time. The author's still tall and upright figure, as upright as his character, must be known to more Carthusians than any other living man. It was a great satisfaction that he was recently interviewed by the prospective biographer of Sir Max Beerbohm, Lord David Cecil, as the only man who now remembered Max at school.

To come to my own small writings : my Winchester book occupied the early months of 1947, when the weather made me thankful for a warm study, and my *Tacitus* appeared in 1952. In the autumn of 1951 I was asked, no doubt at Robert Birley's suggestion, to write the Charterhouse chapter of a book, edited by W. N. Roe of Eton, on *Fifty Years of Public School Cricket*. It would have been absurd that I should do so had R. L. Arrowsmith been available, but he had just become a housemaster and could not spare the time. So I set to work with fifty volumes of Wisden and a pile of *Carthusians* and greatly enjoyed the task.

Dr Johnson once asserted that no man but a blockhead ever wrote except for money. The inference would appear certain, for very little that I have written has been paid for ; and I don't know that I have enjoyed it less for that. I have written an occasional review in *The Oxford Magazine* and other periodicals for more than fifty years, but never been offered any money for them. When I have written it was generally because I wanted to write. My favourite church in this part of Surrey, at Wonersh, seemed to me strangely unknown, and indeed it stands so modestly secluded that one could pass it scores of times without discovering it behind its shielding wall. An article on it in our excellent *Diocesan Gazette* gave pleasure to others besides the writer, so I followed it with one on the famous church of Stoke d'Abernon, which had just been surprisingly enriched with ancient stained glass. That in turn led to others, about ten in all, which meant a good many enjoyable visits, by foot, cycle or car, and a less casual observation of the churches than I had been accustomed to give them.

Towards the end of 1949 a very pleasant task was imposed on me by George Turner, then headmaster of Charterhouse. Sir Frank and Lady Fletcher had found their beautiful home near Dartmouth too remote and isolated for old age and were now living at Shackleford, within three miles of Charterhouse. Sir Frank had suffered a severe stroke, which mercifully affected his speech hardly at all and left that fine brain quite untouched. He was never more to be admired than in the last years of physical infirmity : utterly serene and patient, ready to enjoy his book and his pipe or the talk of friends all day long, with not one of his interests abated. His eightieth birthday was approaching, on 3 May, and George Turner had a proposal to make for its recognition. He suggested that some of his pupils, covering half a century, should be invited to contribute to a memorial volume, either an original composition, or a translation, or some chosen passage likely to appeal to him. George Turner undertook to cover the Marlborough years ; Harry Hardy, late Headmaster of Shrewsbury, stood for Rugby, and I made the Charterhouse selection and arranged for the binding : and with a famous binder, Anthony Gardner, a resident of Chidding-fold, a fine volume was assured. Of the original pieces in the volume one seemed to me outstanding, and I kept a copy of it—the *Ballade of Three Wise Men*, by a Marlburian, Judge Frank Kingsley Griffith. In the nature of things very few can have seen it and, to make it known to a few more, I have his permission to transcribe it here. It is headed :

' " My masters are Plato, Browning and St. Paul." F.F. 1908.'

1.

When I was young and stuffed with pride
    I thought that what was new was best :
My fancy roamed on every side
    And scanned the world from east to west.
' Twas then I heard a voice suggest
    That, after you have tried them all,
You'll find the three who stand the test
    Are Plato, Browning and St. Paul.

2.

New Worlds for Old have now been tried
   (They're hardly Islands of the Blest)—
Marx is a pedant deified,
   And Wells a bore and Freud a pest.
These giants, as I might have guessed,
   Were not so wonderfully tall.
Give me—and you can keep the rest—
   Just Plato, Browning and St. Paul.

3.

Now, to a humble duty tied,
   With chastened soul but undistressed,
I here acclaim my boyhood's guide
   As one in Plato's wisdom dressed,
With Robert Browning's faith and zest
   And charity that crowns them all—
And hug securely to my breast
   His Plato, Browning and St. Paul.

Envoi

Master, you see them here compressed
   In tattered volumes on my wall,
The three I read at your behest,
   Your Plato, Browning and St. Paul.

That I copied into my commonplace book (absurdly so called), and with it one sentence from George Turner's piece : ' If, as I believe, any man is at his best when he is grateful, how ever many, do you think, have you helped to be at their best ? ' I wish I had thought of that !

Many retired schoolmasters endeavour to earn a bit of money by examining. I sent in my name for Higher Certificate Latin in 1949, but never again : it was the most monotonous and most exhausting labour I have ever undergone. All examining is exhausting enough, but it can also be of absorbing interest. Spencer Leeson had invited me to examine for Goddard, the Classical blue ribbon of Winchester, as soon as I was free to do so. When that time came he had already left for his great parish at Southampton, but his successor, Walter Oakeshott, accepted his recommendation and in the first of my two years I had the perfect colleague in Roger Mynors, then Professor of Latin at Cambridge, but since returned to his native Oxford. Thirty years earlier it would have been inconceivable to me that I might one day be a Goddard examiner,

M

or that, as had happened the previous autumn, I should find myself holding forth on the writings of William Morris at a special meeting of the Art Workers' Guild, to mark the fiftieth anniversary of the great man's death. I would as readily have believed that I might some day come to making a bed or washing a plate. (I may say that I do not generally do either.) One other enjoyable piece of examining came my way, for the Moss Prize at Shrewsbury, in March 1948, which involved a stay at that most pleasant school as the guest of the Sixth Form master, Stacy Colman. I had met him and his wife first on a tour to Provence some twelve years earlier. It was now too that I made acquaintance with his Sixth Form colleague, Tony Chenevix-Trench, who returned from a Japanese prison camp to take a specially distinguished First in Greats, and is now headmaster of Bradfield—another most valued friend. Beyond this I have done a little examining at Charterhouse, until the parties concerned decided, quite rightly, that it was more economical to do it themselves.

That I supposed was my final academic task, but it did not prove to be so. In the sutumn of 1955 I was asked to undertake some coaching of University candidates at Prior's Field, and here again I had a delightful job, which unfortunately came to an end at Easter 1957, when for the moment there was no one who needed my assistance. Prior's Field, I may add, is a girls' school near Godalming, founded fifty years ago by the wife of a Charterhouse master, Mrs Leonard Huxley, mother of two well-known sons.

But the appetite for teaching, which to me means sharing with others the things that I enjoy, was by no means sated, and for seven years I gave fortnightly poetry readings in the winter months. Though I enjoy books for their own sake, I enjoy them still more when read with a purpose, and this venture involved a great deal of reading, often of books I had not hitherto known. But for this I should never have tackled that astonishing work, *The Road to Xanadu*, or Betty Millar on Robert Browning, or much excellent Wordsworthian biography, or Professor Sutherland's admirable *Preface to Eighteenth Century Poetry*. The regularity with which friends came from Guildford and Godalming showed that the readings were truly appreciated, and I gave them up after seven years with much regret, when circumstances made it difficult to carry on.

They brought me the most prized friendship of these latter years. The winter of 1951-52 was given to Shelley and Keats, Scott and Byron, when I may remark that I read the poems of

Scott for the first time and found them much more readable than I had expected. One day an unknown lady approached me in the street and said she heard that I gave poetry readings, and very diffidently asked if she might be allowed to come to them. She proved to be a Mrs Howard, a granddaughter of Archbishop Magee and by marriage a niece of Gilbert Murray. It may be remembered that Byron's guardian was the Lord Carlisle of the day, and her knowledge of family history as well as of poetry was a wonderful reinforcement to the ' class '. Unfortunately she and her husband were only a year in Chiddingfold before migrating to a farm near Alton, not easily accessible to one who is not a motorist, and with all the ties that limit the freedom of a farmer's wife who is also a mother. Later meetings have been rare, and I have said that I never see Moira Howard without discovering some new gift—poet, painter, calligrapher, potter, and goodness knows what besides. In earlier days, had not marriage intervened, she would have been Fortnum and Mason's manager in New York.

Lectures too are clearly an educational activity. A year after leaving Charterhouse I was asked to give another course on *Cities of Italy*, and the next term Cecil Harrison, having become a head-master, invited me to do the same at Felsted. It seemed a pity to have the material and never to use it, and I was at all times free of my colleague J. C. Thomson's magnificent collection of slides : so since then I have regularly arranged a few lectures each autumn. They take me to most pleasant places, notably to Malvern every year, and have given me a high respect and admira-tion for the modern headmistress. I shall miss this activity when the time comes to give it up.

One other branch of my education went forward as I had hoped till the failure of M.'s health brought it to an end after 1954. I had realized that if I did not begin to see the north of England soon I never should do so, and in seven successive springs I enjoyed a northern fortnight, which brought me acquainted with the Wall, the Coquet valley and the Tweed, with Dovedale and Southwell, and various parts of Yorkshire, generally but not always new to me. One doesn't visit York or Beverley once only. I was still capable of a good day's walking, though preferably not in a heatwave such as overtook me at Buttermere in 1953 and at Helmsley in 1954. At the last-named place I once more found the value of an Old Carthusian tie. On the evening of my arrival at the delightful hotel known locally as the Mooky Dook, officially the Black Swan, I accosted an old gentleman who was wearing one. He proved to be a

Pageite, one of seven Pageite brothers well known to me by name, and on the Sunday fetched me over to lunch at his beautiful home, Oswaldkirk Hall. I lamented the impossibility of reaching Castle Howard, where Moira Howard had given me an introduction : whereupon the Colonel said he would take me there in the afternoon. Not only so, but we stopped to see the famous and lovely cricket ground of Hovingham, where Sir William Worsley, once captain of Yorkshire, and his family, both sexes, were at the nets ; and as he said that no one should miss Gilling Old Hall—now the Junior School of Ampleforth—we also saw that treasury of Elizabethan panelling and heraldic glass. Truly a crowning day, for that was my last northern holiday.

As another way of seeing England I became a member of the Historical Association, not as a student, but for the sake of the excellently conducted tours, of which I have done three, based on York and Bath and Banbury, a town which strange to say I had never seen. It lies in a region rich in historic houses, and Edgehill, under the tutorship of Colonel A. H. Burne (yet another Wykehamist) is one of the few battlefields I have been able to comprehend.

One of my plans for the pleasures of retirement has not come off at all. I had promised myself occasional week-ends at my Club in Dover Street. But when peace, so called, came the Club stood half-destroyed and, even when some pleasant bedrooms became available, it had ceased to provide meals on Sunday : so it is almost twenty years since last I spent a Saturday to Monday in London. It was an ambition of my youth to become a member of my father's Club, the United University, in Suffolk Street. The height of felicity was on rare occasions to have a meal with him there, and even a night in a hired bedroom close by. The house is the only one I have known that preserved the ancient custom of serving muffins at breakfast. They are romantic no doubt, but I much prefer toast. But it was obvious that I could not afford membership, and every time my name came up for election I asked to be put back at the bottom of the list. Later I was on the books of the Athenaeum, with Emery Walker for my proposer, in days when that club still had a high snob-value. What drove me into the Arts Club in 1931 was the closing of the Civil Service Stores in the Haymarket. That was the traditional lunching-place of my schooldays and then of my children's, and the same waiter served both generations. I am glad to think that on the date when he told me he would complete fifty years of service in the restaurant I remembered to send him a greeting. I loved going to the Stores to ' smell my youth ', and as a meeting-place it served some of the purposes of a club. With my capacity for making things last I still sometimes smoke pipes marked C.S.C.S. When the place closed I made haste to join the Arts Club, now at last, this autumn of 1957, fully restored, but somehow without the charm of the old house I had come to love.

On the other hand one activity which in 1946 I thought of as ended has gone on vigorously. At the age of sixty-five, and without the inspiration of Arthur Trew, I had thought my singing days were at an end, and we sold our Bechstein, for more than we had paid for it second-hand in 1913. But I found that neither voice nor appetite had failed, and through the kindness of neighbours I was given access to a room with a piano in it any morning before lunch. So I keep up the practice of singing a bit more days than not, and it is at least a harmless fancy that I may owe, in part, to this habit the good health for which I have so much cause to be thankful. Many years ago in a Devonshire railway train I found myself talking to a man who proved to be a well-known Carthusian and Corinthian footballer of the nineties. I asked him how he kept fit now and the answer was ' singing '. And did not William Byrd tell us that ' the exercise of singing is delightfull to Nature, and good to preserve the health of Man : it doth strengthen all parts of the brest, and doth open the pipes ' ? I have two excellent accompanists, one amateur, one professional, and have recourse to one or other, or both, more weeks than not. And for one lucky year we had a neighbour, a Mrs Lowe, professionally and in her Wimbledon days Phyllis Grover, whose accompaniment was an inspiration as great as Trew's. Thanks to my good friends I still sometimes acquire a new song, and they in return have acquired many.

In a small way I have become not only a reader of books but a seller of them. We had not been long at Chiddingfold before I was asked to help at a book-stall for the annual Church Fête, an impor- tant source of income, and soon afterwards was required to take charge of the stall. As windfalls of books may come in at any time, so neighbours are always at liberty to pick over the piles which encumber the upper rooms of my garage ; and both church funds and modest libraries, including my own, have profited a good deal. When it becomes known that someone is qualified to make the best of them, it is surprising how many and how good are the books that come along.

All this seems to mount up to a fairly active life, and I have not yet mentioned what since 1954 has been a chief preoccupation, the New Cathedral at Guildford. We attended the laying of the Foundation Stone in July 1936, and I was registered as a ' builder ' in return for some small gift, but took no more than a remote interest in the project. The original estimate was £250,000, and the building was going so well ' according to plan ' that but for the the war the whole structure would have been completed in 1944. But the war left it practically dead for eight years, and when work began again it was miserably half-hearted. It was only in 1953 that a new Provost and a new secretary, a woman of almost portentous energy, brought new life and hope into the work, since when the process of transforming a shell into a shrine, to borrow the Archbishop's words, has gone forward steadily. But it certainly is going the hard way, with the nave alone likely to cost as much as the original estimate for the whole.

When I offered my services in 1954 as a guide one day a week, there was really nothing to show except an exhibition of very limited range in the future Chapter House : choir and crossing could only be seen as a forest of scaffolding by peering from a kind of cage. But in the spring of 1955, with choir and crossing structurally complete, the paving of travertine and Purbeck freestone laid, and the heating at work when required—to the great comfort of long-suffering guides—work on the nave began, and when the Queen and Prince Philip visited Stag Hill on 27 June 1957, the walls, both north and south, had arisen above the tops of the tall windows. On that occasion a long line of guides formed a Guard of Honour, and I was posted on the extreme right in order that Her Majesty might stop and talk to me. One of the excellent photographers of the Guildford School of Art was close at hand, ' to witness if I lie '. This was in recognition of very persistent begging, mainly in support of the admirable Million Brick fund. This scheme was started in October 1954, and at first my heart sank at the demand for new effort. But soon its possibilities impressed me, and the selling of ' bricks ' at 2/6—in neat little books of forty—became an object in country walks and rides, and sometimes at railway stations, or even in the train—in fact, wherever I saw a likely person. But it was long before I realized that the best place was outside our local hostelry, the Crown, towards lunchtime and sometimes before dinner at week-ends. When in June I had reached a tale of 6,400 ' bricks ', or £800, it was obvious that I must set my target at 8,000, or £1,000. At the end of October I was past £900, and then the Law intervened. I was informed that most of my actions were illegal, and that if I ' sold a brick ' in a public place without a permit I was liable to prosecution and a fine. A form was sent me to apply for such a permit, a form devised for those tiresome and complicated flag days with which I should never willingly become involved. No one could have been more friendly than the Superintendent, a keen churchman, who came at my request to see me. And the Chairman of the Committee which deals with such matters is a member also of the Cathedral Council : but neither seemed confident that a permit would be granted. It is always dispiriting when the Law, intended to discourage criminals, is employed to thwart willing service in a good cause : it is not conducive to good citizenship. And it seems ironical that one who in June was exhibited to the Queen as a creditable brick-seller, should be warned off in October as technically a criminal. In the end, after long delay, a permit was refused. No doubt I should be thankful that I was given three years of unmolested usefulness.

I have said elsewhere that begging could hardly be called a hobby ; but Cathedral bricks had almost become one. It has been my lot over a long period to do more than my share of begging and this has been the least distasteful and the most encouraging that I have ever undertaken. It has led to many interesting contacts, and of course to many refusals, but I cannot recall half-a-dozen that need be called rude. And though I have always been a believer in the small gift, this experience has greatly increased my faith in it. Many times I have been told by those who have not visited the Cathedral that it is a hideous building, and it was long before I thought of the correct answer—to have always in pocket a picture of the lovely chancel. That could hardly fail to lead to second thoughts.

My life has been a full and rich and happy one, and yet I am conscious how many good things I have missed. When I repeat the General Confession with my mind, not mechanically with my lips, I incline to deplore the things I have not done as much as those I have ; and like all collectors, great and small, I regret, not the things that I have bought, but the things I have let go. For a good deal of my life the letters L.T.A. would have stood for the Lawn Tennis Association. Since I met them in a context where they meant *Laudator Temporis Acti*, I have been rather shy of them. One who talks too much of the better days of the past is likely to be a bore : but anyone who has in old age to face the year 1958 may be truly thankful to have enjoyed a Victorian boyhood and an Edwardian youth ; and the really fortunate man is one who has enjoyed his work as much as his play, which certainly has been the case with me.

December 1957.

APPENDIX A

SOME COINCIDENCES

SOME years ago I related to Joan and Harold Yeo a few of the coincidences which have so often intrigued me, and was strongly urged to write them down. I wish I had done so, for no doubt some have escaped my memory. ' You collect coincidences, don't you ? ' Robert Birley once said to me, before telling me of an odd one of his own. I wouldn't go so far as that, but they sometimes stick in my mind as worth preserving.

When we first visited Sullington in August 1917, Miss Palmer told me (as I still maintain) that on the centenary of Waterloo her father had preached his father's Waterloo sermon. Canon Palmer had still fourteen years to live, and when he died in August 1931, at the age I think of ninety-seven, I supplemented the notice in *The Times* newspaper with the story of the sermon. This brought me a letter from another daughter, whom I had not met, saying she had never heard of the Waterloo sermon, but her father had certainly preached her grandfather's *Trafalgar* sermon, and she had the copy before her. So that carried the story back to 1805.

It was just at this time that the West Sussex golf links were opened, and I drove down with a friend to try them—and mighty good they were. As the fold of the downs where Sullington lies was within sight, I told my partner the story of the sermon. My caddy listened and then said, ' I cycled over from Worthing to hear that sermon '. The caddy was an elderly man who had long been an assistant in a tailor's establishment, well known to me, at Winchester, and had returned to end his days in his old county. And here he was, nearly twenty-six years after the sermon was preached, to corroborate the story.

There is one book which has amused me so much that for many years I never saw a copy in a second-hand bookshop without buying it to give to someone : it was *Reminiscences of Oxford*, by William Tuckwell, ' the Radical Parson '. Before I learnt the necessity of protecting myself by registering every loan, I lost my own copy and had to replace it. One day I took the fresh copy, unused by me, into school to read certain verses by my father's old friend, R. E.

Bartlett, Fellow of Trinity. Out fell a letter signed 'Grace Bartlett', old Bartlett's daughter.

I have only once read *Antony and Cleopatra* in the tube, and it chanced to be Act IV : of course I was using my Temple Shakespeare. Further down the carriage, on the opposite side, was a man reading a similar small red volume. As I got out before he did, I craned over to see what it was : it was the Fourth Act of *Antony and Cleopatra*.

One day in April 1922, I was writing something which required me to verify the fact that a certain picture (now in the National Gallery) was in a private collection at Milan. I did so by referring to a rather uncritical book on Giorgione written by one Herbert Cook some twenty years earlier. That day we went, for the first time, to stay with friends at Richmond. After tea our host asked if we would like to see Sir Herbert Cook's picture gallery at Doughty House. We did so, and there was the picture in question.

On 28 January 1938, we were at dinner when the house butler, our very good friend Edgeler, came in and asked if he might open the side door and let out the House to see a wonderful display of the Northern Lights, and I enjoyed it as a spectacle I had never seen before. As already remarked, I have never till this year read through my old diaries, or what remains of them, though I have sometimes referred to one to find a particular date or event. That night I took my diary for 1905 to bed, for what purpose I cannot remember : but what I did find, under date 15 November, was this : 'About nine —— called me out . . . to see a most wonderful display of Aurora Borealis, a thing I had never seen before. The effect was very lovely indeed but, alas, very transient. Still for ten minutes or so it was real joy '.

After a visit from my brother one August he wrote to ask if he had left a latchkey behind. A few weeks later, after a dry spell, we had a heavy thunder shower and, wondering if it had made any impression, I took a trowel and struck it into the ground, and in the trowel-full of earth there was a key, which proved to be the missing one.

In days when concert halls were less crowded than now I always tried for the same seat at the Queen's Hall, and several times secured it. On 3 February 1909, I went up at short notice to hear Elgar's First Symphony, then a new work. I wired to my sister, who was going to the concert, to get me a ticket. In the train was a man I knew by sight as conductor of the Berkshire Ladies' Orchestra, who proved very companionable. When my sister handed me my ticket it was for Row 16 No. 28, next to ' my seat ' : and immediately behind me was my travelling companion.

I only once had occasion to write to Henry Howard, of Stone House, near Kidderminster, the Uncle Harry who was rightly a favourite with so many of the next generation. In April 1932 I was staying at Tenbury, within reach of his home, and wrote one evening to ask if I might pay him a visit. Next morning I took train to Church Stretton for a day's walking on the Long Mynd, and posted my letter on the way to the station. When I began the ascent of the slope, past the Long Mynd Hotel, which is the usual approach to the hills, a single figure was visible in the far distance : when after a time it turned back, I found myself meeting Uncle Harry. I cannot remember that I saw any other human being on the hills that day. He told me that he stayed there for a few days every April—presumably to evade spring cleaning in his large and opulent house.

What seems to me the most remarkable of these incidents did not occur to me, but was told me by a member of a well-known Birmingham family, who has often been mentioned in these pages. He said he did not often tell the story, because he disliked being called a liar.

One of his brothers was acting editor, during the editor's holiday, of a daily paper which I presume to have been the *Birmingham Daily Post*. A second brother had reached Birmingham after a night journey and, having breakfasted, looked into the office, where the acting editor had just arrived. Astonished at the pile of unopened letters, he asked what they were all about. 'Anything in the world ' said the other, and tore open one of the top of the pile. It asked a question: was a certain speech of John Bright delivered in May of a certain year, or June ? ' Why should he want to know that ? ' ' I can't say. I suppose it might be a bet '. C.A.V. (the initials will be forgotten by now !) went his way to Shrewsbury, where he was to stay in a certain hotel. Coming down to breakfast next morning, he found only one man at table in the coffee room. Presently another entered with a copy of the paper in his hand and said, ' You pay : it was June.'

After perhaps fifty years I cannot guarantee words or dates, but the truth of the story as a whole I can.

APPENDIX B

TUSCANY REVISITED (1931)

WHEN I told a friend that I was going to Italy in April 1931, and that I had not been there since 1914, he warned me that I should find the country changed beyond recognition. Whether for the better or the worse he did not explain ; but experience showed that, where one was conscious of change at all, it was generally for the better. The introduction to Baedeker, still the most useful of guide-books, cautions the intending traveller that his patience will be sorely taxed. If that was true in 1900, it is far less so now ; for what one is conscious of is a great increase in efficiency, alertness, punctuality, cleanliness. It is no longer, if it ever was, an essential part of Italian charm to be unpunctual and unclean. The train that carried us into Lombardy was late, through an unexplained delay at Domodossola ; but that was the only late train we came across. All others came in and went out precisely at scheduled time, with no more than a single blast on a modern whistle, or a toot upon the more musical little horn. In old days the song of *Partenza ! A Carrozza !* used to be raised long before anyone thought of taking his seat. Further, where trains did not serve our need, long-distance coaches of an almost terrifying efficiency often did, and when neither was convenient, it saved money as well as time for a party of three to hire a private car. What petrol has done to annihilate distance, and the war to alter currency values, my ancient guide-book was a perpetual reminder. It was for a time an amusement to read, ' *Diligence in 2 hours, twice daily*, 1 *franc* ', when you knew that a motor-bus would get you there in twenty minutes : and if the charge was now six lire, that after all is only fifteen pence. The roads you may call good or bad, according to what you expect. Only you must not take refuge in vague euphemisms and say they are no great shakes, or not so dusty ; both propositions would be too palpably untrue. Tarmac has spoilt us in England. Italian motoring is an exciting pastime, but rather exhausting. It is fortunate that on Tuscan roads cars are still, as judged by English standards, not very numerous : in Southern Tuscany the two-wheeled Tuscan cart is as yet far more common. The Italian is sure to be both a rapid and an efficient driver, but if there is a risk to be taken, he does not fail to take it ; and as no signals appear to be in use, his horn is seldom quiet. My companions were two well-seasoned motorists, which I am not, but we were all at one in preferring the ' sweet security ' of trains.

Another recent improvement, which in a town of museums and galleries like Florence must be a very real help to the modest purse, is the opening of all national monuments without payment. The abolition of tipping is now of some years' standing, and the younger generation of travellers may not realize what a deliverance that is. In old days one's departure from a hotel could be genuinely unpleasant. A row of menials was lined up in the hall, and it was a leer and a lira for everyone : but one seldom knew whom one was rewarding, and for what. One is no longer conscious, as we used to be, of a continual oozing of coins from the pocket.

Another marked change in recent years is the disappearance of the beggar. One or two poor waifs might mumble at you from a cathedral doorway, but the swarming and unsightly crowd was gone. Occasionally a child, young enough to know better, would ask for soldi. *Accattonaggio* is clearly a much depressed industry. Readers of the late Montgomery Carmichael's *In Tuscany*, the most charming book on Italy know to me except the *Georgics* of Virgil, may even be a little regretful, and perhaps some Carlo Agnello will one day write a new essay on *The Decay of Beggars*.

As for the language, the same informant had told me that it was changing so quickly that the present generation cannot read their grandparents' letters. I find it hard to take that literally, or to believe that the grandparents would not have more difficulty with *Io Cerco Moglie* than the grandchildren with *I Promessi Sposi*. To me, who have but a smattering of it, the Tuscan seemed its own mellifluous and polysyllabic self. In our blunt monosyllabic northern tongue we speak of a grand dog show and link it with the stark name of *Cruft*. At Florence the same is a *Manifestazione Canina Internazionale*, advertized on a streamer that spans a wide street.

Our first stopping-place was Parma. But Parma is not in Tuscany, and my words must be few. First, a warning. The frescoes of Correggio are over-restored or perished and often invisible, and the reproductions by which we know them in books mostly came not from the originals, but from water-colour copies to the making of which the devoted Toschi, who died in 1854, gave many years of his life. On the other hand, for his *Madonna with St. Jerome* no praise can be too high ; but it stands alone. And one building came as a complete surprise, the great octagonal Baptistry with its five storeys of yellow Verona marble. Begun in 1196, it is a contemporary of its two chief rivals, the Baptistry of Pisa and Dante's *Bel San Giovanni* at Florence. Externally at least it is superior to either, and the name of its great sculptor, Antélami, deserves to be better known.

From Parma the railway runs South-East, parallel with the chain of the Apennines and always close to the line of the Roman *Via Aemilia*. It is not till Bologna, ninety miles on, that it finally turns south and works its way into the mountains by the valley of the Reno. It is a pleasant but, judged by Alpine standards, not a thrilling ascent, and it comes as a relief when, after innumerable tunnels, you suddenly look and see beneath you wide territory spread, and in it a tiny dome. ' Pistoia ' says the waiter in the luncheon-car, and you know you are in Tuscany. Another ten miles and you are there ; another fifty, and both Prato and Florence have been left behind, and there is still a quarter of the day before us when we quit the train at Arezzo.

We had seen no single tourist at Parma and we saw none at Arezzo : but if they do not go there, it is not the fault of a particularly pleasant and friendly-looking town. The birthplace of Maecenas and Petrarch and Vasari stands on a hill of its own, commanding the valleys of the Arno and the Chiana, while the Tiber valley is only a few miles to the east. Florence saw to it that Arezzo, in a position of such importance, should not become too strong. Dante fought in the crippling battle of Campaldino in 1289, and within a century the independence of Arezzo was dead. I suppose few would visit the place now—though they would miss a good deal—unless Piero della Francesca had been born a few miles away at Sansepolcro, and had come here to paint in the choir of San Francesco the history of the Holy Cross in some of the most notable frescoes of the fifteenth century. Piero is a painter whom the present age wisely delights to honour. The good Baedeker, who will give two stars to a Fra Bartolomeo, finds him ' stiff and destitute of gracefulness ' ; but his aesthetic judgment need seldom be taken seriously. The church itself is not of the best. Much finer is *Santa Maria della Pieve*, with its strange many-arched façade and a most stately nave, in which the eye is led up to the high altar on its many steps and the great painting that crowns it, by Giotto's contemporary, the Sienese Pietro Lorenzetti. The Cathedral itself stands at the very top of the hill. It has been strangely overpraised :

for instance by Maurice Hewlett. Apart from the good windows of the east end, it has the usual poverty of Italian Gothic. For six hundred years, like so many great Italian churches, it stood awaiting the completion of its west front, and has received it, a florid atrocity, in the present century. But time will mellow its rawness as it is doing to the façade at Florence, itself not yet fifty years old. The interior is gloomy and disappointing, and some fine Della Robbias have little chance : it is true that they now have their own electric lighting where for four hundred years they had only smoky candles, but no form of art more clearly needs sunlight and air. The most comforting thing in the building is the glass of certain windows by a French contemporary of Dürer, one William of Marseilles. It is a relief to emerge into the daylight and to enjoy almost the best thing Arezzo has to offer, the splendid view of plain and mountain from the ancient walls to the east of the Cathedral. Here, in a spot which a notice requested us ' for considerations of personal security ' not to approach, but where only a lunatic or a deliberate suicide could come to mischief, we sat amid purple anemones and grape-hyacinths, marigolds and Star-of-Bethlehem, to watch the sun go down in glory behind the *Monti della Chiana*, the noblest sunset that any of our twenty-one Italian evenings gave us. Between these walls and the Duomo, in one of those public gardens which are so handicapped in Italy by the refusal of grass to grow into any kind of lawn, stands Arezzo's latest boast, the ambitious group of sculpture erected only yesterday in honour of Petrarch. It is the kind of work that the plain man rather likes, and the admirer of *Rima* and *Genesis* emphatically does not : we may leave it at that. Petrarch by the way was not an Arretine, but was born here, in 1304, though the accident of his father's exile from Florence.

No one should stay at Arezzo without visiting Sansepolcro, away to the east beyond the youthful Tiber. The queerest little railway runs beside the road, but it saves hours of time to hire an excellent Fiat at the modest rate of a franc a kilometre ; and further, this will bring you back by the little medieval town of Anghiari. Most of the way the road climbs above the Torrente Cerfone, through juniper-covered hillsides that, as many travellers have remarked, strangely recall the grey and brown landscape of Piero's own pictures. As you descend into the Tiber valley the scene widens, and the mountains of the Casentino come into view ; among them a single shape which no one who has seen it ever forgets, the crag of La Verna. I think it is Sabatier who compares it to the ark stranded on Mount Ararat. At Sansepolcro the hurried traveller, says Baedeker, may see the points of interest in about an hour. So he may, but he might easily give an hour to the picture that brought him here, Piero's great Resurrection, a fresco not painted in a church, but on a wall of the Palazzo Comunale. When you have sat awhile in the very cold room that contains it, you can return to the sunshine and enjoy the lovely armorial shields, said to be the work of the Della Robbia family, that adorn the outer wall of the Law Court. But before leaving, every man, I hope, will return to take his leave of Piero's masterpiece : it is surely one of the great pictures of the world. And give yourself time to walk up the hill north of the town and look back at the broad valley of the Tiber and the mountains that close in upon it towards Città di Castello. Wherever you go among these hill towns, it is the distant views that live most happily in the memory.

We cannot depart from Arezzo without a word of praise for the Albergo Savoia—almost the only place we stayed at, by the way, which prefers the old Italian name of *albergo* to the modern *hotel*. Nowhere did we meet better food and wine, and the cost of two nights' lodging and five admirable meals came to little more than fifteen shillings a head.

The journey from Arezzo to Perugia through the valley of the Chiana is delightful. Macaulay makes ' sweet Clanis ' wander through corn and vines and flowers, and so it does ; but in his day the district had but recently ceased to be a fever-haunted waste. When you have seen it, you know why Arezzo has set up a statue of Count Fossombroni, scientist and engineer. Macaulay is again in one's mind as the train passes Cortona, which cascades picturesquely down its hill ; but the diadem of towers is a rhetorician's dream. The junction of Terontola was in old days a place of much tedious waiting : now you merely step from one train into another, and in a few minutes you have passed the Umbrian border and are crossing the battle-field on the northern shore of Lake Trasimene. (For present purposes Umbria may be considered as one with Tuscany, both being provinces of Elysium.) I have seen the lake many times, and always it has worn the same cool grey, more satisfying, to one mind at least, than the lusciousness of the lakes of the north. More than a century ago there was talk of draining it, as Virgil's glassy Fucinus has been drained : may that day never come. Perugia lies but a few miles to the east, and to Perugia we gave one half day, no more. Most visitors stay at Perugia, where there is a vast and plutocratic hotel, and merely drop in at Assisi. We preferred to drop in at Perugia, if the phrase is permissible when you must mount several hundred feet from station to town ; for the city stands in the most commanding situation more than 1,600 feet above the sea. The greater things of Perugia can hardly be surpassed ; there is nothing better of its kind than the *Piazza del Municipio*, with the flank of the huge Palazzo Comunale on one side, the Cathedral on another, and between them the great fountain on which worked the most notable sculptors of their time, Niccolo and Giovanni Pisano and Arnolfo di Cambio, designer of the Cathedral at Florence. The visitor must not miss the *Collegio del Cambio*, the hall of the Bankers' Guild, where Perugino is for once at his best, and where the *custode* is a good deal of a humorist : nor the Oratory of San Bernardino, a piece of most delicate colour : least of all the great Etruscan gateway, the *Arco d'Augusto*, to the effect of which Rome and the Renaissance, as well as the Etruscans, have contributed. But the best thing in Perugia, I would boldly say, is the picture gallery, in some ways the most attractive in Italy. Nowhere else can you see so pleasantly the minor painters of Umbria, a fascinating group— Fiorenzo di Lorenzo, Benedetto Bonfigli, Boccati da Camerino, Eusebio di San Giorgio, and many another. All this and more you can see within the limits of one strenuous day.

Truth to tell, there is only one good reason for staying long at Perugia. It is the centre from which the coaches run to a score of places, Gubbio for instance and Todi, that are otherwise only accessible to a private car. I have stayed there three times, and always came away with a sense of relief : there is a hardness and arrogance about the city, which contrasts strangely with the gentle humanity of Assisi, lying plain to view on the flank of Monte Subasio some twelve miles away. At Assisi no man ever stayed too long, or left it without regret. Here you have the charm of Italy at its most magical. Nowhere else, except at San Gimignano, have the streets retained so untouched their medieval aspect ; nowhere else is the spirit of a man dead these seven hundred years so strangely alive. St. Francis indeed is everywhere, yet the place is no mausoleum. Assisi has of late made its mark in league football, and we saw lawn tennis being played, not too well, in the Roman theatre. The *Ars Franciscana*, the local school of needlework, thrives exceedingly : where only one shop kept the stuff in 1914, at least eight do so now, and in every street you may see women sitting at their doors with needle and linen. But the work is not quite what it was. In its early days you could almost choose your pieces

N

blindfold : now it is too often sophisticated. No good purpose can be served by copying a picture or a building in silk. But there is plenty of the best to be had if you look for it, and the prices are very low : you could half fill a suitcase for £5.

Again, in the *Via Portica* there stands the perfect model of a chemist's shop, which in calling itself *Farmacia Inglese* surely pays too high a compliment to this country. Vessels of black and gold, uniform in design, are ranged in cases of the same colour, inscribed with Latin verses derived from the ancient medical school of Salerno, while the ceiling is painted in the most charming taste with the plants from which the drugs are made. Never have I seen a more enchanting shop : to the gratified amusement of the proprietor, Dott. Pietro Cogolli, we paid it four several visits.

But modern things can at times be intrusive. We missed by one night only that detestable institution the *Mille Miglia*, the thousand mile race for motor cars. From midnight till four in the morning these horrid vehicles were shrieking their way up the steep hill and round the hairpin bend into the town, and he who has only heard the English lorry can have no notion of the hell that the Italian racing-car can raise.

Everyone knows that the double church of San Francesco, one church superimposed on another, is one of the great things of Italy, and that, rich with the work of Cimabue and Giotto, and the Sienese Simone Martini and Pietro Lorenzetti, it is indispensable to the study of the early painters. But many seem blind to the wonderful glass of the thirteenth century, which puts this church, if not on a level with Chartres and Bourges, at least hardly below York. Glass contributes more than painting to the beauty of the church. It was founded in 1228, only two years after the Saint's death, and shows Italian Gothic at its best : the side chapels and the admirable Early Renaissance vestibule add charm to an exterior that might have been a little bare. Like all great churches, it must be seen by night as well as by day, and night is by far the better. Many people prefer the Upper Church, because it is lofty and well lighted, but I have no hesitation whatever in giving my vote for the Lower. I have visited it at almost every hour from early morning till after sunset, and I know no more impressive interior anywhere, nor any with a greater sense of peace and holiness. And that holiness, after all, is the strongest impression that Assisi leaves. You feel it at Santa Chiara's church, where you see her body lie, you feel it at the Cathedral of San Rufino, before the font where Francis was baptized ; above all you feel it at the little convent of

San Damiano, which Francis' own hands laboured to repair, and of which St. Clare was the first abbess. Of all haunts of ancient peace this last is the most peaceful. It is almost literally true that not a stick or a stone has been altered since she died in 1253. And a spirit is still abroad there. Nowhere else have I known a beggar, without one touch of servility, pull off his cap, cross himself, and give me his blessing at considerable length, all in return for a coin that represented a minor fraction of a farthing. It was a thing to bring a blush to the cheek of patronage. It is the same everywhere in this astonishing town. The guardians of the sacred things, friar or nun or sacristan, tell the legends of the place with a quiet and disarming conviction that wins a most willing suspension of disbelief : you hear of the repulse of the Saracen host, and it never occurs to you to ask what Saracens were doing in the heart of Umbria.*

The aspect of Assisi is south-west, and the wonderful view may be enjoyed from the balconies of your hotel, the *Windsor* or the *Giotto*. But it is better to climb to the *Rocca*, or Citadel, above the town, and get the full glory of it nearly 1,700 feet up, with Assisi itself included in the prospect. To the right is the great mass of San Francesco's, church and monastery : far below, the little stream of the Tescio winds along in its broad and stony bed, and the great dome of St. Mary-of-the-Angels, covering the spot where Francis died, rises like an exhalation. Beyond is the plain of Umbria, once a mighty lake, and at the back of it springs the main chain of the Apennines. From here, if memory serves, you may on a fine morning identify six famous cities, from Perugia in the north-west to Montefalco conspicuous on its crest to the south.

The best short walk from the city is undoubtedly that to the Carceri, a Franciscan hermitage lying in a gorge of Monte Subasio, an hour's stroll from the Porta Cappuccini. It calls itself a prison : in fact it is a Paradise. The little group of brown-roofed buildings is perfectly set above the ravine, surrounded by a nightingale-haunted wood of ilex, where you may find cyclamen and spurge-laurel and yellow fumitory and, above all, the lovely blue hepatica.

Assisi, as we have said, is not the best centre for expeditions, yet some places should certainly be visited from it. First, without doubt, Montefalco. In the age of horse traffic a day was necessary, now a half day is ample, and the road takes you by Spello, Foligno and Bevagna. At Spello you will stop to see a good fresco by Pinturicchio in the Cathedral, but Foligno lacks charm, and

* In point of fact they were mercenaries of the Emperor, Frederick II.

Bevagna has little besides its enchanting name, more melodious even than the Virgilian Mevania, and the memory of St. Francis : for it was here that he preached his sermon to the birds. It is Benozzo Gozzoli who draws the traveller to Montefalco, though the view of the mountains, very stark and bare, from its walls is as fine as any of these hill-towns can show. The church of San Francesco is now a national monument, containing pictures from various sources, and the general effect is rather cheerless. Yet anyone may be glad to make acquaintance with the local painter Melanzio, seldom to be met with elsewhere ; and there was nothing *triste*, except a broken window, about the choir, which Benozzo decorated in 1452 with the story of St. Francis. It is the earliest of the four great groups of fresco on which Benozzo, the chief pupil of Fra Angelico, may base his claim to his high place among pictorial story-tellers.

At Montefalco we met with a common experience of travellers in an Italian April. We had gone up in the heat of a good English July, but while we sat in the church, the hateful *Tramontana* began to blow, and we returned to Assisi shivering behind closed windows. Fortunately spring had returned next day, when we took train to Spoleto, a journey of some twenty-five miles, marking our southern limit. There is much to see in Spoleto, but the country, not the town, called us, and we entered no building but the *Duomo*. No man could leave that unvisited, though the contrast between the Romanesque façade with its eight rose windows and the Berninified interior is disconcerting. If Spoleto had nothing else to show, its fame would be assured by the splendid frescoes of the apse. They were the last and best work of Lippo Lippi, left unfinished at his death in 1469 and admirably completed by one Fra Diamante. Fra Lippo is buried in the church which he adorned. Our real objective was the woods of Monte Luco, on the far side of a gorge that is spanned by a superb aqueduct, the *Ponte delle Torri*, standing three hundred feet above the water. It is said to date from the twelfth century, that age of mighty builders. From it you can scramble straight up into the woods, and so we did, the more actively to escape from one of the only two unpleasant persons we met in Italy. (Both were clearly touched in the brain.) On this occasion it was an old peasant-woman, a bad lot (*una cattiva*) as she assured us, who had been stealing the water, large bottles of it, from a holy well. Her jargon and mine agreed ill, but I gathered that she wished to associate us with her misdemeanour by inducing us to visit the spot, or alternatively to show us the way to places we did not wish to see by a highroad we did not wish to follow. The raucous voice of the old witch followed us, possibly not with blessings, as we shinned up the steep and densely wooded slope. The flowers went far beyond our botanical knowledge, but they included spider-orchis innumerable, varied by the bee ; Anemone Apennina, genista, cyclamen, hepatica, and a giant spurge. But the place of honour must be given to the homely periwinkle, which grew in sheets. We ate our luncheon in a spot from which the eye raked the whole Umbrian plain to Perugia and beyond.

We travelled from Assisi to Montepulciano by car, a run of two hours and a half : had we gone by train, it would have cost us fourteen hours and then landed us six miles from our destination, for Montepulciano's own little railway has been out of action for some years. The route, by road or rail, leads one to Chiusi, the Clusium of Lars Porsena, a place of no merit, but with, apparently, an unrivalled power of dislocating communications. No wonder Lars Porsena swore. It is as if the present government had left this one spot as a monument of bygone inefficiency.

There is much to take the rare traveller to Montepulciano. The town stands 2,000 feet above the sea, and none has a grander situation or commands more noble wild prospects in every direction. J. A. Symonds has called it the stateliest of Tuscan cities, and certainly it has fine *palazzi*, especially the two buildings designed by Antonio Sangallo in the square before the Cathedral. This Florentine architect was most happily inspired here. Outside the walls stands his church of San Biagio, a very perfect piece of Renaissance architecture in its more sober and classic form ; he also designed the beautiful colonnaded house, known as the *Canonica*, which lies beside it. The Duomo itself contains what must once have been a magnificent tomb, designed by Michelozzo, the architect of the Riccardi Palace at Florence. For reasons unknown it was dismantled in the eighteenth century, and the surviving sculptures are set up in various parts of the church. Even so they illustrate the incomparable quality of the Florentine sculptors of the fifteenth century. The sacristan insists that Donatello had a hand in it, and I hope it may be true. What I remember best in the Cathedral is the pan of charcoal which that same sacristan carried to warm his hands. The day indeed was chilly enough to give added importance to the famous wine at our inn, the Marzocco. If there were nothing else at Montepulciano, it would be worth a journey to drink one of the best of Italian vintages in its native home.

Next morning—it was 17 April—we awoke to the call of the first cuckoo and, what was more important in a dusty land, to the sound of the first rain that had fallen for some weeks. But it soon cleared, and most of the day was brilliant. The daily motor-coach from Perugia to Siena calls at Montepulciano, and by it we proceeded upon our way. This form of travel is stimulating, to say no more, especially when the speedometer is out of order and works in the reverse direction. On this occasion the dial-hand grew particularly lively at a hairpin bend, and once, when we were almost turning in our tracks, it sprang gaily to 90 k.p.h. These long-distance coaches run to a pretty exacting schedule, and punctuality is the rule. Accordingly the driver seldom slows down to pass through a village : he firmly plants his thumb upon the horn and only releases it when the village lies behind him : you fly through them in one long scream. And for the sharp bends on hill-roads made in the days of ox-transport he has little regard. One had the feeling that the speedometer should have registered knots instead of kilometres. It is an advantage of this form of travel that it gives you a glimpse of little-known places, such as Pienza. Here we drew up in a very charming *piazza*, and while the driver was shaved, we had time to visit the Palazzo Piccolomini, with its magnificent *cortile*. It was the home of that Aeneas Sylvius Piccolomini, afterwards abbreviated into Pius II, of whom we see and hear so much at Siena. A well-designed viewpoint in the garden gave us the noble prospect that the clouds had shut out at Montepulciano. Full in face lay Monte Amiata, nearly 6,000 feet of him : to the left was Monte Cetona, and between them rose the lonely basalt fang of Radicófani.

Of the hill-towns of Tuscany Siena is certainly the most brilliant, and it stands second only to Florence in the wealth of its art. To see it fully is a matter of several days, but if you have not got the days at your disposal, you may do wonderfully well with a single long afternoon. My advice is, go first to that great barrack of a church, San Domenico, to get the view, across the valley of Fontebranda, of the Cathedral on its ridge ; there is nothing like it in Italy. Besides, whatever you may leave unseen in Siena, you must not miss the remarkable portrait of St. Catherine by her friend Andrea Vanni, which is preserved in a chapel at the west end of this church. You can see the best of Sodoma here too, but the loss of that would be less serious : a facile and accomplished but seldom interesting painter. Thence a short walk will take you to the vast piazza, the scene, twice every summer, of that famous (or infamous) horse-race, the *Palio*, in which representatives of ten out of the seventeen *contrade* of the city compete for a banner, in medieval costume. The Piazza is shaped like a gigantic theatre, of which the Palazzo Pubblico forms the stage buildings, and beside it leaps into the air the glorious tower of the Mangia, nearly 350 feet in height. You can hardly fail to call it the finest in Italy, unless you chance to have given your heart already to the tower of the Cathedral. That, with its white marble banded with black, has a slim elegance that no other tower in this land of fair towers quite achieves. It has a feminine beauty, while the Mangia is essentially masculine. It was built immediately after the famous Campanile of Venice and tops it by nine feet : in beauty there is no comparison. Competition must surely have been the motive, for none built more ambitiously than the Sienese, till in 1348 the Black Death abated their pride. The Cathedral is built on no mean scale, yet it was to have been a mere transept of the colossal building of which some unfinished arcades yet stand. Everything about this Cathedral would seem to be wrong, yet everything comes off with brilliant success. The façade, much of it restored, is too rich and elaborate, yet it never cloys ; or if for a moment it does, go and see it at night and you will make your peace. The bands of colour in the white marble, both within and without, ought to destroy, yet do not, the vertical character which is essential to Gothic. The interior should by rights be intolerable with the riches of its decoration : yet who finds it so ? The very pavement has an acre or two of *graffiti*, scenes from the Old Testament and a famous series of Sages and Sibyls—surely the only floor in the world that has been the subject of monographs. From the North Aisle you enter the Cathedral Library, to find new splendours. Here Pinturicchio represented in fresco the life of the Aeneas Sylvius Piccolomini who has already been mentioned, and if brilliance were the ultimate test of merit, he would stand at the head of his craft. But not less fine is the array of illuminated missals, some of them bearing famous names, that line the walls below. And when the eye needs a rest, it can find it in the beautiful floor of blue and yellow tiles ; here is simplicity itself.

Fortune had brought us to Siena, all unknowing, on St. Catherine's own day, and all afternoon the Cathedral was humming with activity. And later, as I sat to watch the crowd and listen to the organ, long before daylight had departed, two touches of a switch and the whole building was illuminated. The effect of man's light within and nature's without, seen through the splendid glass of the window above the high altar, was something there is no temptation to forget.

We left after dark and an hour later alighted at Poggibonsi ; whether the town fulfils the promise of its name I cannot say. The omnibus soon whirled us up the seven or eight miles to San Gimignano. As we flew through the dark, I reflected that when last I was on that road, motors were so few that the appearance of one stampeded both our horse and another, insomuch that we were obliged to offer the hospitality of our carriage to a luckless Frenchman, who had been thrown across a ditch into a field. I remembered too the grand sweep of the hat with which our driver accepted a gold half-sovereign as the price and more than the price of his day's hire : it was a coin he had never seen before, and it left him with a bonus of twenty per cent. I suppose an English half-sovereign would be more exciting still in these days.

As a place to arrive at by night I put San Gimignano second only to Venice. You find yourself standing in a great silent piazza, with high dim palaces all about you, and from every point one or more of the mysterious towers that give the place its fame is faintly visible against the sky. Till an orchestra at the Fascist headquarters in a neighbouring street began to practise *Cavalleria Rusticana*, there was hardly a sound except the frequent cry of an owl that must certainly have been Andrea del Sarto's (or Browning's) cue-owl, ' uttering the note we call them by '. Two of these *palazzi* are now hotels, and it is pleasant to recommend the *Cisterna*, then in the first year of its new phase of life. No doubt the shell of the building is, like its neighbours, a good five hundred years old : five centuries hence I trust it may still be giving the same welcome to the foreigner, and at a cost as reasonable as to-day. A man could live here, and live well, for two guineas a week. And what a place for a holiday, or to work in. I always hope that when Mr E. M. Forster described it so brilliantly in *Where Angels Fear to Tread*, he did it *in situ*. You could get an endless variety of walks over hills of scrub-oak and fragrant wormwood : you could see little rarely-visited towns like the charmingly named Colle di Val d'Elsa and Pomarance and Boccaccio's home at Certaldo : and lastly you could enjoy the beauties of San Gimignano itself without the thought that is always at the back of the passing traveller's mind, ' I shan't see this again tomorrow '. For besides possessing in its architecture more of the charm of unspoilt antiquity than any town of Tuscany, it has also more than its share of good painting. Benozzo Gozzoli is here again at Sant' Agostino's with his life of

St. Augustine, better and riper work than at Montefalco ; and the
same church has one of those lovely altars in grey stone gilded, by
the Florentine Benedetto da Maiano, who did a good deal of work
here. The Collegiata, as the Cathedral is called, has only one show
piece, the chapel of Santa Fina, that unpleasant little saint who died
at fifteen after lying on a board till it adhered to her flesh. It is an
early work of Ghirlandaio, and I do not know that he ever bettered
it. But the whole church is full of frescoes by Sienese primitives
and would afford entertainment for a week. Where else does one
meet Barna da Siena ? And the still earlier Bartolo di Fredi is
not much better known. The place is described, at least in advertise-
ments, as *San Gimignano delle Belle Torri*, and of these towers
it is said at one time to have possessed fifty-six. If that is true, it
must have presented a startling spectacle indeed : the surviving
thirteen are remarkable enough. Individually they have no beauty
but what age and wall-flowers supply, but from every point they
group in some fresh way, and seen from a distance, whether of one
mile or ten, the effect is magical. The outstanding building is the
Palazzo Comunale, dating like most things in this astonishing town
from 1300 or thereabouts. In the great new-built Council-chamber
Dante spoke as ambassador of Florence : he came a few years too
soon to see the magnificent fresco by Lippo Memmi which has
adorned it since 1317, but the vivid representations of charging
knights may possibly have been there already. Here too is the little
picture gallery, containing far more good than bad, which is not
usually the case with the galleries of the smaller towns. From a
window of the Palazzo we watched the Sunday market in full swing
below, and subsequently bought excellent ties for less than 1/6
apiece : a green golf-umbrella cost about 3/6. I hit on another shop
which displayed good ties for sale and bought one, fatuously calling
it a souvenir of San Gimignano. The proprietor thereupon showed
his name upon the end ; it was Baldi Narciso, and I noted with
satisfaction that the bald Narcissus bade fair soon to become a fat
Adonis of forty.

There is a daily omnibus to Volterra, a city which twenty years
ago cost a real effort to visit. Certainly the far-famed hold scowls
pretty grimly on the surrounding hills. It stands seven hundred
feet higher than San Gimignano, with a view that may extend even
to Corsica if you are lucky. I have never seen a bleaker town :
five miles of Etruscan wall do not make for amenity. It seems only
right that Walter de Brienne's stern fortress should be now a house
of correction. If on the day of our visit it blew hard and at times

rained, there are those who say that it always does so here. The
local product is sculptured alabaster, but one's sympathy for a
depressed industry was rather dried up by the vulgarity of the work.
Rock-salt is another export, and boric acid from the volcanic springs
of Larderello : hence the distant cloud of vapour that catches the
eye as one stands on the southern rampart. But the place has
a more humane industry, and a surprising one. At Martinucci's
in the Via Guidi you may buy the most delightful toys : little
wooden figures of local make, Pinocchios of every size, and all the
characters of that excellent children's newspaper, the *Corriere dei
Piccoli*. A priceless *Arcibaldo* survived the journey to England,
only, alas, to fall into a nursery fire. These things may of course
be bought in the toyshops of Florence, but it is always better sport
to go to the fountain-head. Greater arts are not absent in Cathedral
and Baptistry, but the place seems too austere a home for the work
of Mino da Fiesole, gentlest of Florentine sculptors. If Etruscan
cinerary urns excite you, you can see more than six hundred of
them here. It is interesting to see how often in this region the old
Etruscan cast of countenance has survived—the rich brown colour,
the deepset eye, the prominent cheekbone, the beaky nose. There
was one transport official who displayed the type in perfection, and
to one of us his name came in a flash of inspiration : he was
Tarquinius Super-Bus.

For our unwilling departure from San Gimignano the motor
once again proved more economical in time and money than the
train, and we drove to Florence by way of San Casciano and the
Certosa. But not to stay, for a few hours later we had left by
omnibus for the Casentino. These few hours had been quite
enough to make us crave for the country. The plain fact is, the
internal combustion engine has ruined this lovely city. It was
always noisy, but not as it is now : there was nothing unpleasant
in the cracking of the *vetturino's* whip and the clop-clop of hooves
on the pavements ; they were part and parcel of a less harassed age.
The ceaseless yell of the high frequency horns, blown with very
high frequency indeed, and as a rule without cause, is frankly
intolerable. Rome, as the columns of *The Times* attest, is as bad.
Must one fear the same in the future for Arezzo and Assisi ?
I am grateful to Florence for many happy memories, and no doubt
she contains, in street and church and gallery, more beautiful things
than any city of her size in the world, but I have no wish to go there
again.

There is little more I need say. The Uffizi has of late been sifted, rearranged, and reinforced from the Accademia, and all that is not Italian moved elsewhere : consequently, as a collection purely of Italian painting, it stands alone and unrivalled. Only one great name is missing, Fra Angelico, and you will learn the reason when you visit San Marco's, the convent where the master (the servant rather) lived and laboured. The exquisite things that he painted in cell or lunette, above all the great Crucifixion, always made it the most lovable spot in Florence : but now, in addition, all his panel pictures have been brought together in one large gallery, and the place is paradise itself. If anything heartens me to face the racket of the Florentine streets again, it will be the knowledge that this haven of peace awaits me.

The weather was not too kind to us as our bus left Florence for Bibbiena : rain fell continuously and darkness came before its time. This was unlucky, for it is a magnificent ride over the Consuma Pass, as we found on our return journey three days later. The Casentino is the upper valley of the Arno, bounded on its western side by the great massif of the Prato Magno, which, rising to 5,000 feet, looks down on the whole course of the youthful river, as it runs south-east for many a league, works its way round the southern end of the mountain, and then flows north-west to Pontassieve, where it turns westward to Florence, and ultimately to Pisa and the sea. You may reach the district by rail from Arezzo at its southern end, or by road from Florence and the north. The wisest traveller, with time at his disposal, would take train or omnibus to Pontassieve, thirteen miles out, and then use his legs. The road over the Consuma rises to nearly 3,400 feet, and for miles he would descend with the whole of the Casentino and its surrounding mountains spread before his eyes. Bibbiena is a poor little town, but the Albergo Amorosi-Bei meets all reasonable requirements, and I need hardly add that it is cheap. In fact three days' supply of excellent wine cost me the same, within a penny or so, as two commercial ham sandwiches and a small Worthington on the Channel boat, and just over half what the smallest *fiasco* of Chianti would cost in Soho. It is an admirable centre for the walker. La Verna is not eight miles away, and Camaldoli and the Prato al Soglio above it, from which, if you are lucky, the view may extend to both seas, are within a day's expedition with a little aid from a bus. Unfortunately the weather, as had happened to me twenty-six years earlier, balked us of Camaldoli ; but the short walk to Poppi, with its remarkable castle, the most conspicuous feature in the whole district, did well enough : and the stripling Arno, with its border of poplars tenanted by innumerable whitethroats, is as lovely a stream to follow as heart could desire. The gold of those poplars in a stormy sunset was the most beautiful thing we saw in Italy. Another day we let a charming mountain stream, the Torrente Teggina, lead us to the remote hill-village of Quota. But to the traveller fresh from Assisi, La Verna, the mountain home of St. Francis, given him by the Count of Chiusi in 1213, is what matters most. It stands 3,700 feet up, on the side of that crag of Monte Penna whose shape, once seen, can never be mistaken. It is accessible by a good road, and now even boasts a hotel close at hand. Every spot in and about the monastery holds its place in the Franciscan legend, and the welcome of the monks was as genuine in 1931 as in 1905. The monastic church contains perhaps the finest of all Della Robbias. As we sat before them, a storm without plunged the building half in darkness : next minute the west door was thrown open and with a banner at their head, the monks entered, in procession, chanting a litany, and falling on their knees in the nave, sank into that ghostlike stillness which only the monastic orders can achieve. It was astonishingly impressive. Nature dealt with us bountifully that day. Wordsworth's cuckoo was there to greet us, though he had migrated lower down the mountain. We walked up the mountain in shirtsleeves, lunched cowering under a wall in a heavy snowstorm, crowded round a blazing faggot in the monastery, watched, as we descended, a thunderstorm advancing from the Prato Magno, and were ushered into Bibbiena by a wonderful double rainbow. Nature was kind again on our return journey to Florence. Gears gave some trouble as we climbed the long road of the Consuma, but it was a comforting reflection that if we stuck we should be in a pretty pass. One might do worse than be forced to wait an hour or two on an April evening in a mountain lawn of hellebore and primrose and purple crocus. To approach Florence at sunset over her eastern hills is to see the city at her wonderful best. It might not be easy to arrange, but it would be worth a good deal of trouble to get that impression before any other.

The journey from Florence to Pisa is brief and uneventful, though no journey in Tuscany can be without interest. Pisa itself you may see very tolerably in a short day, if you give your time to the great things and let the lesser go. The obvious course is to take a tram straight to the *Piazza del Duomo* and stay there till the need of luncheon becomes imperative. Afterwards, sun yourself on the Lungarno till you are satisfied, and then give the rest of

the day to the Cathedral group. Time spent on the parapet of
the river, or the ledge below it, will be well repaid. The Lungarno
here is far finer than at Florence, less picturesque but more ample
and stately, and the river flows in a larger sweep. Of the three
giants of Pisa, the Cathedral was begun in 1063, nearly a century
earlier than the rest : the Baptistry in its first form came next :
the Campanile followed in 1173, but neither was completed before
the middle of the fourteenth century. Add the Campo Santo, the
great cloistered burial-place, which was not begun till the Gothic
manner had already superseded the Romanesque, and you have in
this one place nearly four centuries of great building. All alike are
of white marble, apt even now to be dazzling on a sunny day.
They are enclosed in a vast green space, and from the south-east
corner it is possible to enjoy an uninterrupted view, at an adequate
distance, of the whole wonderful group : I know no such architectural *coup d'oeil* anywhere. It is not faultless : there is some
weakness in the exterior Gothic decoration of the Baptistry, and
the Leaning Tower would be handsomer if it did not lean.
Internally, the Baptistry must take pride of place as pure architecture, and it is enriched with Niccolo Pisano's great pulpit, finer
work than he did at Siena, and the wondrous font, sixteen paces in
circumference, carved and inlaid with mosaic, as ornate as its only
rival, at Parma, is plain. That another sense besides the eye may
have its delight, the Baptistry is blessed with a marvellous echo.
The *custode* gives tongue in a quavering falsetto, and the sounds
become heavenly music and melt and tingle into silence in the dome
above.

There is so much of the sublime at Pisa that a touch of the
ridiculous comes almost as a relief, and in the Cathedral we read
with pleasure the following notice addressed to our compatriots.
' It is severely forbidden to ladies indecently dressed the entrance
into the Cathedral and Baptistry, and the sa-me is equally forbidden
to gentlemen without jacket or shoes '. Why ' sa-me ' ? This
comes second, though a good way behind it, to the notice in Milan
Cathedral once recorded by Sir David Hunter Blair : ' The
Brothers so called of Mercy ask some slender arms for their
hospital. They harbour all kinds of diseases and have no respect
for religion '. There is also unconscious humour in the bronze
door of the south transept, with its naive tales from the Bible ;
but you laugh with the artist, old Bonannus, not at him. It is the
only survivor of the original doors of 1180, and the progenitor,
when you come to think of it, of Ghiberti's astonishing *tour-de-force*

at Florence 250 years later. As so often, the primitive craftsman really has the better of it : his design is lovely, and no one can accuse him of asking too much of his material. One curious feature in the Duomo I cannot remember to have observed before. As you look towards the west, you notice something peculiar, but most pleasing, in the effect of the stained glass : it then occurs to you that outside you had not been conscious of any western windows at all. On leaving the building you will discover that the architects, unwilling to break up their splendid colonnades, covered the windows with louvers, so that only close observation reveals them. So you *can* both eat your cake and have it too.

Some people prefer the Campo Santo to all the other buildings.* If so, it is not that Pisan Gothic is superior to Romanesque, far from it : it is probably that in the great cloister nature is allowed to do so much, a hundred yards of grass sprinkled with buttercups and orchis, roses and lilac-bushes, all enclosed in a marble tracery of unusual grace and lightness. The inner side of the containing walls is frescoed throughout, but who would not flinch at 400 yards of pictures, even if they were well preserved ? At Pisa you may take a rest from painting, and be content with the mistress art. Yet here you have Benozzo for the last time, much the most distin- guished of the company, even in decay. We had already seen him on a big scale at Montefalco, at San Gimignano, and in the Riccardi Palace at Florence, practically the life-work of a very fascinating painter. It is a reminder that our northern galleries, even Burlington House on an occasion of unique privilege, cannot give us the best of Italian painting : the early painters at least were happier when they had a wall than when they had a panel to work on.

From Pisa to Lucca is a matter of fifteen miles only ; and when you have crossed the open plain, with the Pisan mountains away on the right, and entered the valley of the Serchio, the richness and beauty of the scene are a delight : I would as soon travel those few miles in spring as any in Italy. Lucca, like Pisa, is a city of the plain. Yet the mountains stand all about her, and a walk round the circuit of the ramparts that Vauban designed gives the best views of town and country alike. The meadows below are pink with ragged robin, or blue with bugle, and on the glacis you may find bee-orchis and white squills and pale blue flax. The place has nothing to show so thrilling as the Pisan giants, but I prefer

* On 27th July, 1944, the roof was hit by a stray shell and set on fire. The roof was destroyed and the frescoes gravely injured, but I am assured that the place is now as beautiful as ever.

it as a whole : it is more of a country town and less of a great city, and its streets and squares have a satisfying combination of the homely and the picturesque. The best spot in the town, and one of the most romantic in all Tuscany, is the little square west of the Cathedral : in front the arcaded façade, with columns of infinite variety in design and colour ; at its corner the beautiful tower, and at right angles to it the Archbishop's palace, patched and stained in every gradation of red and pink and white, with yellow wallflower wherever it can get a hold. Lucca produced one sculptor almost in the first flight, Matteo Civitali, and the Cathedral is full of his work. But the building contains one treasure, of earlier date, which stands quite alone in beauty, the tomb of Ilaria del Carretto, a bride of the house of Guinigi. She died in 1405, and her monument is the work of Jacopo della Quercia, who carved it when Donatello was only twenty years old and all the other great sculptors of Florence were yet to come. Without fear of contradiction I would say that none of them has surpassed it, ' a perfect form in perfect rest '.

We had wondered why there should be a warning posted in the Duomo against the introduction of bicycles. We learned the reason when we visited San Frediano's, the second among the churches of Lucca, and found it full of them. We found it full of votaries too, for, as Fortune had taken us to Siena on St Catherine's Day, so she had brought us to Lucca for the *festa* of the city's patroness, Santa Zita. And she lies in the great church that bears the name of a sixth century Irishman, founder of Lucca's first cathedral. There were stalls without for the sale of flowers, mostly wild narcissus from Altopascio, and all morning the crowd filed through her chapel, kissing the altar and holding out their flowers to the little withered, glass-protected figure behind it.

We spent our last afternoon in climbing Monte San Giuliano, a shapely, clean-cut hill, rising to about 1,500 feet above Ripafratta. The view certainly rewarded our pains, and so did the flowers, especially the orchises, great red fellows of one or more species that we failed to identify. In the plain to the south lay Pisa, and the seaward view embraced the flat green coastland almost from Viareggio to Livorno, with the mouths of the Arno and the Serchio in between. We were looking down on the waters that drowned Shelley, and the shore where his body was burned by Trelawny and Byron. Of more immediate interest was a football match down in the valley by Ripafratta. It was a curious experience to watch through the glasses a goal scored from a corner kick (*un calcio d'angolo*) and, I thought, with the player's head (*un bel colpo di testa*) an hour's walk from where we sat.

The morrow found us seated in the train that slowly climbed out of Tuscany and descended towards Bologna, with a sense, like two earlier exiles from Paradise, of wandering down 'into a lower world, to this obscure and wild.'

In reading through these notes I am not unconscious of a plethora of superlatives, but I offer no apology. Many years ago I came under the spell of Tuscany, and have learnt, as happens not too often in life, that my youthful impressions were not wrong. The charm of the land is incomparable.

APPENDIX C

FRANCE ON 25 GUINEAS (1952)

CROSSING the Channel one morning in May, I read a well-informed 'middle' in *The Spectator*, under the title *France on £25*. It seemed worth putting on record the experience of one particular traveller, and the 25 guineas of my title includes the cost of the crossing between Newhaven and Dieppe, not merely of food and lodging and petrol in France itself. The car went with us on the outward journey, but on our return we reached Dieppe in time to send it by cargo-boat, a saving of about £3. 10s. 0d. in cost. The length of our stay was limited not so much by 'the Chancellor's dole' as by the time that the Managing Director could afford to be absent from his business. The Managing Director was he who did all the work and nearly all the driving. His wife, the Cordon Bleu, talked accomplished French and catered for our admirable picnic lunches. The two old people had merely to enjoy themselves—not a difficult task. We left perforce on a Saturday and returned on a Monday : not the best of days, for the first meant an overcrowded boat and the latter meant two successive days, Sunday and Monday, on which French banks do not open. We brought home £35 in uncashed cheques—remember that an extra £15 is allowed for the car—so we could have stayed several more days in France had circumstances permitted. We had travelled 860 miles of French roads.

Our first stop was to have been at Beauvais, but the representative of the A.A. at Dieppe warned us against looking for accommodation in a badly battered town. So we stopped instead at Forges-les-Eaux, a dull little town which once had some vogue as a watering-place, brought into being by Anne of Austria, mother of Louis XIV. The house she occupied still exists on the verge of an unpretentious public garden at the back of the Hotel de Ville. There is also an *Etablissement* and a casino, but who takes what at Bath Mr Smauker called the 'killibeate' I cannot say. We had heard of two hotels, and tried the *Lion d'Or* (*J. Entwistle, propriétaire*). The rooms were homely but adequate, and dinner when it came truly magnificent. France gave us eight good dinners and one bad one, but this was the best. And an inscription in the

room where we enjoyed our coffee and *croissants* next morning,
' *Un repas sans vin est une journée sans soleil* ', is one that all sensible
travellers in France will take to heart. In May 1952 we lacked
neither *vin* nor *soleil* on any day, two things that still are cheap.

We came to Beauvais in mid morning and left after a couple
of hours, which with things as they are is sufficient. For this
astonishing Cathedral, this sublime folly, has yet to recover its
dignity : most of the windows are still boarded up and the general
condition is shabby. We arrived in the middle of a service which
also lacked dignity : there was too much singing of the hymn tune
Hanover, none too melodious, as a priestly solo. It is a building for
which figures must speak. Begun in 1225, only choir and transepts
were ever built, with a spire that outtopped by a hundred feet the
400 feet of Salisbury. This fell, not surprisingly, in 1573. The
interior height of the vaulting is 152 feet, the exterior ridge no less
than 225 feet. The vault fell twice before a re-planning of the
supports gave it stability. We rightly think of Westminster Abbey
as a lofty building, but its vault-ridge is only 102 feet above the
pavement. Of our cathedrals the highest vault is at Salisbury, and
that is 84 feet only. We left the place with relief and turned our
faces southward for Chartres.

Our only stop, except for a roadside lunch, was at the Château
d'Anet, near the Ivry of the famous battle, Henry of Navarre's
or Macaulay's. Though it suffered sorely in the Revolution it is
still a splendid place, built at the order of Henri II about 1550 for
Diane de Poitiers, Duchesse de Valentinois—*le Dianet*, as her friend
the poet Ronsard called it. Diane is one of two famous French-
women whose name follows us to Touraine : the other, of a very
different type, is of course St. Joan. For the latter, anyone who
travelled these roads with some knowledge of her history would
find that half the town-names of this well sign-posted land recall
her name. Rouen and Orleans, Chinon and Poitiers go without
saying. But it begins before that. At Dieppe she stopped on her
last journey to Rouen. At Compiégne she was taken prisoner.
Her principal judge was the Bishop of Beauvais. At Verneuil her
beau duc, D'Alençon, was made prisoner in battle. Châteaudun
was the stronghold of her friend the Bastard of Orleans, Dunois.
Tours and Blois, Bourges and Loches, Romorantin and La Charité—
we hear of her at every one, and a dozen more besides.

The country, while naturally more advanced than England,
still had the freshness of spring, though there were cherries in
the shops and the roses were in bloom. With showers about, the

air had an April brilliance. The contours of the fields, without timber and hedgerows, told one that this was France, not England ; and the emptiness of the cultivated land, so often surprising to the townsman, was very marked until, further south, we came more into a region of vineyards, where properties tend to be small and workers more frequently visible. I am told that in England the ordinary ratio of workers to land is one to fifty acres, which certainly leaves room for concealment. The flowers were not those of an English spring. Broom was everywhere, gorse nowhere ; and we never saw bluebells or cowslips or belated primroses, ' orphans of the flowery prime '. Only the fields of buttercups, their gold tinged with the red of sorrel or the pink of ragged robin, reminded us of home. Nothing caught the eye more than the tall blue sage (*Salvia Verbenaca*), which is not uncommon in England, but hardly to be found fringing the road for miles together. To one who knows nothing of trees the woods too seemed alien, partly perhaps because they appeared less neglected, and partly through the surprising prevalence of the acacia, everywhere in full flower, and becoming more and more common the further south we got. Flowers play as important a part in a French village as in an English, though we never saw a cottage garden such as Devon or Sussex will show. They grew right against the houses that front the road itself, with no enclosure between—great clumps of pinks and oxalis and often heuchera : and climbing roses and clematis were in their glory. Of the birds that make our woodland ring loud and long, only the nightingale seemed common : his song was everywhere. The willow wren, the wood wren, the chiffchaff we heard seldom or never ; and of the two birds which thirty years ago I came to associate specially with Touraine, the redstart and the siskin, I neither heard nor saw a single one.

In mid afternoon we sighted the Cathedral of Chartres rising on its low hill above the wheatfields. We had expected to stay at the *Grand Monarque*, recommended to us by one who had known it more than sixty years ago, and whose good fortune it had been in youth to visit such places in the company of Ruskin or Morris. But we had heard of it as grown vastly expensive, and it seemed wiser (and certainly was) to consult the *Syndicat d'Initiative*, in an office close to the west end of the cathedral. This advice we offer to all travellers : unless you know where you are going to stay and have booked your rooms, always consult the *Syndicat*. Here and at Bourges and at Tours we got just the help and advice we needed : it saved us much trouble and, without doubt, expense.

Unless you are going to stay long enough to enjoy full *pension*, it pays best to go to an *hôtel meublé*, that is a hotel without a restaurant, and you can dine at the place of your choice, again acting under advice. We were sent to the *Jehan de Beauce*, a name that recalls the designer of the great screens in the cathedral and of its north-western spire. We found all that we could wish, and two good restaurants within a few yards.

A great many people know of the Cathedral of Chartres as a thing unique in Europe, or the world. York Minster and the church of San Francesco at Assisi retain nearly all their original glass, but neither can compete with the French work of the thirteenth century. The mere figures are astonishing—125 windows, with the three great roses and 47 lesser ones. The combination of great architecture, great sculpture, and marvellous glass make a whole unrivalled anywhere. And its glory is not of the thirteenth century only. The west wall with its three windows and the sculptures of the *Portail Royal* alone survived a disastrous fire in 1194, and these early windows, glazed a little before 1150, are even lovelier than the work of fifty or a hundred years later. Turn from their soft glow to the blaze of the *Rose de France* in the north transept, and the five great windows below it—all the gift of St. Louis, who came to the throne in 1226—and it will be surprising if you do not prefer the earlier work. And it may well be the same with the sculpture, that you will prefer the tall figures with the archaic smile and the drapery that recalls the *Korai* of the Acropolis Museum at Athens—only that the Christian sculptures have an element of mystery which the Greek do not possess—to the thirteenth century statuary of the great north and south porches which Sir Thomas Jackson has called the greatest work of Gothic art.

There is another church, St. Pierre, that must on no account be missed. It can be reached by a short walk through winding streets, but it is better to go by the river, the Eure, with its pleasant bridges and a fresh view of the cathedral. Here not all the windows had yet been replaced, but the glass of the splendid apse, dating from just about 1300, is even more radiant than in the apse of the cathedral itself.

We left towards midday and reached Orleans in time to eat our lunch on the south bank of the Loire, here first seen, looking across at the city and watching a tern fly up and down the river. We made one more stop before Bourges, to investigate a yellow flower beside the road. It proved to be a beautiful yellow cistus, growing in profusion over a stretch of many acres, as I have seen a white one cover a whole hillside in a Greek island. We saw it nowhere else. At Bourges we once more sought the counsel of the *Syndicat d'Initiative* and were sent to the *Hôtel des Etrangers ;* and next day, on seeing the Vauxhall outside the office, a courteous official came out to ask if we were satisfied. Our rooms had what seemed a quiet outlook, within sound of a cuckoo (as at Forges-les-Eaux), but the peace was shattered four times in the hour by a very villainous church clock, striking in cracked semitones. And at Bourges quiet was very necessary. May, it appears, is a month of *foires*. At Chartres there was a good old-fashioned fair, amusing to many and offensive to none. But at Bourges loud-speakers spouted song at every street-corner, and later at Tours and Saumur we met the same—only worse.

The Cathedral of St. Etienne at Bourges is only less wonderful than Chartres, and if you chanced to see it first you might say that no lovelier glass could be dreamed of anywhere. And even seen second it might well be claimed that, as a building, it is not inferior. In the great French churches the *jubé*, or rood screen, has almost always disappeared, and Bourges has no transepts. And here as elsewhere the absence of innumerable memorials to unimportant people with which our own cathedrals are cluttered leaves the mistress art of architecture to speak for itself. And so, within, the unchecked vista from west to east, or east to west, is magnificent ; and without, from the public garden where we ate our lunch, you can enjoy the unbroken line of roof and window and buttress ; while by descending some steps you may appreciate the wonderful apse soaring above you. Every great church we saw emphasized the loss involved in the English preference for a flat east end. The wide west front, with its five portals, is less easy to see : there is no place that gives a really satisfactory view. The whole of the east end is full of thirteenth century glass, hardly inferior to Chartres and much, though not all, of it a good deal easier to see : the windows are so low that by standing on a chair one can even use an exploring finger. And from outside one can appreciate what an enormous amount of lead went to the making of these early windows, built up from very small pieces of glass. When viewed at short range from outside, such a window looks more like a sheet of lead than a sheet of glass ; and to understand how such a thing can become a miracle of glowing jewellery one must study the meaning of the term ' irradiation '.

The other building in Bourges that must not go unvisited is the house of Jacques Coeur, the rightly famous merchant prince who was Master of the Mint to Charles VII (St. Joan's Dauphin), and after doing infinite service to his country fell a victim to royal treachery and aristocratic jealousy. In it were incorporated two towers of the Roman wall : the town was once the Gaulish Avaricum, as Julius Caesar had cause to know. It was long the *Palais de Justice* and now is a place for visitors, with much to show them. It was good to see a mason, a master of his craft, carving a gargoyle to replace one that was no longer safe.

Bourges was our furthest south : from here we turned west, that is homeward, and our sixth day was the most varied of all. At Blois we once more lunched on the bank of the Loire, after a rather weary progress round the celebrated château. I am glad to have seen the famous staircase sometimes attributed to Leonardo da Vinci, but really designed by Delorme, the architect of Anet ; and there is a fine equestrian statue of Louis XII over the entrance. But the chief subject of a prolix guide is the history, replete with topographical exactitude, of the murder of the Duc de Guise in 1588. It is a topic of which one may easily tire : after life's fitful fever why should he not be allowed to sleep well ? This was the only showplace from which we were glad to escape.

Very different were our feelings at Chenonceaux, perhaps the loveliest of all the great houses of Touraine. The building was begun in 1515, and twenty years later it became the property of the Crown. Henri II gave it to Diane de Poitiers, but after his death she was compelled by his Queen, Catherine de Medicis, to exchange it for Chaumont. Its special charm is that it is built, for the most part, on the arches of a bridge across the Cher. Here Mary Queen of Scots spent her honeymoon, though not as our Baedeker told us in 1599. Our only guide, by the way, was a Baedeker of 1896 vintage, belonging to that departed world in which a dinner at the best hotel might cost four francs, *vin compris*, and the hire of a cab was one franc an hour. Now one can earn 25 francs by returning an empty bottle when you have drunk the wine.

From Chenonceaux our road led us by Amboise, with its great château lowering above the town, another stronghold with a bloodstained history. And so to Tours, a place of whose quiet dignity I had the pleasantest memories from thirty years ago. This time we found it frankly intolerable with noise and crowding, and when the demands of one-way traffic brought us a second time to the doors of the *Syndicat*, regardless of the trouble we had already given them, we asked if they could recommend any place outside the town. Some telephoning followed and we were told we could have rooms at the *Grand Monarque*, Azay-le-Rideau, sixteen miles further to the south-west. Nothing could have been better. It gave us a little town, or large village, instead of a big one, and a more convenient base for the things we wanted to see. And the hotel, as we learned by pleasurable experience, is noted for its cookery, and the white wine, beautifully iced, was not only the best we met anywhere but much the cheapest, approximately a shilling a bottle. Further, there was a quiet garden in which to sit. Its château, like Chenonceaux, is a place of Renaissance amenity, not a fortress. On our third and last night it was flood-lit. So on that night were others in this land of châteaux, and we saw signposts on the roads marked *Route des Illuminations*. But it brought no undue crowd to Azay. On the previous night a military band had marched into the town to give a concert in the *Place*—a rare event, we were told. We arrived just in time to hear a very military rendering of Beethoven's great *Ode to Joy* from the Ninth Symphony.

Our programme for the second day allowed us to eat an admirable déjeuner in the hotel, after giving the morning to the enchanting château. After that we set out for a short expedition to Candes, Fontevrault and Chinon. It was our policy to follow minor roads, and rivers where we could, and at one place we accepted in faith the sign *Bac Irrégulier*, none of us knowing that the word *bac* means ' ferry '. And a charming road it was, often fringed with a beautiful mauve campanula which we had not seen elsewhere. It brought us in due course to the *bac*, which we crossed in company with a lorry, and found to our satisfaction that there was nothing to pay. Candes is a village at the junction of Vienne and Loire, with a fine church built, 800 years later, over the cell where St. Martin died in 397. His body was carried off by boat, under cover of night, by the people of Tours, and the event is recorded in a modern window that is a remarkable tour-de-force in the representation of night. There is a richly sculptured south porch, with the vault springing from a central pillar, like some of our own chapter houses. Beyond the church an arrow points the way to a *panorame*, and it was well worth the climb to the flowery clifftop to see the view of the Loire, a splendid river to think of with Rhine or Rhone rather than with ' our poor Thames ' or Severn.

At Fontevrault the famous monastery has been for 150 years a *maison centrale de détention*. Its once magnificent church contained the tombs of two of our kings, Richard I and Henry II, and two Queens, and still has certain fine sculptures. But as we found we must wait longer than was convenient for admission, we went our way, contented with a glimpse of the noble Romanesque tower. Less time at Fontevrault meant more at Chinon, where a visit of two hours is far too short. The castle, which is really three castles, extends in ruins over a plateau high above the town and its river, the Vienne, with tree-clad glacis between, ' the haven of every bird ', and valerian and bugloss to temper its severity. The central one is the *Château de Milieu*, on the site of the Roman fortress of Caino, and its great hall is the place where in March 1429 Joan identified Charles, who had concealed himself in the crowd of courtiers, and gave him the famous greeting : ' *Gentil Dauphin, j'ay nom Jehanne la Pucelle.*'

Our last day before we finally turned homeward was given to Angers, a drive of about 70 miles. We took one more château on the way, Langeais. This lacks the urbanity of Chenonceaux or Azay-le-Rideau, for it belongs to an earlier age, built after 1450 at the order of Louis XI : it is therefore a medieval fortress. But a visit to it is indispensable and, within, it has more of amenity than any. Most of the châteaux are furnished after a fashion with pictures and tapestries often of mediocre quality, though Azay holds a fine collection of the so-called Rhodian, really Turkish, ware. But at Langeais the generosity of its last owner, M. Jacques Siegfried, filled the rooms with really fine works of art and utility— I refer to the enchanting kitchen equipment—and then presented it to the *Institut de France*. A large photograph of this munificent benefactor is the one thing in it which dates.

There is only one compelling cause for visiting Angers, the *Musée des Tapisseries*—and we found it closed. But we were not wholly frustrated. Those who saw the entrancing exhibition of French tapestries at South Kensington in 1947 will recall the great Apocalypse series, woven in Paris towards the end of the fourteenth century. These are now, as in earlier days, to be seen hung in the cathedral. Others may be seen, in such leisure as a guide permits, in the restored chapel of the castle ; and some day the whole collection is to be brought together there and in a building not yet under construction close by. When that is done, Angers and the Cluny Museum in Paris will be the two places of pilgrimage for this most lovely art. Apart from this, there would be no need to enter the castle ; it is best to see it only from outside, with its mighty walls and towers which, though cut down to the same level as the walls, yet leave it the most impressive medieval fortress I have seen. And the abundant growth of valerian makes it as beautiful as it is stern. Angers has not one of the great cathedrals, a huge aisleless church with a bad west front, certainly not a place to love and hardly to admire. Yet here again there is splendid early glass, especially the Zodiac of the rose in the south transept. The organ case is a feature which seldom gets due notice, but here the great caryatids on the west wall refuse to be ignored. And then there are the tapestries : but they will be far better in their gallery, hung at a lower level.

Returning by a different route we passed through Saumur, much in need of a cool drink, for the weather was as hot as at that moment in England. But Saumur was intolerable, and we fled. And we were to see one more château, of a different kind. Keeping an eye open for a place of refreshment, we saw on a gate, by the village of Parnay, a notice *Maison de dégustation*, and turned in. There outside a charming old house, the Château de Marconnay, we drank a pleasant light beer, though the proprietor, M. Paul Loitière, regretted that we should not choose the *vin rosé* which he regarded as appropriate to the hour. He then showed us his pleasant old rooms, one of them displaying a complete frieze of bottles, each with its great glass beside it ; another was hewn in the rock. Cave dwellings indeed are still frequent in the cliffs of the Loire valley, and the word troglodyte is not unknown to Baedeker.

We returned to Azay by the *bac* at Candes and left for home next morning, with much to see on the way. Le Mans is an unattractive industrial town but has a superb cathedral, no anti-climax to eyes fresh from Chartres and Bourges. The glass of yet another wonderful apse is of the same age and quality, and some may even prefer the great Romanesque nave to the Gothic. A service was in progress and we sat down unobtrusively at the west end, where I found myself just below the Ascension window, which may possibly be the earliest stained glass in Europe. We realized in due course that the service was a Confirmation, with much pulpit exhortation and rather undistinguished music, till suddenly the congregation began to uplift its voice in *Auld Lang Syne*—the tune, that is : to the words we held no key. Naturally, seeing the places we visited, stained glass was a major preoccupation, and here we found something that we met nowhere else. The Chapel of St. Joan, in the south choir aisle, is full of modern glass of real quality, telling the story of the Maid—vigorous, dramatic, and excellent in colour.

Our next stop, unpremeditated, was at Verneuil, where the splendidly romantic late-Gothic tower of the church drew us from the car. We had yet another cathedral to see, Evreux, which demands much more than a fleeting visit. Here yet again is fine glass, but of the fourteenth and fifteenth centuries, not to be compared with the jewelled fabric of an earlier day. Our journey ended at La Bouille, finely situated on the Seine below Rouen, at the southern end of one of the great loops of that most tortuous river. Here our hotel and our dinner were by no means what we had been led to expect : the hotel clearly catered for a different kind of guest on a fine Sunday evening. Yet here too we met from a harassed and overtasked Madame the same courtesy we had met everywhere else. For the second time we had allowed ourselves to run short of money, and banks are not open on Sunday evening nor yet, as it appeared, on Monday morning. But it did not add to the worries of Madame when we could not meet our bill : we were merely invited to send the money from Dieppe. Would our own hoteliers be equally accommodating to French travellers ? This was the second time we had been guilty of improvidence, on both occasions when the bank was closed. On the first occasion a very gracious Madame rang up the manager, who replied that he would be pleased to see us if we would excuse his gardening clothes.

From La Bouille, if you avoid a long detour by using the *bac* (free as usual), it is only a short run to Dieppe and the boat. As we approached the English coast, the sun disappeared and we were greeted with thunder and lightning, the storm which brought the May heatwave to a close.